THE DEVIL IS IN THE DETAILS:
EXAMINING MATT MURDOCK AND DAREDEVIL

THE DEVIL IS IN THE DETAILS:

EXAMINING MATT MURDOCK AND DAREDEVIL

EDITED BY

RYAN K. LINDSAY

SEQUART RESEARCH & LITERACY ORGANIZATION   EDWARDSVILLE, ILLINOIS

The Devil is in the Details: Examining Matt Murdock and Daredevil
Edited by Ryan K. Lindsay

Copyright © 2013 by the respective authors. Daredevil and related characters are trademarks of Marvel Comics © 2013.

First edition, February 2013, ISBN 978-0-5780-7373-6.

All rights reserved. Except for brief excerpts used for review or scholarly purposes, no part of this book may be reproduced in any manner whatsoever, including electronic, without express consent of the publisher.

Cover by Alice Lynch. Book design by Julian Darius. Interior art is © Marvel Comics; please visit marvel.com.

Published by Sequart Research & Literacy Organization. Edited by Ryan K. Lindsay. Assistant edited by Hannah Means-Shannon.

For more information about other titles in this series, visit sequart.org/books.

Contents

And a Blind Man Shall Lead Them: A Foreword 1
    by Ralph Macchio

A Different Daredevil 3
    by Will Murray

Grabbing the Devil by the Horns: Daredevil and His Early Rogues Gallery 13
    by Matt Duarte

Being Mike Murdock.. 21
    by Timothy Callahan

Daredevil and the Missing Father: Why Fathers Matter in Super-Hero Origins. 32
    by Forrest C. Helvie

There Will be Blood: Daredevil's Violent Tendencies... 45
    by Henry Northmore

Science Fact! 58
    by Stéphane Guéret, Marie-Laure Saulnier, Manuella Hyvard, and Nicolas Labarre

Daredevil: Not Ready for Primetime?... 71
    by M. S. Wilson

The Life and Times of Foggy Nelson 79
    by Christine Hanefalk

Blind Dates and Broken Hearts: The Tragic Loves of Matthew Murdock........... 98
    by Ryan K. Lindsay

Daredevil and Spider-Man: Dark Alleys and Bright Lights................................ 147
    by Vinny Murphy

Daredevil and Punisher: Polar Opposites? 156
    by M. S. Wilson

What Fall from Grace? Reappraising the Chichester Years 166
    by Julian Darius

.22 Caliber, a Girl's Gun: Vanessa Fisk and Freedom of Action 192
    by Kevin Thurman

When Things Fall Apart in Hell's Kitchen: Postcolonialism in Bendis's Daredevil
.... 197
    by Jon Cormier

Daredevil: Intermediate Super-Hero Filmmaking.. 208
    by Geoff Klock

The Only Way is Down: Brubaker's Saga as '70s Cinematic Noir 219
    by Ryan K. Lindsay

And a Blind Man Shall Lead Them: A Foreword

by Ralph Macchio

There's always been something special about Daredevil — about Matt Murdock, really. In those heady days when the Marvel Universe was aborning in the early Sixties, you might have wondered how the adventures of a blind super hero wouldn't have gotten lost in the shuffle. C'mon, you had thunder gods and mutants and hulks, not to forget a certain star-crossed teen with spider powers. So why did Daredevil survive and thrive amidst such awesome competition?

I believe it was because Matt Murdock was such a real flesh and blood character. I truly felt I knew him and understood him. Sure, DD had a great costume, quirky villains, and a good supporting cast. Frankly, lots of characters did. However, unlike those other stalwarts, Matt Murdock made me a nervous wreck! This guy was blind, for heaven's sake. He'd swing from building to building like Spider-Man, battle the Stilt Man or whomever — but he couldn't see! Yes, he had a radar sense and his other senses were enhanced, but that still didn't placate me. I worried about my hero. I cared about him.

And Daredevil's heroism, even among super heroes, was second to none. I'll never forget him desperately clutching at the ankle of Prince Namor, the Sub-Mariner, in issue seven, begging him not to attack mankind. Namor was taken with DD's courage that he temporarily abandoned his vendetta against mankind and returned to the sea. Brilliant stuff from Stan and illustrator Wally Wood. It forever endeared me to the scarlet swashbuckler.

Decades later, I was privileged to first assist on and then edit *Daredevil* during the revered Frank Miller and Nocenti / Romita Jr. runs. It was gratifying beyond words to have overseen such extraordinary high points in the fascinating life of Matt Murdock.

And I say Matt specifically, because more than any other comic book character, this hero's saga is much more about the man beneath the mask than about his costumed alter ego. If you recall the pivotal story "Born Again" or "The Man Without Fear," Matt was hardly in costume during the events of either tale. It was all about this man, this utterly fearless man.

In the first issue of *Daredevil*, Stan Lee and Bill Everett gave us an origin that I've long felt was perhaps the best in the Marvel pantheon. There was a whole movie packed in those twenty two some pages. It was rife with potential. And later, Frank Miller expertly expanded upon that initial story, carefully adding elements to the origin, yet always emphasizing that at his core, Matt Murdock has, since childhood, struggled mightily against great, almost overwhelming odds to achieve his destiny. He may be the most truly human of all the Marvel super heroes, and that's saying something. I believe that's why he holds such a special place in the hearts of Marvel readers. He just gets to you.

Right now, under the guidance of editor Steve Wacker and writer Mark Waid, *Daredevil* is very much a talked about title. After almost five decades of nearly continuous publication, this singular figure is compelling to an entirely new generation of readers. As I said, there's just something about him. And may it ever be so. Hang in there Matt. We're with you through thick and thin.

A Different Daredevil

by Will Murray

If Marvel Comics publisher Martin Goodman and his editor Stan Lee had gotten their way, Daredevil fans would soon be celebrating the 50th anniversary of a revival of one of the most successful super-heroes of the Golden Age of Comics – a circus acrobat who fought crime in a blue and red uniform – as reimagined by the stellar team of Stan Lee and Steve Ditko.

The year was 1963. *The Fantastic Four* and *The Amazing Spider-Man* were Marvel's top super-hero sellers. Thor, Iron Man, Ant-Man, and the Hulk were in their formative period as the second-string. The Marvel Universe? It didn't exist as we know it now. But Martin Goodman wanted more super-heroes. So he instructed Stan Lee to replicate the sure success of the FF and Spider-Man. Out of that conference came the X-Men. No doubt those specifics were a product of a typical Lee-Kirby brainstorming session.

But Goodman also gave Lee a clear directive for a second Spider-Man. He had been keeping track of the legal status of the old Golden Age super-heroes of consequence. Charles Biro's phenomenally popular *Daredevil* had fallen out of trademark. It was up for grabs. Anyone could do it. In later years, this strategy led to Marvel's appropriating Magazine Enterprises' Ghost Rider and trademarking a new Captain Marvel. But this was the first try.

Goodman instructed Lee to revive *Daredevil*. With his face-concealing mask and striking uniform, he might have seemed like a natural twin to Spider-Man, despite his lack of superpowers. Over at DC Comics, they were rethinking and

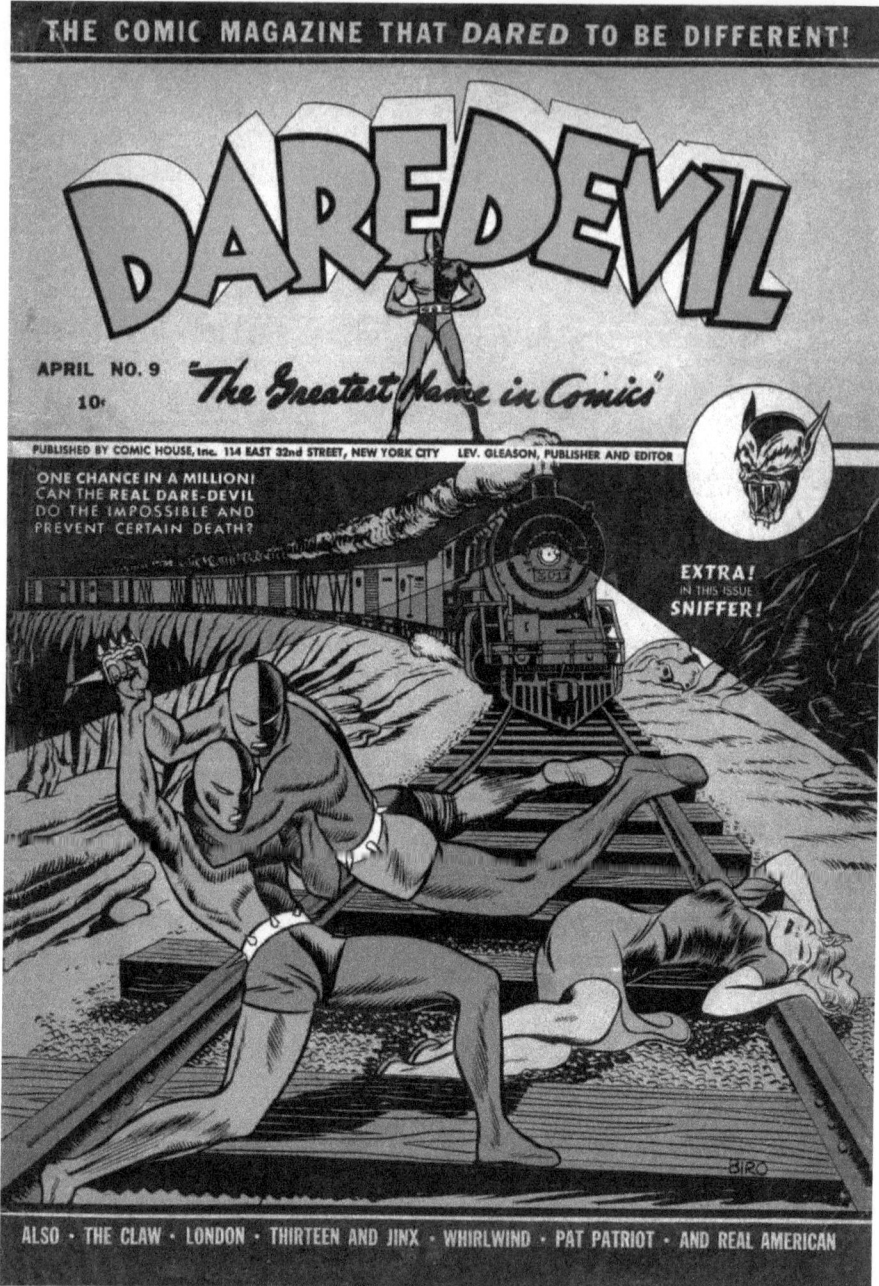

The cover to *Daredevil Comics* #9 (April 1942), starring the Golden Age character published by Lev Gleason. Art by Charles Biro.

modernizing their retired heroes with spectacular success. It was the dominant comic book trend.

Stan Lee was a company man. His personal feelings – if any – about the task assigned to him were unimportant. He reached out to the artist who helped make Spider-Man the overnight success it was. Steve Ditko turned him down cold. Reportedly uninterested in co-creating a clone of his own character, and possibility turned off by the prospect of copying someone else's creation, Ditko wanted no part of any Daredevil revival.

"I was sorry," Lee recalled to *Wiz-Bang*. "Steve would have been great. But I was lucky to get Everett."

Lee next turned to the creator of one of Marvel's earliest superstars, the Sub-Mariner. But Bill Everett, too, balked at the task. However, he was willing to discuss ways to make it work.

"I know [Stan] had this idea for Daredevil," Everett told *Alter Ego*. "He *thought* he had an idea. And we tried to talk it over the phone, and it just... wouldn't work. With a long distance phone call, it just wasn't coming out right, so I said, 'All right... I'll take a day off and come down to New York.'"

Out of that conference came the template for the Marvel version of *Daredevil*. By this time, Lee had been convinced that all but the name should be discarded. Goodman was primarily interested in masthead names, anyway. He firmly believed that was what sold magazines.

The original Daredevil was Bart Hill, a young mute, who lost his voice due to traumatic shock over the murder of his parents. Although that aspect of his personality was later abandoned, it was a unique trait for a super-hero. Since Lee liked heroes with flaws, this may have provided the impetus to make Marvel's version of Daredevil its first handicapped hero. It's highly unlikely that Lee, who loved to write dialogue, seriously considered making the new Daredevil a mute protagonist.

Jack Kirby had been called in to help refine the character. "Kirby had a lot of input into all the looks of all these things," Lee explained. "If I wasn't satisfied with something and Kirby was around, I would have said, 'Hey Jack, what do you think of this? How would you do it?'"

Kirby's recollection was different. He told *Comics Feature*, "All of them came from my basement. The Avengers, Daredevil, the X-Men, all of them."

The original yellow and red Daredevil costume appears to have been designed by Jack Kirby, with some assistance by Everett, who inked the concept sketch. But this is unconfirmed. It was clearly modeled after an old-style gymnast's tights, however.

"Originally, I wanted him to be a great gymnast," Lee remembered. "So I thought maybe I'd make him a circus acrobat. But I somehow decided that was a little unoriginal."

The Golden Age Daredevil was armed with a boomerang. That, too, was dispensed with. Marvel's DD would carry a policeman's billy club instead.

"Well, I don't think I was thinking of the boomerang," Lee stated. "I needed some reason for him to swing from building to building. It well might have been Kirby's idea. It could have been Everett's. I don't remember. Maybe Kirby decided he should have the club, but I remember it was me who felt the club should have a wire that came out of it. See, I wanted him to be able to go from building to building. He couldn't fly, and he couldn't stick to the wall like Spider-Man. And I thought if he had this little wire that he could throw, I could combine it with the billy club."

Everett later recalled that this was Jack Kirby's idea. Matt Murdock's blind man's cane folded, converting into an all-purpose billy club. The wire was a later development.

For an origin, they resorted to the same quasi-scientific trigger that had given so many of Marvel super-heroes great powers: radiation. After a can of radioactive waste strikes young Matt Murdock in the eyes, he loses his sight — but soon discovers his other senses are amplified. More significantly, he acquires a Radar Sense that informs him of his surroundings.

In his preface to the *Son of Origins of Marvel Comics* reprint of *Daredevil* #1,[1] Lee remembered being inspired by Banyard Kendrick's stories of blind detective Captain Duncan Maclaine. Perhaps he never read the pulp magazine *Black Book Detective*, whose long-running hero, District Attorney Anthony Quinn, after being blinded by acid and having a double cornea transplant, regains his senses with a twist. He can see in the dark. Donning a Batman-style costume, he fights crime as the Black Bat. Daredevil is closer to the Black Bat than he is to Duncan Maclaine.

Stan Lee recognized that Everett developed this part of the character perfectly. "He was terrific," Lee praised. "I was so pleased that he was interested in doing this. He put in all these little things that made it seem so

---

[1] All references to *Daredevil* are to the first series, unless otherwise specified.

believable, as I remember it. Like how he could sense things, and why he was a great acrobat because you get your balance through your ear. As I recall, he did little shots of Daredevil doing different things so the readers could understand how his blindness was helping his other senses take over. And I thought he made the character very believable. He had a way of drawing these things so that made it very clear to the reader how everything worked."

A little-known insight into all this is that Everett's daughter was legally blind. No doubt real-life experiences informed the artist's sensitive portrayal. However, the true origin of DD's Radar Sense may be that it's a variation of Spider-Man's Spider Sense, which had already manifested in his own strip.

Both *The X-Men* and *Daredevil* were scheduled to debut in the summer of 1963. Everett penciled the first issue – all except the cover, which doubled as the splash page. It appears to be Kirby's original concept sketch. But Everett had trouble making the deadline due to the fact that he had a day job. When it became clear he could not make the deadline, Lee was forced to create a fresh book from whole cloth with Jack Kirby. Thus was born *The Avengers*, which replaced DD on the schedule.

Everett kept plugging away, and the months passed. Eventually, Lee took the partially-drawn art away from Everett and threw Sol Brodsky, George Roussos, and Steve Ditko onto the unfinished pages in a rush to get them to the printer. It was an eerie echo of the events surrounding *Daredevil Battles Hitler* #1, back in 1941. In the rush to get that first issue out, probably to cash in on the Hitler cover to the best-selling *Captain America* #1, publisher Lev Gleason ordered that book produced over a frantic weekend. George Roussos had also participated in that marathon creative storm.

Daredevil #1 debuted with a 2 February 1964 release date. In any event, Bill Everett was off the book. Joe Orlando picked up the strip, with Vince Coletta inking it in a gritty style that foreshadowed Frank Miller's treatment two decades later. Orlando left after only three issues because Lee kept rejecting pages and sequences in an effort to make the nascent character work. They were working Marvel-style (in which the writer would script based on already-produced pages of art), and when Lee would receive Orlando's pencils he often saw the need to rethink Orlando's interpretation of the agreed-upon storyline. Since he wasn't being paid for the unused pages, Orlando, in frustration, walked off the book.

Enter Wally Wood.

"I don't remember if I was still with *MAD*," Wood told Mark Evanier. "If I was, I figured it wasn't for long. Ran into Joe on the street, I think. He said he'd left the strip. I figured I'd go up and see Stan Lee. It was work."

Lee was excited to get Wood. He thought Wood's style was similar to that of Orlando's, thus ensuring a certain continuity to *Daredevil*'s look. They did two issues, in which the only alteration Wood made was to change Daredevil's chest insignia to the familiar double "D" that survives to this day.

Once they settled in as a team, Lee asked Wood to help him revamp the book, already floundering as a bimonthly. Reader mail was running against the predominately yellow costume. Reportedly, consideration was given to putting the Marvel Daredevil in the Golden Age costume last seen in 1951.

"[Lee] didn't know what to do with it," Wood recounted. "The book was nothing. He said, 'Make this work. You'll be a rich man.' You know, a cut of profits, a cut of merchandise... I was stupid. I went home, drew up all these model sheets and sketches. Gave him a new costume. Lee loved it all. Why not? I was doing all the work. I was doing everything. Just like Jack, writing the story, letting him put his name on it. I never got the bonus, never got the cut of profits, nothing."

"I wasn't happy with the original costume," Lee explained. "I can't remember why. I remember I asked Wood if he could redesign it. I think I wanted to play up the fact that the last part of his name was 'devil.' And you think of the color red for fire, and so forth. We didn't have any characters who had an all-red costume."

Many of Wood's concept sketches survive, and can be found on the web.[2] They include high-tech augmentations of the redesigned billy club, and elements never used such as "hearing-ear" headphones, an infra-red sniperscope helmet, and other special electronic gear. Only radio antenna built into his cowl horns and a shotgun mike and tape recorder concealed in Daredevil's cane were ever shown. A bulletproof chest was considered, but ultimately discarded. The retractable wire for the cane was implemented at this time.

The culmination of their brief collaboration came in the issue which introduced Daredevil's striking scarlet outfit. "In Mortal Combat with... Sub-Mariner" appeared in issue #7 (April 1965). It depicted Daredevil being bested

---

[2] http://wallywoodart.blogspot.com/2011/09/marvel-concepts.html

by the seemingly invincible Sub-Mariner while heroically refusing to admit defeat.

In his introduction to the reprint of that classic story in *Marvel's Greatest Superhero Battles,* Lee wrote:

> "In Mortal Battle [*sic*] with Sub-Mariner" is one of my all-time favorites. The reason is, when two super heroes battle each other, the toughest task for any writer is to figure out how to have one combatant win without deglamorizing the other by having him lose. I mean readers hate to see their favorite costumed character lose, no matter who he's fighting. Yet, we can't have every battle between two heroes always end in a tie. [...] Obviously, in strength alone, Matt Murdock could never be a match for the super-powerful Sub-Mariner. How then do we stage a story in which he can give a good accounting of himself against so mighty a foe? This was the problem that gave me the most concern. I knew that the story plot demanded a battle between the two heroes, but how were we to do it in such a way that it would seem believable? How were we to do it while still keeping them both in character? And, most important of all, how were we to do it so that the Lord of Atlantis didn't come across like an arrogant bully, and the Man Without Fear wouldn't come across like an ineffectual, bumbling weakling? Well, needless to say, I think we found the way.

Between the redesigned outfit and the compelling story of the overmatched Man Without Fear standing up to the powerful Prince Namor, Daredevil had crystallized as a feature. He quickly crossed over into *The Fantastic Four*, though artist Jack Kirby inadvertently drew the old yellow-garbed DD, and Wood had to ink in the updated costume.

Daredevil soon went monthly. Lee was so thrilled with Wood's work that he wanted to assign him the Sub-Mariner strip he was planning to introduce in *Tales to Astonish*, as well as the Human Torch, whose feature was in trouble in *Strange Tales*.

Neither would come to pass. Creative differences led to Wood following in Orlando's wake. His final issue was penciled by Bob Powell, with Wood only inking. Wood wanted to take over scripting, but Lee reasserted his authority over the ongoing storyline (in the second part of the Fellowship of Fear sequence). This led to Wood's departure.

The next artist in line was Dick Ayers, who may have seemed like a natural choice to Lee. Ayers was then drawing the Lee / Kirby revival of the Western hero, the Two-Gun Kid. In that incarnation, the Kid was frontier lawyer Matt Hawk. If one were looking for another influence on Daredevil, one could say that lawyer Matt Murdock was modeled on the unmasked Two Gun-Kid. Thus Ayers made sense.

Dick Ayers drew the first three pages of issue #12 (January 1966), co-starring Ka-Zar. But Lee wasn't happy with them. He showed the opening to John Romita, who had just returned to the company after a stultifying stint drawing romance strips for DC Comics.

"Stan showed me Dick Ayers' splash page for a Daredevil," John Romita noted in a 2001 interview. "He asked me, 'What would you do with this page?' I showed him on a tracing paper what I would do, and then he asked me to do a drawing of Daredevil the way I would do it. I did a big drawing of Daredevil. It was just a big tracing paper drawing of Daredevil swinging. And Stan loved it."

The book was his. But when Romita turned in his version of the Ayers pages, Lee was not quite satisfied with the artist's storytelling, so he got Kirby to lay out the book. That worked. Romita fell into the Marvel style of fast-paced storytelling, and Daredevil came back to life.

As Lee told *Wiz Bang,* "I'll tell you, Romita was the perfect replacement for anything. I mean to me he was the perfect artist, second only to Kirby. And only in the sense that Kirby was more imaginative and spectacular than Romita. As far as actually drawing a strip, where you simply couldn't fault any of the shots, where it just told the story beautifully and perfectly, Romita was the guy."

It was supposed to be a stop-gap two-issue stint but Romita found the character growing on him. He decided to stay on the feature. Had the timing been slightly different, Daredevil might have veered in unexpected creative directions.

"Soon as I got the assignment on *Daredevil*," Romita recalled to Jim Keefe and John Mietus, "I got a call from two DC editors wondering if I wanted to do Metamorpho. I said that I was already committed, so I never got the chance to see what I could do with the DC super-heroes. It's one of my regrets."

Remarkably, Romita had been a fan of the original Daredevil. He told *Alter Ego*, "One of my favorite companies was Lev Gleason. Charlie Biro's stuff [for Gleason] appealed to me. His Daredevil was my favorite character. He wasn't blind; he just had that split red-and-blue costume... I told that to Stan in '65, and he said he thought Biro was a genius. I maintain that Biro did a lot of the stuff that Stan did later, but it wasn't noticed, even though he was putting a lot of personality into his comics."

It looked as if the strip had found another perfect artist.

Once again, events were working to undermine the development of *Daredevil*. In 1965, Steve Ditko abruptly quit *Spider-Man*, leaving Lee in the lurch. Kirby was too busy with *The Fantastic Four* and *Thor*. Don Heck had his hands full with *Iron Man* and *The Avengers*. Ayers was out of the question. In those days, Lee was understaffed in the artist department.

So he turned to John Romita, a reluctant recruit at best. Thinking it a temporary assignment, he gave it his best shot. It was more than good enough. Still, it wasn't what the artist wanted to do. Romita was heartbroken.

"I really hoped I could get back to Daredevil," Romita admitted in 2009.

> Somebody had told me that sales had improved while I was on it and I was feeling great. I was saying, 'Hey, wouldn't it be nice if I could move *Daredevil* up to one of the top sellers?' But I never had a chance to find out. So that run on *Daredevil* was like a blissful period of six months that I enjoyed myself tremendously. I loved that character. I still to this day think that Daredevil is the best character that Marvel has.

Once again, Stan Lee needed a new *Daredevil* collaborator. This time it was the returning artist who had been given the Sub-Mariner strip Wally Wood had walked away from. Gene Colan signed on to pinch-hit for just one issue, #20 (September 1966), but that single effort turned into an unprecedented 80-issue run. Finally, the Man without Fear had a permanent artist.

Once he made the commitment, Colan strove to put his own artistic stamp on the Man Without Fear. "I wanted to change his costume to make it black, just with little spots of red showing through it," he reminisced to *Alter Ego*, "but Stan wanted me to leave it open for color, which I thought lost the dynamics of the character… made him look almost weightless."

The Wally Wood Daredevil remained the standard. With the exception of interludes and variant costumes, it continues to be the version of the character the public recognizes.

The early history of Daredevil is a story of interrupted collaborations, creative roads not taken and many, many misfires. What if Ditko had said yes to Daredevil at the beginning? What if Wally Wood had stayed on the strip? Or Romita? All of these choices fed into the definitive Daredevil swinging through the 21st century.

It's also interesting to see how Stan Lee's ideas were shaped by the different artists with whom he paired himself. Had Ditko and Everett separately resisted Lee's original thinking, might we today be reading an utterly different *Daredevil*?

Consider this: simultaneous with *Daredevil* #3 back in 1964, Lee, obviously hopping to boost sales on the struggling new super-hero, crossed Daredevil into an issue of *The Amazing Spider-Man* drawn by his first artistic choice, Steve Ditko. Lee pitted Daredevil against the Ringmaster and his Circus of Crime, under the big top. The cover depicted Daredevil as an aerialist on a circus trapeze, looking right at home in his original acrobat's costume! Was this Lee testing whether his original concept might still be the way to go?

Consider also this anecdote: in the early 1980s, Mark Evanier was present at a network conference for a Daredevil Saturday morning animated TV series wherein Stan Lee pitched a reimagining of the Man Without Fear – a carnival phrase if one was ever coined – as a circus performer and human cannonball who drove around New York in a special truck equipped with a circus cannon that would catapult him up onto rooftops, where he would do battle with his foes *à la* Spider-Man...

We could have ended up with any number of different Daredevils. We ended up with this one. Our one.

Works Cited

Morris, Brian K. "They Depended on [the Super-Heroes] To Keep Us Afloat." *Alter Ego* #52, Mar 2006.

Murray, Will. "Daredevil Origins." *Wiz-Bang*, Apr 2003.

Murray, Will "The Untold Origin of Daredevil." *The Official Overstreet Price Guide* #37. Gemstone Publishing.

Keefe, Jim and Mietus, John. "Interview: John Romita." Keefe Studios. www.jimkeefe.com/studio/romita/interview.htm

Lee, Stan. *Origins of Marvel Comics*. Simon and Shuster, 1974.

Lee, Stan. *Marvel's Greatest Superhero Battles*. Fireside Books, 1978.

Romita, John, quoted in *The Men Without Fear: Creating Daredevil*. Video documentary. Spark Hill Productions, 2003.

Thomas, Roy "Bill Everett Interview" *Alter Ego* #11, 1978.

Van Hise, James. "A Talk with the King. Jack Kirby" *Comics Feature* #44, May, 1986.

Thomas, Roy. "Fifty Years On The 'A' List. A Candid Conversation With Marvel Artist/Art Director Supreme John Romita." *Alter Ego* Vol. 3 #9, July, 2001.

Grabbing the Devil by the Horns: Daredevil and His Early Rogues Gallery

by Matt Duarte

Stan Lee doesn't have a very deep imagination.

Which is not to say he has a small or limited imagination. The man's output in the early to mid-'60s is more than enough proof he was a creative force to be reckoned with, having had a hand in developing some of the most memorable heroes and villains of the era, many of which would live on for decades in the public consciousness. Daredevil, the Man Without Fear, was one of the characters created during this time.

Some other creators have a deep pool from which they bring forth fantastic and unimaginable creations. A deep well of murky waters dwells inside their minds, a font of imagination which would take years to explore and discover properly and fully. Stan Lee was never one of those creators. If one were to choose a word to describe Stan Lee's sense of imagination and creative output, it would have to be "wide." He was probably more concerned with the number than with the quality of his ideas. In those early Marvel days, Lee was responsible for writing more than a handful of ongoing titles, including such popular titles as *The Amazing Spider-Man, The Fantastic Four, The Avengers,* and *The X-Men*. By sheer necessity, he would only give the most general outline to his artist collaborators, who would often bring their own concepts to the percolator of ideas that was '60s Marvel. The visuals were produced first, and Lee would add his dialogue to the finished pages. Later, people would dub this the Marvel Method.

Going back to the water analogy, Stan Lee's imagination would be more along the lines of a flood meadow. Expansive and overreaching, but nonetheless overtly shallow at certain points. One of those points was Daredevil's rogues gallery, which has not reached the same level of recognition or acclaim as the other villains created in that same time period. Looking at the first issues of the series, we can see Daredevil's formative start as a super-hero placed him up against some less than memorable villains. An analysis of the first dozen issues shows how weak and weird Daredevil's villains were.

Things did not bode well from the start. In Daredevil's very first appearance (*Daredevil* #1, Apr 1964), he didn't fight a super-villain, unlike other characters' debut issues in the same era (the Fantastic Four faced the Mole Man; the X-Men battled Magneto). Instead, the first issue of the Man Without Fear's series was all about his origin story, and the only heroics involve fighting a group of small-time crooks who work for the Fixer – a man who technically is Daredevil's first antagonist. The connection that Daredevil shares with the legal system, with Matt Murdock as an attorney-at-law during the day, made him ideally suited to be matched up with mobsters and thieves, as opposed to criminals bent on world domination. The Fixer set a long precedent of Daredevil having to fight corruption and greed. This concept of fighting a systemic problem, rather than a costume, was something later writers would pick up on, perhaps most notably Brian Michael Bendis in his seminal run on *Daredevil* Vol. 2 during the early to mid-2000s. Back in the '60s, though, readers were starting to get accustomed to the idea of colorful villains as the usual antagonists of costumed crusaders. A gangster in a suit and tie just didn't cut it. As if to prove such low-key assumptions right, rather than demanding a bombastic fight, the Fixer died of a heart attack in the final pages of the comic and has never appeared again.

Daredevil #2 (June 1964) featured a match-up between Daredevil and Electro, a character who had previously appeared in the pages of *The Amazing Spider-Man*. The electrically powered rogue was the first super-powered villain the Man Without Fear would ever face. More importantly, he started a precedent for Daredevil "borrowing" Spider-Man's antagonists. While it's true that back in those early Marvel days, when all the heroes lived in the same city, there was a strong cross-pollination between the villains, the relationship between Spider-Man and Daredevil's rogue gallery is stronger. It would culminate years later when Wilson Fisk, a.k.a. the Kingpin and originally a Spider-Man villain, became one of Daredevil's most recognizable recurring foes. As for Electro being used in *Daredevil*, it certainly didn't help expand the world of rogues Daredevil would come to build antagonisms with.

It wasn't until *Daredevil* #3 (Aug 1964) that Daredevil was finally able to match wits and muscle with a super-villain created solely for his benefit. Unfortunately, that villain happened to be Leland Owlsley, a.k.a. the Owl. On the surface, nothing's wrong with the Owl as a Daredevil foe: he's a businessman who cooked his books and who, faced with the possibility of persecution by the authorities, decides to give up his veil of legitimacy and turn into a fully developed underworld leader. The problem arises from the fact that his whole visual appearance and modus operandi is not particularly creative: a short, rotund, but imposing man who physically resembles his avian namesake, with a vast fortune he amassed as a legit businessman. In other words, he is greatly reminiscent of the famous Batman villain the Penguin, who at this point had already been established for over 20 years. Was this resemblance intentional? Was Stan Lee trying to draw parallels between Daredevil and Batman? Or was he simply perhaps borrowing too much inspiration from the Distinguished Competition? Only he would truly know, but the Owl never reached the same level as other villains and antagonists from the era, despite being Daredevil's first super-villain and appearing repeatedly over the years. He has certainly come nowhere close to the famous heights of Oswald Cobblepot. For comparison's sake, that same month in the pages of *The Amazing Spider-Man* #15 (Aug 1964), readers witnessed the first appearance of Kraven the Hunter, a remarkably popular villain for the web-crawler.

With *Daredevil* #4 (Oct 1964), the Man Without Fear struck out again with his choice of villain. Zebediah Killgrave, a.k.a. the Purple Man, turned out to be a great match for Daredevil, since he was able to emit powerful pheromones that could control the minds of the people around him. Killgrave cut an imposing figure with his purple-toned skin, unusual facial features, and matching purple suit (demonstrating the old adage that villains work well with secondary colors). With his own hypersensitive senses turned against him,

Daredevil had to do some lateral thinking in order to defeat the Purple Man. Despite a great visual image and some interesting (and frankly, dark) moments in his first appearance (such as when he almost forced Matt Murdock's sweetheart Karen Page to jump off a building), Killgrave never really stuck around as a recurring villain for Daredevil, only making a handful of appearances sporadically over the years. The potential was there, but the yield was not what some might have hoped.

The first appearance of the flamboyant and fiery foe called the Matador arrives in *Daredevil* #5 (Dec 1964). Wearing a traditional colorful bullfighting outfit, Manuel Elongato made a change in career, from participating in one of Spain's oldest traditions to a life of crime, in retaliation for the mocking he received in his previous profession. When you have a main character who has two horns on his head, it's only logical he would end up battling a bullfighter. The visual is just too obvious to pass up, and Stan Lee does not disappoint, providing plenty of fights between the Man Without Fear and Matador – until the fearless foe is head-butted by the horned vigilante. Bullfighters are used to surviving in an environment where agility is key to a long life expectancy, and where the right movement means the difference between life and death. Daredevil is used to this lifestyle, as he swings and leaps through the high rise buildings of New York City. Even though the obvious links are there, Matador would only appear a couple more times over the years before eventually retiring.

Daredevil had to battle his first super-villain team-up, the Fellowship of Fear, in *Daredevil* #6 (Feb 1965). The group didn't prove to be very popular; it never appeared again. This is perhaps explained by the motley crew of villains making up the villainous roll call: the Eel (a slippery safe cracker who had previously fought the Human Torch), the Ox (a strong man who was originally part of the Enforcers, a group of Spider-Man villains), and Mister Fear. This latest one is of particular interest, since he became one of Daredevil's recurring foes – although several different characters have sported the mantle. Using a chemical of his own creation, Zoltan Drago could send people into fits of fear and phobia, including the so-called Man Without Fear. While this would be the making of a legendary foe for Daredevil, Mister Fear bears a dangerously close resemblance to (once again) a Batman villain: Scarecrow, who also uses a fear toxin of his own creation to inflict terror upon his victims. In the space of half a dozen issues, Stan Lee managed to create two separate characters that were

The Matador makes his first appearance on the cover to *Daredevil* #5 (Dec 1964). Art by Jack Kirby and Wally Wood. Copyright © Marvel Comics.

closely similar to the Distinguished Competition's foes. Ox has appeared subsequently but he has hardly earned the status of legendary rogue. The Eel... is not worth addressing, sadly.

After a battle with the anti-hero Namor, the Sub-Mariner (*Daredevil* #7, Apr 1965), Daredevil would meet another of his long-time yet small-time foes, Stilt-Man, in *Daredevil* #8 (June 1965). As the name implies, Wilbur Day uses a pair of technologically advanced stilts to commit high-altitude crimes, such as robbing helicopters and terrorizing high-rise buildings. The vertical villain was well-suited to battle Daredevil, since he provided plenty of opportunities to show the Man Without Fear swinging around town. Stan Lee perhaps noticed this and featured Stilt-Man quite often during his tenure as writer on the title. Stilt-Man appears a record four times in those early years. Nonetheless, Stilt-Man has not aged well, and as the years passed, his popularity decreased. The whole stilt-leg schtick was only so useful for a variety of very specific situations. Frank Miller famously had Turk, a loser and low-life, easily beat Stilt-Man and steal his technology in the pages of *Daredevil* #186 (Sep 1982) – 'nuff said.

If all of Daredevil's super-powered foes so far have been harmed by too few and sporadic appearances, Duke Klaus Kruger has the dubious honor of appearing in one lone issue throughout nearly 50 years of publication: *Daredevil* #9 (Aug 1965). That one issue was more than enough to establish Kruger as being in the style of a far more popular villain: Doctor Doom, the leader of Latveria and recurring foe of the Fantastic Four. The similarities between the two are astonishing: they both are leaders of small Eastern European countries (Lichtenbad, in the case of Kruger), which they rule with a mixture of an iron fist, an enormous ego, and an army of electronic automatons. Kruger also happened to attend college with Matt Murdock, just like Victor Von Doom shared educational facilities with Reed Richards. As if realizing that the semblance between his two creations was too much to be sustained, Stan Lee decided to mercifully kill Duke Kruger at the end of the issue, and he has never been heard of again.

Having faced his fair share of costumed villains, it was time for Daredevil to meet "the strangest foes [he] has ever faced," as the cover of *Daredevil* #10 (Oct 1965) proudly boasted. That illustrious claim might actually have a point, though not necessarily in a positive way. The Ani-Men were a group of con-men and thieves dressed in animal-like suits who were recruited by the Organizer, a mysterious underworld leader. Made up of Ape-Man, Bird-Man,

Cat-Man, and Frog-Man, each one with the physical characteristics of their totemic animal, this team of criminals fought against the Man Without Fear over the course of two issues. No explanation was ever given as to why they had to wear animal suits, leaving the reader to assume a sense of theatrics overruled everything else. It has to be said, however, that fault for the particularly uncreative Ani-Men does not lie fully with Stan Lee: Wally Wood, the artist, was in charge of the writing duties for the first part of this caper. The collective villains do not deliver much excitement, so it's not surprising that each villain on his own is embarrassingly silly and unmemorable. The Ani-Men have only appeared incredibly sporadically in the Marvel Universe since their creation, with perhaps their greatest claim to fame being their appearance in *X-Men* #94 (Aug 1975), in the "All-New, All-Different" era of the X-Men. (That was also the very first issue of legendary X-writer Chris Claremont.) The Organizer, a.k.a. Abner Jonas and the man behind the Ani-Men, faced a more ignominious fate among Daredevil villains: he never appeared again. The black-hooded villain shared many similarities with another villain who would follow in his path, the Masked Marauder, who would torment Daredevil some six issues later and reappeared several times during Stan Lee's tenure on the series (*Daredevil* #16-19, #22-23, and #26-27). Perhaps this shows that Lee quite liked the idea of an organizing crime boss who used super-powered thugs to commit crimes, wreck havoc, and fight do-gooders. He liked it so much, he used it twice. Perhaps he had to, because he knew he didn't do it justice the first time.

Daredevil #12 (Jan 1966) made the scarlet swashbuckler face an actual pirate called the Plunderer. Little is known about the pirate; Matt Murdock runs into him while on a vacation cruise. After the fight, the Plunderer even recognizes Daredevil's talents and invites him to join his band of pirates on a trip to the Savage Land. While the match-up between the Plunderer and Daredevil is a good one (agility versus sheer force), it becomes completely derailed by Plunderer's connection to Ka-Zar, who guest-stars in this and the following two issues (*Daredevil* #13-14, Feb-Mar 1966). What starts as a pirate story with lots of possibilities for swashbuckling action thus becomes a sci-fi romp through the Savage Land, not exactly Daredevil's natural habitat, nor the right place to use a pirate. The Plunderer went on to appear dozens of other times, but only once again as a Daredevil foe – in the pages of *Daredevil* #24 (Jan 1967), once again with Ka-Zar as a guest star.

When looking at this cacophony of villains whom Daredevil battled in his early days, it's surprising to see how many of them have faded into oblivion or relative obscurity. If one compares the same number of *Daredevil* issues against those of *The Amazing Spider-Man*, the difference in quality of foes is astounding. In the same number of comics, Spider-Man faced the likes of the Vulture, Doctor Octopus, the Sandman, the Lizard, the aforementioned Electro, Mysterio, the Green Goblin, and (if you count him as a foe) J. Jonah Jameson. Four of those early Spider-Man villains have become well-known enough to appear in film, while absolutely none of Daredevil's early villains warranted an appearance in his self-titled 2003 film. Not even the Fixer, who was instrumental for Matt Murdock's origin as a super-hero, made the cut. The filmmakers decided to use the Kingpin instead, accompanied by the Frank Miller creations Elektra and Bullseye.

It's interesting to consider why Daredevil has stood the test of time alongside his Silver Age compatriots. The quality of villains to showcase Daredevil's heroism were severely lacking in ingenuity or longevity. An eclectic smattering of suits, bland enforcers, strange animal themes, and anachronistic losers made for an underwhelming and quite forgettable opening dozen issues. There are likely a variety of reasons why none of these Daredevil villains have truly taken off. Stan Lee was putting in long hours, and it's not surprising that his batting average dwindled by the time he got around to organizing his thoughts for issues of *Daredevil*.

However, there is a silver lining to the situation of Daredevil's early foes catalogue being particularly poor. Perhaps aided by this lack of clearly defined antagonists, Matt Murdock became the true reason to read *Daredevil*, and this, in turn, led to the rise of Matt Murdock as his own worst enemy. But that's a story for another day.

Being Mike Murdock

by Timothy Callahan

It all begins, as these sorts of things sometimes do in the Marvel Universe, with Spider-Man. The wall-crawler gets the blame – just as *The Daily Bugle* has repeatedly reminded us, and rightfully so. Who is this masked menace to swing down on his web-line, stirring up trouble for a noble blind lawyer dressed in red tights? What right does this interloper have to break the sanctity of a secret identity when lives are at risk? Did Spider-Man imagine, for even one second, that the domino effect of his meddling would lead a good-hearted man to concoct a lie so preposterous, so astonishingly unbelievable, that innocent civilians would be forced to risk their lives, and their sanity, to unwittingly cover up the truth?

Surely Spider-Man couldn't have known how far Daredevil would go to pretend that Matt Murdock, sightless lawyer, is not the costumed "Man Without Fear" who coincidentally becomes involved in rooftop scuffles with the same criminal element he interacts with during his day job.

Still, Spider-Man kicked off the chain of events that led to Matt Murdock's most ridiculous cover-up. Spider-Man, unknowingly, helped give birth to Mike Murdock – imaginary twin brother of Daredevil's secret side – and for a brief, shining moment it seemed that nothing would ever be the same again.

Mike Murdock may have only lived for a brief 17 issues, but he blazed like a comet during that short span, burning into our memories forever, even if he's been barely mentioned since. Yet he's important to the Daredevil legacy, and he's an essential window into the Man Without Fear's psyche in the early days of his adventures and in all the tragedy that would follow. Mike Murdock may be long gone, but he will never be forgotten.

Who is Daredevil?

The origin is a familiar one, sent to Hollywood and projected around the globe thanks to Mark Steven Johnson's not-so-critically-acclaimed 2003 movie *Daredevil*. In that film, as in the original 1964 comic-book version by Stan Lee and Bill Everett, young Matt Murdock knocks a blind man out of the way of an onrushing vehicle and pays a lifelong price. The vehicle carried radioactive chemicals, splashing onto the teenage Murdock's face, blinding him in the process. Like the pedestrian he saved, Matt Murdock would never see again.

Murdock soon finds his other senses have increased dramatically, and as he bounces around the gym in *Daredevil* #1 (Apr 1964), wearing nothing but black undershorts, boxing shoes, and blind-man sunglasses, he thinks to himself:

> It's as though nature made all my senses far more powerful, to compensate for my blindness! / I wonder... could the *radioactive elements* which struck my eyes have anything to do with my increased powers?? Stranger things have been known to happen!

Indeed they have, particularly in the Marvel universe, where radiation might give you the proportionate strength and speed of a spider, or transform you into a hulking green monstrosity, or turn you and your pals into elemental forces. Matt Murdock, though, just ended up blind and super-sensitive.

But that didn't stop Murdock from turning into a super-hero when the moment called for it, as seen later in *Daredevil* #1 when he throws on the yellow and black tights before tracking down his father's killer and bringing him to justice. "Whenever I don this costume," says the recent law school grad, "I'll no longer *be* Matt Murdock! But I'll need a *new* name! What if the kids in the old neighborhood could see me now!! The kids who taunted me...called me 'Daredevil'! *Wait!* That's *it!*"

Daredevil springs into action, using his cane as an all-purpose weapon against the forces of evil, and soon confronts his father's killer and gets him to confess in front of the authorities.

The story complete, Matt Murdock's thirst for vengeance sated, you might think the Daredevil persona would be put aside, never to be needed again. But this is comic books, and two months later, Daredevil is back in action in *Daredevil* #2 (June 1964), so vehemently protective of his costumed identity that he would do nothing to jeopardize it, even if that means he'll forgo treatment for his blindness.

Now operating out of the law offices of Nelson and Murdock (as was established by the end of the first issue of the series), Matt Murdock's supporting cast features two integral characters: Foggy Nelson and Karen Page. Law-partner Foggy Nelson acts as the eternal foil throughout the *Daredevil* series, providing turns as a straight man, when needed, and as comic relief when Matt Murdock is in a more serious mode. Secretary Karen Page is the love interest, creating friction between the two lawyers, and providing a body regularly in need of rescuing for the hero.

It's Page, in *Daredevil* #2, who introduces the idea that Matt Murdock may not face blindness forever. She has written to an eye specialist in her hometown. Murdock might regain his sight after all. Though he may appreciate the gesture on Page's part, Murdock wants nothing to do with the operation. He plays it off as not wanting Page to get her hopes up, but his thought bubble reveals the truth behind his decision to ignore treatment: "I must continue to refuse the operation, for I'd rather be blind and be *Daredevil*, than be an average normal man."

That statement, transcribed on paper through writer Stan Lee and letterer Sam Rosen, captures the essence of Daredevil. Matt Murdock will go to any lengths to maintain his super-hero swashbuckling identity, to continue to dance across rooftops and sock criminals in the jaw. He's willing to remain blind forever, as long as he gets to keep playing Daredevil.

Daredevil, as he's presented in the opening issues of the series, seems more than a logical outgrowth of Matt Murdock's characterization. Young Murdock is precocious and studious, yet when he adopts the Daredevil persona, he becomes blustery, sarcastic, even mean. True, he may be facing off against criminal underlings, and they may neither deserve nor expect politeness, but Daredevil taunts and ridicules without restraint. He seems unusually obsessed with mocking others for their weight – a characteristic of Daredevil's personality that will come back in our later exploration of Mike Murdock. But first, let's look back at some of the things Daredevil says and does in his earliest adventures, when his persona was first revealing itself to the reader.

In the very first issue of *Daredevil*, our title character scraps with some thugs, and mercilessly taunts the chubbiest one as he catapults the criminal into the air: "If it's *exercise* you want, fatso... you've come to the right guy!" On the following page, as Daredevil jumps over the same opponent, the hero shouts, "Bite your tongue, porky! Think what a *loss* that would be to the world!"

Daredevil's cruel super-hero arrogance isn't limited to his interactions with the criminal element, as we see also in *Daredevil* #1 when the costumed hero first meets the police. "The name's *Daredevil*," he declares. "Remember it! You'll be hearing it again... I *promise!!*" Then he jumps over the subway turnstile and disappears.

This is Matt Murdock, blind lawyer, dressed as a super-hero. And this is how he talks in that role. In his civilian identity, he doesn't talk like that at all. He's tight-lipped, conservative, and overly hesitant about almost everything. It's almost as if his Matt Murdock identity is the character his father wanted him to become — the nice, pleasant, upper-class lawyer — while the Daredevil identity is the back-room brawler who his father actually raised. Battlin' Jack Murdock may have been an innocent victim in the eyes of his son, but he ran with a tough crowd, and the life and death of a low-rent boxer seems more in line with the way the Daredevil persona behaves than the starched-collar lawyering of Matt Murdock himself.

Yet because of the nature of the comic book medium, we can distinguish between self-identity and displayed identity. The heavy use of thought bubbles in the Silver Age show us what the characters are thinking, while their actions and words show how they present themselves to the world. Stan Lee was certainly unashamed to show thoughts and spoken words in contrast to one another, fully taking advantage of the dramatic irony so easily present in the medium since decades earlier when Superman began hiding himself inside Clark Kent's jacket and tie.

If Daredevil is, in any significant way, Matt Murdock's true identity, then we can look to the hero's thought balloons for such indications. But it's not as simple as looking for clear indications of who's "real" and who's not, because Stan Lee uses Daredevil's thought balloons almost purely for exposition. It's not a matter of looking to see if Murdock-as-Daredevil's thoughts align with Murdock-as-lawyer's thoughts, or if either match up with what those two personas say out loud, because Lee presents a complex characterization that can't be peeled apart that easily. As Daredevil, Murdock thinks purely in terms of plans or describing the context for what's going on. As Matt Murdock, in lawyer garb, he thinks about what his senses indicate, but mostly he focuses on what he needs to do to protect his identity. Basically, he continues to think about the lies he must support as Matt Murdock. How he can't tell Karen Page the truth. How he can't just change into his super-hero costume when a threat presents itself. Etc. As Daredevil, he thinks about action, not deceit.

Perhaps it's a rather straightforward dual identity scenario, after all, but Stan Lee would complicate things even further within a few years. Mike Murdock was due to arrive on the scene in 1967, but only out of desperation.

Enter Spider-Man

A key plot point for the creation of the Mike Murdock identity kicks off nine issues before the character appears. In *Daredevil* #16 (May 1966), Spider-Man guest stars, and (as was so often the case in comics of that era – and every era that followed) the two heroes swap punches. Unlike most super-hero team ups, they never actually got to the sweet spot of "let's team up and fight the bad guy." They just traded blows – and barbs. A typical exchange: "I'm *fed up* with being an easy target for any character who has a *hostility complex!*" shouts a lunging Spider-Man, to which Daredevil replies, "*I'm* getting fed up with being pushed around by some neurotic who does his thinking with his *fists!*"

Later in that issue, Matt Murdock vehemently defends Daredevil – who, this early in his career is still a mystery to some and often suspected to be in cahoots with criminals, which is why Spider-Man is quick to try to beat him up – and our leading lawyer says to Foggy Nelson, "I *know* that *Daredevil* has no connection with the *Masked Marauder!* He *can't* have!"

Foggy, surprised by the normally even-tempered and bland Matt Murdock's reaction, replies, "Okay, Matt -- we were only *talking!* No need to fly off the handle! But *tell* me something -- how can you be so *sure* about Daredevil?"

This is where Murdock first truly realizes his secret identity is more precarious than he ever imagined, which perhaps should have occurred to him earlier, since it's an amazing coincidence how Daredevil gets involved in all the same cases and characters as Murdock's law firm. So here's what Murdock thinks to himself, finally: "Uh oh! I've got to be more <u>careful!</u> I almost gave myself away!" And his quick cover-up to Foggy, to explain how he would be so confident that Daredevil would have nothing to do with the villain du jour? A simple, "I don't know, Foggy! -- Just a *hunch* -- that's all!"

For a trial lawyer, Matt Murdock is embarrassingly bad at being convincing. *Daredevil* #16 ends with Spider-Man (then spelled "Spiderman," without the hyphen, which persisted throughout many of his early Silver Age Marvel comics) bursting through the window of the Nelson and Murdock law offices. Somehow, his spider-sense also has the ability to detect when Daredevil is nearby, and the buzzer in his head goes off like crazy when he swings past that particular window.

Spider-Man assumes Foggy is Daredevil (because it can't be the blind guy or the girl, so obviously it's the chunky guy who looks nothing like Daredevil physically). As Spider-Man gets ready to punch Foggy in the face, he calls Foggy out: "Alright, horn-head! The masquerade's *over!* Now, this is where I learn the *truth* about you!"

By the end of the opening scene in *Daredevil* #17 (June 1966), Spider-Man leaves (after everyone pretends to have no idea what he's talking about). But all this provides is an opportunity for Foggy to act coy, as if he might just secretly be Daredevil. He knows doing so will get Karen to notice him more. Matt Murdock doesn't comment on how pathetic that is, when he probably should; though, let's be honest, he has since used the same move a zillion times to pick up women.

Daredevil #17 features a ridiculously virtuoso bit of writing by Stan Lee on page 3, where Karen, Foggy, and Matt are all in a single panel, cranking out their own thought balloons about what they think is going on. The cluttered results are hilarious. It adds up to seven total thought balloons in a single panel, which even Stan Lee comments upon in the footnote caption box: "Seven thought balloons in one panel... undoubtedly a new world record! —Sensation-monger Stan!"

The subplot takes a bit of a back seat for half a year, and remains mostly ignored while Daredevil concerns himself with more pressing matters like the Gladiator, the Owl, and the escalating threat of the Masked Marauder. The accusation from Spider-Man doesn't kick back to the forefront of the story until the end of *Daredevil* #24 (Jan 1967), when Karen and Foggy open a letter addressed to Matt. Karen Page provides the context: "It's from *Spiderman* -- he says he *knows* that Matt is -- Daredevil! But tells Matt not to worry -- he won't reveal his secret! / Oh Foggy -- can it -- be *true?*"

Keep in mind that at no point in issue #16-17, or anytime between then and *Daredevil* #24, does Spider-Man ever really find out Daredevil's identity on the comic-book page. Last we saw of him, he thought Foggy was Daredevil. You can suppose, off-panel, that he went back to Aunt May's house and reflected a bit, then wrote a wildly dangerous letter that just goes to show how reckless Spider-Man can be about revealing secret identities.[1]

The Life and Death of Mike Murdock

In *Daredevil* #25 (February 1967) — a.k.a. the single greatest and most significant single issue of the series until Frank Miller started writing it in 1980 — Foggy and Karen confront Matt about the letter from Spider-Man, and we get the most ridiculously hilarious, and psychologically telling, conversation: Matt says, absurdly, "Okay, group -- I can see that I can't keep the *truth* from you any longer! You're forcing me to tell you about -- my twin brother!"

That's the decision he makes. He fabricates an until-now secret twin brother, as if that will somehow get him off the hook.

Matt Murdock, supposedly trustworthy lawyer, continues to dig this hole of lies all the deeper: "I've never *told* you about him before," he says, "because he asked me *not* to! His name is -- eh -- *Mike* -- Mike Murdock - and he's a *dead ringer* for me!"

Foggy, though, will have none of it, because he is actually a professional lawyer and not an imbecile: "Come *off* it, fella! I *roomed* with you all thru college -- we were *buddies* -- we confided about *everything* -- and you never *mentioned* a brother!"

But this is Matt Murdock we're talking about, a man who has already spent two years of comic-book time establishing his lack of ethics, as he ends each lawyerly day by going out on vigilante patrol at night, gathering evidence, and tampering with court cases. Matt Murdock sticks with his preposterous lie: "I, eh -- I couldn't, Foggy -- Even in those days he was a *loner* -- always practicing to be an *adventurer* -- he never wanted *anyone* to know about him -- and, since he was my own *twin brother*, I kept his secret -- all these years!"

Foggy is still suspicious of Matt's claims and continues to believe the obvious truth. Matt, in a simplistic gambit to throw his partner off the scent, points out the fact he is, in fact, blind and Daredevil is clearly not.

Thus, Matt reveals himself to be unexpectedly reasonable after the rest of the goofiness he was spouting. No one can counter the blind rebuttal, but now

---

[1] In recent years, Spider-Man has made similar errors, before, during, and after *Civil War* (July 2006 - Jan 2007) and the lead-up to the still-controversial "One More Day" story arc, in which he turned to the demonic Mephisto for help with his secret identity problems.

Foggy wants to meet this brother. This "Mike" Murdock. Because, once again, Foggy is a lawyer and rightly demands to see the evidence for himself.

Instead of confiding in Foggy, or pretending to be joking and admitting he has no idea who Daredevil is, Matt Murdock shows the true attributes of a Man Without Fear (or Man Without Common Sense), and so he thinks, "I was a *fool* for lying! Now he wants to *meet* a brother who doesn't *exist!* But, I've got to bluff it thru *somehow!*"

Right! Because if comic books have taught us anything, it's that the best solution to a tricky situation is to concoct a completely absurd alternate identity and then try to pass yourself off as your own twin brother who is also secretly a super-hero.

Matt Murdock's mental problems and trouble handling reality did not begin when Elektra died under Frank Miller's watch, or even when he went into outer space in the Steve Gerber issues. No, his mental instability was always there, from the Stan Lee days onward. Mike Murdock is just the first indication (after his original costume choices) that something is wrong with Daredevil's psyche.

Stan Lee and Gene Colan give us, in *Daredevil* #25, one of the greatest single panels in all of Daredevil's history. After some side business with the villainous and none-too-threatening Leap-Frog, we cut back to the law offices of Nelson and Murdock. And who should be sitting with his feet up on the desk when Foggy and Karen walk in? Mr. Mike Murdock, wearing the following ensemble: wrap-around green sunglasses, a white fedora with a yellow feather, an orange-checkered sports coat, a yellow vest, and a western bow tie.

His first words (in response to Karen's surprise at seeing someone who is clearly Matt's identical twin brother – as opposed to Matt just wearing different clothes): "You can say *that* again, doll! Ol' Matt's the one with the *brains* -- but *I'm* the family *pussycat!* / The name's *Mike*, gang -- and try not to *applaud* -- I'm almost as *shy* as I am *glamorous!*"

Matt's strategy, to preserve his own secret identity, is to act as loud and insulting as possible as Mike Murdock. Of course, he now has a second secret identity to preserve, but it's clear he didn't think that far ahead. And because Mike Murdock talks a lot like Daredevil (while Matt Murdock, in his suit and tie, is always so hesitant and conservative), it seems that Mike Murdock helps provide another clue about Matt's "true," or at least default, identity. Mike Murdock has the cadence of Daredevil himself, with his boisterous arrogance. No wonder he slipped into the role so easily. No wonder he even decided to come up with this preposterous scheme in the first place.

This "true" Matt Murdock, calling himself Mike Murdock, gets to actually say what's been on his mind all along. He hits on Karen Page relentlessly, while Matt always presented himself as super-shy about it, even though Matt's thought balloons showed how much he wanted to make a move on Karen. And most tellingly, the Mike Murdock persona insults Foggy (who is, remember, his very best friend in the whole world) at every turn, mostly focusing on Foggy's weight. And as we've seen, the Daredevil persona also cracked fat jokes whenever the opportunity arose. This "true" Matt is an insensitive blowhard, let's be honest.

Mike Murdock's zings toward Foggy, in *Daredevil* #25 and in the issues that followed: "You're just a bundle'a *personality*, eh, tubby?" and "...let me warn you, my chubby friend..." and "Atta boy, chubbins!" and, well, it just goes on and on like that.

The most disturbing thing is that Matt's plan works, and Foggy and Karen fall for it immediately even though they never once think to wonder, "Wait, where's Matt, and why isn't he here to introduce us to this brand new person who looks exactly like him?" Nope. Instead, Karen puts the nail in the coffin of reason: "*Foggy!* This means -- Matt was telling us the *truth!*"

Karen Page ends the debate, just by accepting the reality presented to her, as unbelievable as it may be.

Stan Lee and Gene Colan provide more insight into Matt Murdock's truly fragmented mind, and his glee at playing multiple roles, in *Daredevil* #26 (Mar 1967), when Matt actually chooses to put on the Mike Murdock outfit, just for fun. "Just for kicks," says Matt Murdock, changing out of his Daredevil costume in his apartment, "I'll become Matthew's frantic, fast-talkin' *twin brother!* / I'm beginning to *enjoy* the role of madcap *Michael Murdock!* / I guess I'm really as big a ham as '*he*' is!"

He's doing it not to protect his identity, but just because he enjoys playing the façade, and he admits it's closer to his preferred, hammy behavior.

Matt Murdock is mentally unstable, perhaps bordering even on psychotic in his willingness to layer the fabric of lies in his relationships with others. And that underlying concern, sparked by the appearances of Mike Murdock in year three of the *Daredevil* series, informs every other *Daredevil* run that followed, in the work of Frank Miller and David Mazzucchelli, Brian Michael Bendis and Alex Maleev, Ed Brubaker and Michael Lark, and many more.

Matt Murdock enjoys being the obnoxious Mike Murdock so much that he contemplates giving up his Daredevil persona, suggesting that persona's true function. From *Daredevil* #26 (Mar 1967). Art by Gene Colan. Copyright © Marvel Comics.

But Mike Murdock, as much as we learned about our hero through the appearance of this fabricated boor, wasn't meant to last, and even Matt gets tired maintaining his loudmouth, brightly-clad civilian alter-ego. As such, he kills Mike (himself) off in *Daredevil* #41 (June 1968). As Murdock indicates, dressed as *Daredevil*, via thought balloon: "I just *thought* of something! – The nuttiest idea I've ever *had!* / But if I can pull it off... it'll end my *triple-identity* bit... *forever!*"

His brilliant, "nutty" plan? To blow himself up after a fight with the villainous Exterminator and company, and secretly escape the explosion, but leave the tattered front double-D logo of his costume where Foggy can find it.

And it works! Foggy, who was being held captive by the villains, finds the red piece of fabric and says, out loud to no one, "This is all... that's *left* of him! Mike Murdock... gave his *life*... to save *mine!*"

So much for what we may have believed about Foggy being the intelligent and reasonable lawyer in the office.

Because – and here's the kicker – Daredevil appears in the very next issue of *Daredevil*, and Mike Murdock never appears again, and somehow Matt Murdock is able to just say the equivalent of "Oh, that must be some other guy who took his place!"

That's it for Mike Murdock. And that's it for Foggy and Karen's suspicions about Matt Murdock's secret super-hero identity – at least for a while.

The series would eventually get a whole lot darker, mostly when the 1970s gave way to the 1980s, but also when writers realized that Matt Murdock was more than just a swashbuckling super-hero – he was a man who had a documented history of psychotic episodes, as characterized by the entire invention of the Mike Murdock persona. And if that was indeed something closer to his true persona bursting through, he must have even bigger issues of repression after he decides to stick with the uptight Matt Murdock secret identity.

Mike Murdock was fun while he lasted, and what he told us about the true nature of Matt / Daredevil provided a subtext that would inform *Daredevil* ever since. The long-lost twin brother is still nowhere to be found. Matt Murdock may act differently now. He may have put his past behind him, or pretended to. But beneath it all is an obnoxious, fat-guy-insulting, sleazeball of a lout, just waiting to reappear. Mike Murdock may have died in 1968, but he's still there, bouncing around in Matt Murdock's head.

Daredevil and the Missing Father: Why Fathers Matter in Super-Hero Origins

by Forrest C. Helvie

In their collaborative series of interviews that comprise *The Power of Myth* (1988), Bill Moyers relates to Joseph Campbell the story of his first viewing of *Star Wars*: "The first time I saw *Star Wars*, I thought, 'This is a very old story in a very new costume.'" Looking carefully at George Lucas' original trilogy, it's clear to students of Campbell that Lucas did his homework in his adaptation of the hero's journey Campbell discusses in his seminal work *The Hero of a Thousand Faces* (1949). The result is a synthesis of both contemporary science fiction and timeless mythology.

Of course, Lucas wasn't the only person to blend works of present-day fiction with the mythical traditions of generations past. By the time *Star Wars* was released in May 1977, the comics industry had been providing the world with retellings of the old myths in new costumes for nearly 40 years. One of these old myths that both Lucas and early comic creators adapted for their contemporary audience was the hero's search for the father. While this motif isn't necessarily addressed in *every* comic hero's origin, Superman, Batman, and Spider-Man – the three most well-known comic heroes – *do* incorporate this motif into their respective origin stories. This poses a question for readers: why is there such interest in the relationships between the most successful super-heroes and their missing fathers?

Before delving into a discussion of fathers and their influences on comic book super-heroes such as Daredevil, it's important to address a few practical concerns in order to avoid imprecise generalizations. First, despite Joseph Campbell's attempts to apply his mythological understanding to myths from around the world, they are best applied to Western mythology and cultures (universal grand narratives are problematic). Furthermore, this discussion of atonement with the father – while not exclusive to other demographics – does not profess to apply neatly to all men and women of all backgrounds, even if it does attempt to speak to certain shared experiences. Looking at the greater body of super-heroes in comics, particularly DC and Marvel comics, super-heroes are more likely to be Caucasian heterosexual males of Western origin, from the United States in particular, and Matt Murdock is no exception. A simple survey of the comic super-hero movies that have made it to the silver screen confirms this: Batman, Superman, Spider-Man, Iron Man, Thor, Captain America, Green Lantern, and Daredevil – to name just a few – all cast heroes of this general demographic in their leading roles. Therefore, it's problematic to discuss this notion as a universally shared experience, given the limited demographics of the heroes themselves.

This is not to say there are no exceptions to the trend of Western, white, heterosexual super-heroes. Diversification of super-heroes, in order to better represent an increasing variety of readers, has been going on for decades. Black Panther, Blade, and the Falcon often serve as early examples of diversity, and the recent addition of Miles Morales as the new headliner of *Ultimate Spider-Man* serves as an encouraging contemporary example. However, one cannot escape the cultures in which these heroes were initially introduced, which was not as greatly concerned (or only just beginning to become concerned) with inclusivity and diversity. As such, much of the discussion will assume that the comic super-hero audience is one that generally resembles the heroes themselves. Furthermore, this analysis will primarily concern itself with the relationship between the masculine, male[1] Matt Murdock to his father, and

---

[1] I differentiate masculinity and maleness to underscore the separation between behavioral traits (masculinity) and biological gender (male); these terms are often used interchangeably, when there are, in fact, distinctions between them.

may make some general assumptions from an Anglo-Western perspective. It is exciting, however, to think of the new and progressive discussions that will follow in the years to come as comic super-heroes continue to diversify and address human experiences from different gender and ethnic perspectives.

Fathers, Sons, and Atonement

Because many comic super-heroes originally published in the United States possess predominantly Western characteristics, it's no surprise to see how they fit into the discourse of Western mythology. From *The Odyssey* to the *New Testament* and the medieval tales of the Grail Knights, the quest for one's father is a motif that regularly occurs in numerous Western myths, and within this quest, the notion of atonement is a central motif. Put simply, this recurring theme places the son in a position apart from the father for various reasons, and it's the role of the son-hero to overcome a series of challenges before he can take his rightful place alongside his father. These challenges can either be placed before the hero by the father or be the same challenges the father surmounted in the past. Regardless of how these challenges originate, they constitute a sort of initiation, which drives the hero's journey. Not only do these challenges create a separation between father and son, they also serve as the means of bridging this gap. In much the same way as the Greek term *pharmakon* means both "poison" and "remedy," so too does the journey into manhood – and by extension, "super-manhood" – provide both the cause and cure for man's separation from his father. In terms of comics, this challenge ultimately sets the stage for the birth of a new and exciting super-hero.

In the early 20th century, this arc was embedded in the earliest and most important comic titles: *Action Comics* and *Detective Comics*. Both Superman and Batman stand above and beyond the average men with whom they interact on a daily basis, and yet, neither hero's father is alive to continue guiding them. Superman's father – a brilliant Krpytonian scientist – died when his planet exploded moments after he sent his lone son hurtling into space. Thomas Wayne – noted philanthropist and a skilled doctor – died after unsuccessfully defending his wife and son from a mugger on the streets of Gotham City. It's no surprise Superman would then spend his life protecting the planet Earth from destruction on numerous occasions, while Batman would dedicate his life to preventing many similar crimes being perpetrated against fellow Gothamites. Each of these heroes attempts to fill the role of protector in an even greater manner than their fathers who preceded them. From his inception, the male comic-book super-hero has linked the search for atonement with the loss of the father to form his life's mission. As comics continued to grow in popularity, this search for atonement would continue to prove fruitful territory for creators to explore in new and even more colorful super-hero comics.

DC Comics dominated the super-hero genre throughout the years prior to and following World War II. Marvel Comics quickly rose to prominence during the early 1960s and established itself as the House of Ideas through its unique and creative heroes. By the mid-1960s, Marvel had established its dominance in the super-hero market with titles such as *The Fantastic Four*, *The Incredible Hulk*, *The X-Men*, *Journey into Mystery* (featuring Thor), *Tales of Suspense* (featuring Iron Man and, later, Captain America), and *The Amazing Spider-Man*. In 1964, Marvel introduced another hero in the form of a blind attorney, Matthew Murdock, a.k.a. "Daredevil." Although Daredevil's origins included the requisite exceptional circumstances that created other heroes – exposure to a radioactive chemical – Murdock's transformation is far more understated as heroes such as the Fantastic Four, the Incredible Hulk, or Peter Parker.

Following in the Father's Footsteps

Unlike more traditional initiation stories of the son following in the footsteps of the father, Daredevil's origin, as portrayed in *Daredevil* #1 (Apr 1963), provides a slightly different take on the old motif. Jack Murdock issues a different challenge for his son to earn his place as a man: "I've no future... nothing I can do but become a punching bag for younger men! / But I won't let that happen to *you*! You're gonna *study*... become a lawyer, or a doctor... you'll *be* somebody... the somebody that I can never be!" As Matt grows older, he receives affirmation from his father not from fighting with others but through success in his studies. He is determined to please his father, as shown by his thoughts: "I can't defy dad, after all of his sacrifices! I've got to be the son he wants me to be!" Despite this attempt to find manhood through an overt rejection of the father, however, Matthew is found, only one page later, applying himself to a thoroughly rigorous training regimen. After all, "it is only natural that the son of Battling Murdock should take to vigorous training in the way a duck takes to water!" With the bookish Matt taking to physical training in a that emulates Battling Jack, Stan Lee seems to suggest it's natural for sons to want to emulate their fathers.

Despite Battling Jack Murdock's disavowal of his success as a man through physicality, that ends up being perhaps one of the most powerful lessons he provides his son the night of his final prizefight. Jack (and the reader) realizes his previous fights were fixed by the mob, and despite being told to throw the fight, he embraces his role and life as a fighter: "I've always trained *him* to do his best... I can't disappoint him now!" The final exchange between father and son reaffirms the father's place as his son's epitome of manhood when Matt exclaims, "You *did* it, Dad! You proved that *nothing's* impossible if a man has the courage! If a man's not *afraid*!!" Instead of rebuking Matt for openly celebrating his display of physical prowess, Jack tells him, "I wanted you to be proud of me, Matt." The father-son relationship is affirmed in this final panel, and the final example of manhood placed before the son is that of the warrior who successfully navigates the harrowing challenges placed before him through a combination of mental endurance and physical superiority. This seems to set the standard which the soon-to-be super-hero will aim for, as seen later in that same issue.

Matt respects and makes good on his earlier promise to his father through starting his own law practice after graduation. This sets the stage for providing Matt with the drive and motivation to become Daredevil: "I can't break that promise I made! And yet, with my agility, my extra-sharp senses, there is so *much* I could do! I can't let all my powers go to waste! *Wait!* I *have* it! / I'll see to it that Matt Murdock never *does* resort to force... but somebody *else* will!" In perhaps a nod to classic Freudian notions of repression and displacement, Lee and Everett show Matthew as he begins to compartmentalize aspects of personality. He goes on to create a separate identity to allow him to *both* respect Jack's spoken wishes *and* honor the father's final lesson by becoming and surpassing him as a warrior. According to Freud, displacement refers to the notion that emotions linked to troubling and problematic thoughts and actions are then censored (or repressed) by the individual's subconscious. In essence, they are moved or displaced from the conscious to the subconscious mind (see Felluga). In this light, Matthew Murdock represses a desire to allow himself the place as avenger to his father's death; instead, he displaces these troublesome feelings and creates the Daredevil persona to deal with these desires.

Lee had already found success with the psychologically scarred Peter Parker, he adapted this for Matt Murdock. It's the dual trauma of Matt Murdock's exposure to the radioactive waste and the murder of his father at the hands of the Fixer that makes trauma theory an especially useful lens to better understand the rise of the Man Without Fear as a response to Matt Murdock's search for atonement.

Trauma and Its Effects[2]

In medical terms, psychic trauma arises "when a sudden, unexpected, overwhelming intense emotional blow or a series of blows assaults the person from the outside. Traumatic events are external, but they quickly become incorporated into the mind" (Terr). Other clinicians explain how "it is not the trauma itself that does the damage"; rather, it is the manner in which the mind of the individual finds itself without the necessary resources and abilities to navigate the traumatic experience that gives rise to long-term difficulties (Bloom). From these two perspectives, one can surmise that these sudden external events serve as a catalyst for an internal shift, which places the victim under a state of duress for a variable period of time. Furthermore, trauma acts as a "source that marks and defines... individual identity" as much "as racial or cultural identity" (Belaev), though certainly originating from a far more negative experience than one's race or culture. Therefore, one might begin to understand how trauma creates a lasting shift within the individual's psyche, the effects of which will remain a part of that individual's conception and performance of self. Although this is a somewhat cursory view of a very complicated condition, it should provide a basic understanding of what is referred to as "trauma" and the effects it has on the traumatized victim.

In her medical study on trauma, psychiatrist Sarah Bloom notes "we are physiologically designed to function best as an integrated whole... [and] the fragmentation that accompanies traumatic experience degrades this integration and impedes maximum performance." This seems to point towards the significance often placed on the individual's place and need for community—the need on the part of people in a community for unity and integration in their everyday experiences. It is then reasonable to assume that, in a sense, a

---

[2] This section is adapted from an earlier essay I wrote on Spider-Man's origins and trauma theory, "The Loss of the Father: Trauma Theory and the Birth of Spider-Man," found in *Spider-Man, Spider-Women, and Webspinners: Critical Perspectives*, edited by Robert G. Weiner and Robert M. Peaslee (2012). Elsewhere, Weiner offers an interesting discussion on the application of trauma theory and Captain America in his "Sixty Five Years of Guilt Over the Death of Bucky." (*Captain America and the Struggles of the Superhero: Critical Essays*, 2008).

traumatic experience is one that introduces some form of fracture in those affected and causes a displacement from the community. When placing this notion of trauma against an analysis of popular comic-book super-heroes, it's surprising to note how many seem to have elements of trauma incorporated into their various origins and their driving concern to protect their respective communities, as opposed to seeking personal benefit from their powers.

Daredevil: A Response to Trauma

In October 1993, Frank Miller and John Romita Jr.'s *Daredevil: The Man Without Fear* hit comic-book stores, and the first cover image highlighted the traumatic origins of the red-clad super-hero. Painted against a dark background, the reader sees a ghost-like image of Daredevil looking off into the distance, while a young boy kneels in the foreground cradling a battered and bleeding body. The following splash page presents this same boy alone on a fire escape, while the closing panel of the final page ends with a "Blam!" as the Fixer's goons execute the defiant Battling Murdock. Clearly, isolation and tragedy mark Matt Murdock from early in his life, and this point is reinforced in the series from the very first images the reader encounters to the very last panel of the first issue.

Interestingly, Miller makes a stronger point than Lee in his depiction of Jack Murdock's lesson to his son about how to truly become a man. Where Lee dedicates his first issue to establishing Daredevil's roots, Miller allocates six issues – two of which focus almost exclusively on Murdock's years with his father, the murder, and his pursuit of the Fixer and his gang. Within the first issue, Miller reinforces the point Jack makes to Matt. "You've got to be something *special*. You've got to be *nothing* like *me*," the elder Murdock emphasizes. Matt violates his promise to be different, however, when he confronts a schoolyard bully to solve his problems, and his father responds violently to his disobedience by hitting him. While Matt chooses to "study the rules... study the laws," he also finds solace and release at his father's gym spending "endless stolen hours. / At the *bag*...when his *fists* are like *machine gun fire* – drowning out his angry sobs." Ironically, Jack Murdock uses violence to correct his son's use of violence. Instead of reinforcing the desired lesson that Matt should use his brain instead of brawn, Jack drives home the point to his son that force is a viable option to enforce the rules. While Matt respects his father and continues with his studies, eschewing further public confrontation, the traumatic experience of Matt's father hitting him causes him to find a physical outlet in the very place his father would have most wanted him to avoid.

Of course, this painful rejection by his father wasn't the only instance of trauma in young Matt Murdock's life. Soon after this altercation, Matt saves an older gentleman crossing a street who did not see a fast-moving truck barreling down on him. Knocking him out of the way, Matt is covered in radioactive material spilling from the truck, and he begins to encounter other side effects, aside from blindness, as a result of the accident. Although Lee's origin story merely glosses over the introduction of Matt's newfound heightened sense of hearing and physical prowess, Miller uses this as an opportunity to bring Daredevil fully into the mythic tradition with the introduction of the mystery man, Stick. Serving as a mysterious mentor who seems to be grooming Matthew with some role in mind, Stick proceeds to provide Matt with a means of not only coping with the loss of sight, but with discovering he is still a fully functioning person capable of being more than just a member of a community. He can be a protector of the common good: "Quit feeling sorry for yourself. Get up. / If you're *good* enough, I'll make you a *warrior*." While the counselor trope is easily identifiable here, what is less obvious is the role Stick plays in reaching out to the traumatized young man. Matt was literally separated from his sense of belonging through his loss of sight, and to a lesser extent, the lack of masculine validation from his father (in rebuffing his physical response to bullies). Stick helps Matt to move past the trauma of feeling "useless" as he runs the boy through a grueling training regimen that would challenge anyone who had full use of his or her senses. Stick helps Matt feel more like a member of the community, but he also offers Matt the possibility of becoming a warrior like his father and a man in his own right.

At the end of this first issue, the motif of atonement with the father and following in the footsteps of one's parent is reinforced in Battling Jack Murdock's final fight. Although the elder Murdock initially impresses upon the reader that his "fists" have gotten him nowhere in life, he brazenly declares to the Fixer's thug that "I'm thinking *my boy* is *out* there – in the *audience* – and I'm thinking about how I told him *one thing* worth a damn." Yet it wasn't so much the lesson that Jack *told* Matt about not using his fists; instead, it was the lesson he *showed* his son every night he stepped into the ring: "I told him to *never* give up. *Never*. It's time I showed him his dad may be a *loser* – but he's no *quitter*." Romita's artwork reinforces this lesson: the young boy, in the panel directly below the battered old warrior, stares forward intently, as though to better hear what his father is saying to him – and not the hired thug. The fight begins in the bottom double panel, and the last round of Jack's life commences.

The father's brutal death following the fight leaves an empty space for a new warrior to step in and fill. Just as Matt responded to the traumatic loss of his sight and change in his physical abilities through training with Stick, so too does he respond to the traumatic loss of his father. Miller and Romita proceed to lay the groundwork for the way in which Matt Murdock will strike out on his own to hunt down the perpetrators of his father's murder, and then become entangled with the thrill-seeking and dangerous Elektra Natchios. (This is in addition to setting up the future rivalry with the Kingpin.) In each of these instances, Matt seems to demonstrate risk-taking behaviors often associated with victims of trauma, in which "decisions tend to be based on impulse… geared towards action and often the action taken will be violent" (Bloom). Matt engages in dangerous behaviors that certainly appear impulsive. Furthermore, he seems to fit an interesting take on one clinical response to trauma, referred to as "Victim to Victimizer," when he turns the tables on the criminals who killed his father and traumatized him. As Bloom discusses in her study of adolescent responses to trauma: "In an attempt to regain control over their lives, traumatized individuals assume the role of victimizer so they can assert some level of control over their lives and the world around them." In this instance, however, the Daredevil persona emerges as a means of revisiting this trauma on those who traumatized Matt and his family; more importantly, Daredevil provides a means to address the fractures in the community the criminals create. In this light, the super-hero serves as a response to trauma – the fracturing of community – caused by those criminal members of society. The empty space left by Battling Jack Murdock is then filled by the warrior Matt Murdock creates from his traumatic experiences: Daredevil, the Man Without Fear.

Of course, Miller and Romita Jr.'s *Daredevil: The Man Without Fear* isn't the only comic series to deal with Matt Murdock's atonement quest. In 2001 and 2002, Jeph Loeb and Tim Sale teamed up (not for the first time) to create *Daredevil: Yellow* (the first in what would become a series of color-based Marvel origin mini-series). Although Loeb sets each issue up as though Murdock is writing a love letter to his lost love, Karen Page, it is the story of a

The cover to *Daredevil: Yellow* #1 (Aug 2001). Art by Tim Sale. Copyright © Marvel Comics.

son trying to find atonement with his father that drives the narrative. While the letter boxes in the opening pages address Karen directly, the reader sees Daredevil swinging through NYC only to land in front of Battling Murdock's old stomping grounds – Fogwell's Gym. We cannot ignore the conversation Murdock is having with Karen in this "letter," yet it would be at least as negligent to overlook the longing with which he reaches out, with his ungloved hand, to the poster of his father. Although lost love is at the forefront of Matt's mind, there appear to be greater unresolved issues hidden more deeply in his mind regarding "Kid" Murdock[3] that are making their way to the surface.

While Loeb's retelling doesn't drastically differ in its plot from Miller's or Lee's works, he offers a few key differences that reinforce Matt's search for atonement with his father. Aside from cover images, Daredevil doesn't appear in costume in *The Man Without Fear* until the final two pages (in a dramatically rendered double-page spread). Loeb and Sale, however, bring their rendering of Daredevil to the reader right away, but they also share how Matt Murdock created the costume – and by extension, the persona – of Daredevil at the end of the first issue. This is an especially important scene in understanding the importance of atonement for Matt Murdock. Following the acquittal of the Fixer, Matt returns to his father's apartment: "just opening his old footlocker after what had happened was overwhelming. / I found his robe. His boxing shoes. Even his under gloves." The younger Murdock then proceeds to take up his father's boxing garb and fashions a suit he could wear to fight crime: "I sat in his chair and I could almost feel his hand on my shoulder telling me I was going to amount to something special." On one level, Matt is reminiscing about when his father spoke to him in years passed; however, this also works on another level. As he stands dressed in his original yellow-and-red suit, Matt recognizes that "Battling Jack raised [him] to be a fighter, and now it [is] time to step into the ring." Matt recognizes that to find atonement with his father, he will need to become Daredevil, and this certainty leads him to feel as though his father is there in the room guiding him. It's a poignant moment, and while the reader

---

[3] In *Daredevil: Yellow*, Loeb has the Fixer refer to Jack Murdock as "Kid" Murdock (instead of his previous moniker of "Battling" Jack) in mocking reference to his old age (a reference only made in a passing headline in *Daredevil* #1). This serves to emasculate the elder warrior by referring to him as a child who needs his fights fixed. It underscores the theme of heroes moving from childhood to adulthood by becoming warriors capable of defeating their foes through their own abilities.

later discovers it was Karen Paige who inspired Daredevil to dress in red, it was Battling Jack who inspired the young boy to answer the hero's call and become a man.

Loeb and Sale end their retelling of Daredevil's origin story (in the sixth issue) in the same way they opened it. While Daredevil speaks directly to Karen, professing his continued love for her in the final splash page, the artwork itself shows no hint of Karen Page — only the newly renamed "Battling Jack's Gym" as an homage to the fallen warrior who was Daredevil's inspiration. Looking down on the newly renamed gym, Daredevil smiles to himself, thinking, "I finally found a way I could honor my father beyond wearing his colors." He then swings off into the city to fulfill his role as not just warrior but protector. Although the love story embedded in *Daredevil: Yellow* is certainly an important element, far more of that is communicated through text than is shown in the art. The journey of a young man trying to come to terms with the traumatic murder of his father, however, is played out dramatically and powerfully, in both Loeb's writing and in Sale's rendering of the story, as the story follows Matt Murdock's journey to becoming a hero grounded in tragedy, as well as to physical and emotional strength.

Conclusion

Myths attempt to explain the various facets of the human experience. Western mythology's use of the atonement motif provides a means for writers and mythmakers to discuss the trauma many readers experience in their initiation into adulthood, particularly as they relate to the relationship between male heroes, their fathers, and their growing sense of masculinity and self. Daredevil serves as an example of positive masculinity and manhood through his journey to become a hero and, by extension, an adult — as well as through his attempt to seek atonement with his father and rise above the traumatic experience of Battling Jack's murder. He relies upon his other senses and newfound enhancements to achieve this sense of fulfillment, and rises above the trauma of his loss of sight as well. While readers may not be exposed to a radioactive isotope and find themselves imbued with powers like Matt Murdock, they too can use their gifts and abilities to find atonement with their elders and become successful, heroic adult members of the community. Although Daredevil might not be one of the most well-known super-heroes, his story contributes to the modern myths found in American comics in a meaningful and relatable fashion that makes him worthy of our consideration.

Works Cited

Balaev, Michele. "Trends in Literary Trauma Theory." *Mosiac* 41.2 (2008): 148-167. *Academic OneFile*. Web. 23 June 2010. Online.

Bloom, Sandra L., M.D. *Trauma Theory Abbreviated.* Philadelphia: CommunityWorks, 1999. PDF file.

Campbell, Joseph. *The Hero of a Thousand Faces.* Princeton: Princeton UP, 1973. Print.

Campbell, Joseph and Bill Moyers. *The Power of Myth.* New York: Doubleday, 1988. Print.

Felluga, Dino. "Modules on Freud: On Repression." Introductory Guide to Critical Theory.31 Jan. 2011. Purdue U. 6 Dec. 2011. <http://www.purdue.edu/guidetotheory/psychoanalysis/freud3.html>. Online.

Helvie, Forrest. "The Loss of the Father: Trauma Theory and the Birth of Spider-Man." *Spider-Man, Spider-Women, and Webspinners: Critical Perspectives.* Eds. Robert G. Weiner and Robert M. Peaslee. Jefferson: McFarland, 2012. Print.

Lee, Stan, Bill Everett, and Joe Orlando. *Marvel Masterworks: Daredevil vol. 1.* First Printing. New York: Marvel, 2010. Print.

Loeb, Jeph and Tim Sale. *Daredevil: Yellow.* First Printing. New York: Marvel, 2002. Print.

Miller, Frank and John Romita Sr. *Daredevil: The Man Without Fear.* Second Edition, First Printing. New York, Marvel: 2010. Print.

Terr, Lenore. *Too Scared to Cry: Psychic Trauma in Childhood.* New York: Harper, 1990. Print.

There Will be Blood: Daredevil's Violent Tendencies

by Henry Northmore

Blood drips from the walls, mutilated bodies are scattered around the church. Six nuns lie dead and the corpses of several vagrants lie scattered amongst the pews, their cadavers skewered with seemingly innocuous objects: a serving tray cleaving a head in two, a fork to the brain, impaling by a walking stick. At the altar, a young woman lies in a pool of gore. Her name is Karen Page. This is what happens when you mess with Bullseye (*Daredevil* Vol. 2 #5, Mar 1999).

This grisly tableau could have been ripped directly from EC's *Vault of Horror*, not a mainstream super-hero title, but over the years a rogues gallery of mass murderers, serial killers, and psychopaths have stained the pages of *Daredevil* with blood. Broken, battered, bruised, driven to the edge of sanity, with a string of dead lovers and acquaintances, Matthew Murdock has faced some of the most vicious villains in the history of comics. And he hasn't come out the other side unscathed.

A History of Violence

Daredevil's dark origins are steeped in violence. Growing up in Hell's Kitchen, he was persistently bullied by local kids, even taking on the name

"Daredevil" from their sarcastic sneers. His principal role model, father Battlin' Jack Murdock, was a brawler (a boxer and a gangland enforcer) who was killed for refusing to throw a fight. This is often retold as a noble stand against corruption, but ultimately all this macho posturing achieved was leaving his son an orphan. This is the environment where a young Matt Murdock spent his formative years, a world bristling with testosterone where fighting was normalized.

As Frank Miller states in his introduction to *The Man Without Fear* (1993):

> It's a wonder he isn't a villain. He's got every excuse. Born to poverty. A broken family. A childhood spent in a squalid slum. Hounded and taunted and beaten by schoolyard bullies. To top it all off he gets struck in the eyes by toxic waste and blinded for life. Blinded, bullied, impoverished. Surrounded by calamity.

Matt bottles up his emotions; when he does give into impulses, he's heavily chastized (we know his father hits him on at least one occasion). Therefore, he represses his anger, locking it down deep inside, ignoring his problems and letting them fester. It's no wonder they eventually boil over as an adult. Even before he becomes Daredevil, Matt seems addicted to danger. He always wanted to fight back, training in secret against his father's wishes, and throwing himself across the nighttime rooftops of New York City. His affair with Elektra Natchios at Harvard is a mix of terrifying risks and adrenaline-fuelled passion that ends the first time he ever wears a mask in a botched attempt to rescue Elektra and her father from terrorists. He wants to be the hero, yet the situation only yields a dead father and a fatally wounded love (*Daredevil* #168, Jan 1981).

Death (the murder of his father) and vengeance are his main motives for donning the costume. When Matt seeks his revenge, in his first ever public appearance as Daredevil (in issue #1), the Fixer dies. Chased down by a stranger dressed as the Devil, he suffers a fatal heart attack, much to Murdock's chagrin: "I remember thinking 'don't fall down before I get to hit you,'" he recounts (in *Daredevil: Yellow* #2, Sept 2001). He wanted that moment of physical reckoning. This isn't about retribution, this is retaliation. Daredevil's actions, from the very beginning, come from a dark place.

Logically, this should be the end of it all; with his father's killers brought to justice, he should hang up his billy club. But Matt can't resist the lure of locking horns with the underworld. He may have promised his father he'd use brains over brawn, but unfortunately it has proven almost impossible for Murdock to break the cycle of violence, exploiting a fairly flimsy loophole to get round this vow: "I'll see to it that Matt Murdock never *does* resort to force... but somebody *else* will[...] / whenever I don this costume, I'll no longer *be* Matt Murdock" (*Daredevil* #1, Apr 1964). These are not the actions of a well-balanced individual.

Pulp Fiction

Like most characters from the '60s, Daredevil's crime fighting career started off innocently enough through confrontations with the likes of Stilt-Man and a rag-tag band of animal-themed super-villains. All long-running comic titles are part of a collective writing process; this can lead to schizophrenic and contradictory storytelling. Therefore, a definitive history of any character is almost impossible to determine, and so most heroes that have stood the test of time have a defining era that sets the tone for the rest of their shelf life.

Frank Miller's influence on the series cannot be overlooked. Throughout his run, one sees a young artist and writer honing his skills, taking chances, taking *Daredevil* into far more graphic territory, and firmly establishing him as a "street-level" hero and *Daredevil* as an adult-orientated title.

As he told comicdom.com in 2006:
> I never planned to draw super-heroes. My favorite genre has always been crime fiction. So there I was, bugging New York publishers with a very young version of what would become *Sin City* many years later – and there the editors were, explaining that all they published were guys in tights. It was adapt or die time, so I adapted. With *Daredevil* I found the perfect vehicle... I was able to do my kind of crime comics. I followed the example of Will Eisner's *The Spirit*. He gave his hero a mask to keep the publisher happy. Me, I had a blind guy in red tights.[1]

The consequence of this new style was less fantastical villains than those faced by the likes of the Fantastic Four, the Avengers, or the X-Men. Out went the spangly costumes and in came thugs, criminals, and ninja. It's this key moment, when *Daredevil* became a crime comic rather than a super-hero adventure, that imbued the title with a more violent sensibility.

Daredevil suits this type of story; his super-powers are more grounded in our world and nowhere near as formidable as many of his contemporaries. They give him an edge without turning him into an all-conquering superman.

---

[1] archive.comicdom.gr/interviews.php?id=17&lang=en

For too long, super-hero comics were aimed at a family audience; they were being left behind by the other contemporary arts. Miller treated his audience as adults; his run on *Daredevil* helped the entire medium find a more mature voice (though he certainly wasn't the only creator walking this path). It was one of the steps in repositioning comics as an artform that could be taken seriously. It was a different approach that had more in common with novelists like James Ellroy or a filmmaker like Martin Scorsese.

Subsequent writers have often felt the need to follow Miller's lead and up the ante to continue the shock factor. As in movies, the sequel has to be nastier and bloodier. To quote Randy (Jamie Kennedy) from *Scream 2* (1997): "There are certain rules that one must abide by in order to create a successful sequel. Number one: the body count is always bigger. Number two: the death scenes are always much more elaborate – more blood, more gore – carnage candy."

Following Miller was a thankless task, yet this gritty edge eventually attracted some of the best writers in comics. However, it wasn't until the relaunch in 1998, with indie filmmaker Kevin Smith on writing duties, that the series really felt like it was fully back on track. Now enjoying the freedom of Marvel's more "adult" Marvel Knights imprint, the violence didn't take long to flow back onto the pages. This was soon followed by Brian Michael Bendis's justly acclaimed four-year tenure with artist Alex Maleev, who gave way to writer Ed Brubaker in 2006. These were writers who built on Miller's groundwork, taking the story in their own direction while staying true to the book's established mood, tackling real-world issues filtered through the Marvel Universe.

This more realistic take on super-heroes embraced the idea that if you use violence you must expect it in return. When you fight crime, crime fights back, and in the real world that will involve guns, bullets, beatings, and death.

Twins of Evil

There are two villains who have become Daredevil's main adversaries: the Kingpin and Bullseye. Their history has become so interwoven with Matt Murdock's that they are almost inseparable; apart from Foggy and Black Widow, they are the two longest relationships in Matt's life.

Since Frank Miller brought Wilson Fisk back to New York in 1981, the Kingpin has become Daredevil's primary antagonist. A cold and calculating genius housed in the body of a man-mountain, he's the perfect example of the kind of enemy Daredevil faced under Miller's new regime. This is organized crime, extortion, murder, drugs, gambling, prostitution, and not sci-fi theatrics or trips to the Savage Land.

It's easy to argue that Fisk is the instigator in this ongoing war – you break the law and you must expect the punishment due. Although published in 1993 in our timeline, Daredevil's first encounter with Fisk involves the Kingpin's child trafficking (a truly reprehensible crime) in *The Man Without Fear* (1993). To deal with despicable acts of this magnitude, Matt creates an alter ego who can side-step the judicial system. Once he pulls on his mask, due process goes out the window; he's judge and jury. The Kingpin would be appalled to learn that he helped create Daredevil.

There have been physical confrontations, but the Kingpin usually plots Daredevil's downfall from afar, always lurking in the background, an ever-present threat, hiring a string of hitmen and assassins (from Typhoid Mary and Elektra to Bullseye and the Twin Killers). Fisk doesn't care who gets hurt as long as he gets what he wants. As Daredevil so succinctly puts it: "*Wilson Fisk* is simply the single most *evil* and *dangerous* man I've ever *known*" (*Daredevil* #297, Oct 1991). By branding him in this way, Matt positions Fisk as almost inhuman. Therefore, he can be treated as such, almost absolving Matt of any guilt for his later actions.

The events in "Born Again" (*Daredevil* #227-233, Feb-Aug 1986) show a particularly sadistic streak as Fisk proceeds to take apart Matt Murdock's life piece by piece, destroying his business, his reputation, and finally arranging his murder. Obviously, Matt survives, so Fisk sends in a U.S. Army experiment, Nuke, to finish the job. It's wanton wholesale destruction; Nuke is happy to unload his arsenal of weapons on the inhabitants of Hell's Kitchen, setting the streets ablaze and mowing down men, women, and children in a hail of bullets. Dozens of innocent bystanders are killed in the crossfire, but it's hard to blame Nuke for his actions; he's a frazzled Vietnam vet who blindly follows orders. However, the Kingpin only employs such drastic methods because he is afraid: "The *Kingpin* of *crime* will *aim* this Nuke at the man he is learning to *hate*. / The man he is learning to *fear*" (*Daredevil* #232, July 1986). Despite the torture he's been put through, Daredevil seems unstoppable. It's a fear born out of Fisk's own arrogance; he's so used to his machinations going to plan that he's instantly thrown when Matt's body goes missing. His fears are fuelled by paranoia, but his reaction and its consequences are very real.

Under Miller's guidance, they seem perfectly matched. The Kingpin introduced a more serious level of crime and violence to Daredevil's world, but Murdock was perfectly adept to deal with it. Matt is happy to respond in kind. "Last Rites" (#297-300, Oct 1991 - Jan 1992) is very much a reversal of the events in "Born Again," as Murdock coldly dismantles Fisk's empire. To an impartial observer, these events are just as cruel; it's reciprocal retaliation. Changing the victim doesn't change the nature of the act itself. A "hero" can be just as vindictive and malicious as a "villain." Fisk deserves punishment, but here Murdock recognizes the effectiveness of the Kingpin's callous tactics and employs them to fulfill his own objectives. It's not often a hero will stoop to his opposite's low, going so far as to even copycat him, and it's a sure sign the good man within is bending, if not outright breaking.

While the Kingpin is the puppet master, it was usually Bullseye who got down and dirty, as the man who inflicted the real damage. Created by Marv Wolfman, Bullseye kills a man with a pen straight through the jugular within five panels of his first-ever appearance in *Daredevil* #131 (Mar 1976). The only reason he's an assassin is because it's an easy way to make a buck from his homicidal impulses. It's almost impossible to calculate how much blood there is on Bullseye's hands. There is a confession to 360 "cold blooded murders," but he's killed many, many more since *Elektra Lives Again* was first published in 1990. While much of the mini-series *Bullseye's Greatest Hits* (2004) is revealed to be an elaborate fabrication, there are still hints of his real past, and the hatred of his father is set up as a major motivation for his future actions (diametrically opposed to Murdock's devotion to his father). Great arch-nemeses must fit their hero, and Bullseye is the other side of violence – both in what he's received and what he expresses. He revels in violence, whereas Matt still seems repentant about it all. Bullseye is Matt unleashed.

Through the years, Daredevil and Bullseye have forged a strange bond. Bizarrely, despite their battles, Matt has saved Bullseye's life. After beating him unconscious, he pulls Bullseye's body from the path of an oncoming train (*Daredevil* #169, Mar 1981). Murdock is left conflicted by this act of compassion: "I wanted to hear your bones splinter beneath its wheels. I wanted to hear you scream – and die" (*Daredevil* #172, July 1981). But at this point, he has the strength to resist giving in to his base desires.

There are two pivotal events in their relationship. Firstly, the murder of Elektra. This is a nasty close-quarters kill, as Bullseye thrusts Elektra's own sai through her heart (*Daredevil* #181, Apr 1982). Bullseye takes glee in her death partly because he knows how much it will hurt Daredevil; unsurprisingly, the loss hits Matt hard. Driven by anger when they fight, he purposefully lets Bullseye fall to his apparent death (although it only leaves Bullseye crippled). This is when the cracks really start to appear in Matt's psyche; he's so consumed with rage, he forgets his own self-imposed limits.

Predictably, he can't help but confront his paralyzed opponent. DD's game of Russian roulette with Bullseye (in *Daredevil* #191, Feb 1983) is a defining moment in their relationship:

> What am I giving people by running around in tights and punching crooks? What am I *showing* them? / Am I showing them that *good wins out*, that *crime does not pay*, that *the cavalry is always on its way* – / – or am I showing them that any idiot with fists for brains can get his way if he's fast enough and strong enough and *mean* enough? / Am I fighting violence – or *teaching* it?

This impassioned monologue has the tone of a confession and proves how self-aware Murdock is of his role in his own downfall. Dressing up as a demon and beating the tar out of criminals is going to have repercussions. In the case of Bullseye, Matt has to accept some responsibility in molding him into the perfect enemy:

> How many times have I [Bullseye] scrambled to the top of the heap, just to have you bring me down... and send me back to this stinking cell... / I hate you. / You've hurt me. You've ruined my reputation. But that's not the worst of it. Now nearly[...] one thought sits in my gut, and burns, and burns... / you saved my life. (*Daredevil* #181, Apr 1982)

Daredevil has inflicted more physical abuse on Bullseye than the other way around, besting him in nearly every encounter – thus, the villain's anger grows and grows.

The second key moment in the two's relationship is the murder of Karen Page. And Bullseye's weapon of choice? Daredevil's very own billy club, making it all the more personal. This event has repercussions for the rest of Murdock's life. He never really recovers, even contemplating suicide directly after her death (*Daredevil* #6, Apr 1999). Two lovers, both killed by the same man, is a terrible burden for any hero to bear. As Foggy points out:

> The only two women in your life that you ever gave a damn about – / – died violently at the hands of the same man. / When it comes down to it, this life you've chosen brings you nothing but a vicious cycle of pain[...] You

created it[...] It starts[...] every time you put on that costume. (*Daredevil* Vol. 2 #34, Aug 2002)

By choosing the life of a costumed vigilante, Murdock accepts a life of violence, but he also makes the same choice for everyone he knows. He unwittingly invites them into a world inhabited by violent thugs, butchers, and immoral felons. If Daredevil and Bullseye weren't locked in this constant struggle for supremacy, Elektra and Karen Page would not have died. Death is now a part of Matt's life, and he can't help but act accordingly. It's impossible for him to view his adversaries in the same way again. He knows what they are capable of, so he reacts faster and stamps down harder.

Murdock has tasted the bitterness of grief; this constant exposure to violence has chipped away at his humanity. It has affected his moral compass and intensified Daredevil's own use of force. Kevin Smith and Glenn Fabry's *Daredevil / Bullseye: The Target* #1 (Nov 2002) directly deals with Daredevil's anguish, his scream of pain as he fights the urge to dish out greater punishments on his foes:

> It's been three years since she was murdered and I still haven't fully recovered[...] Anyone who crosses my path that night... / Finds themselves at the receiving end of my grief... / And that grief is fully realized... / As violence. / They get a small taste of the beating I've been rehearsing for three years[...] The physical manifestation of the hatred I've been nursing... / Just for him. He calls himself Bullseye. / I call him the Antichrist.

Not only has Bullseye killed two of the most important people in Matt's life, he has changed the hero irrevocably, dragging Matt down to his own level.

The Descent

Kingpin and Bullseye have had a massive impact on Daredevil's life, and their malevolent deeds have changed the landscape, increasing the levels of violence on both sides of the equation. Other villains had to up their game to compete. When they reappear, they are radically different from their original incarnation – nastier, meaner, and more cruel.

Jeph Loeb's *Daredevil: Yellow* (2002) is a masterful retelling of the first four issues of *Daredevil*. It's a new take on his first encounters with Electro, the Owl, and the Purple Man that hits all the same notes but from an updated perspective. Matt even reminisces about the old times, acknowledging how high the stakes have been raised: "Villains would talk a lot back then. / They didn't leave innocent women in a pool of blood[...] The ones in costumes never used to kill anybody" (*Daredevil: Yellow* #4, Nov 2001).

The world is changing, and Daredevil has to race to keep up. The Owl has morphed from a pompous corrupt businessman (in his first appearance) into a vile vindictive killer who'll (in Brubaker's hands) happily beat a guard to a bloody pulp in a messy prison break (*Daredevil* Vol. 2 #118, June 2009). Mr. Fear starts as a slightly spooky villain but unleashes a wave of senseless slaughter across New York during "Hell to Pay" (*Daredevil* Vol. 2 #95-105, May 2007 - Apr 2008), including a particularly nasty massacre in Chinatown, turning both Gladiator and Matt's wife, Milla Donovan, insane in the process. Even a bit player like Leap Frog is recast as an abusive father in "Wake Up" (*Daredevil* Vol. 2 #16-19, May-Aug 2001), and the seemingly innocuous Mysterio becomes a deadly rival in "Guardian Devil" (*Daredevil* Vol. 2 #1-8, Nov 1998 - Jun 1999). This is no longer costumed swashbucklers exchanging pithy dialogue; chivalry is dead. Matt needs to alter his methodology to counter the increased threat these villains pose, but he also uses this as justification for releasing his own wrath. Both sides are guilty in this power struggle, creating an unwinnable arms race where both sides lose.

It certainly hasn't been a one-way street. Matt often goes beyond what most heroes would consider acceptable. Daredevil used to question suspects, whereas now he regularly dishes out beatings and even resorts to torture to get information. How many times has Josie's Bar been trashed for a lead? In recent years, he's become ever more unpredictable. His contact with "normal" society dwindling, he's spent so long surrounded by lowlifes that the ugliness has started to rub off. Once he could control his cravings to lash out, but now he joins in the mayhem. Bullseye was left disfigured after their savage clash in Vol. 2 #49 (Sep 2003), with Murdock carving a target symbol into his forehead, screaming into his face, "You serve no purpose in this world!! [...] You mean *nothing*!!" Matt's reaction is so extreme, due to Bullseye threatening Milla, that he cannot cope with the prospect of losing a third woman to the same man, and what he discovers is that this violent reaction works. It gets results. This is another step in our hero being dragged down, and it's followed by many further launches down that slippery slope between vigilante hero and recklessly violent danger. Matt severed the nerves in the Owl's arms and legs, leaving him paralyzed (Vol. 1 #500, Oct 2009); while the Kingpin has been ruined several times, including being very publicly beaten and ridiculed in the climatic fight of Vol. 2 #50 (Oct 2003), with Matt even taking on the mantle of the Kingpin at the end.

Daredevil tortures. From *Daredevil* Vol. 2 #104 (Mar 2008). Art by Michael Lark, Paul Azaceta, and Stefano Gaudiano. Copyright © Marvel Comics.

This is a double-edged sword: it removes Fisk but it creates a power vacuum. In many ways, Daredevil takes on the role of "the criminal." If he stood back and examined his actions, he'd be shocked to see how similar they are to Fisk's. Ben Urich refers to "six straight weeks of terror and violence against the underworld" in *Daredevil* Vol. 2 #56 (Mar 2004) as Daredevil establishes his rule. The targets may be different, but Murdock's methodology is almost identical. His relationship to violence has changed: once it was entirely negative, and now it's becoming positive. His initial motivation to become Daredevil was to put a stop to violence in society; now, he sees it as the most direct solution to his problems. It's rapidly becoming his default setting.

In *Dark Reign: The List – Daredevil* (Sept 2009), Bullseye detonates a bomb that kills 107 tenants in one split second. He doesn't even break a sweat. It's one of the worst atrocities Matt has witnessed. His world has literally started to crumble, and his fragile psyche soon follows suit. Ever since he saved Bullseye's life, Murdock has felt a level of responsibility for the villain's future actions, and this is the final straw.

This pain builds as he takes over leadership of the Hand. The Matt Murdock of 1964 would never sink to such depths. He sets up a totalitarian state policed by his own clan of ninja (*Shadowland* #1-5, Sep 2010 - Jan 2011). He was once part of the pantheon of heroes New Yorkers in the Marvel Universe came to accept as part of life. They used to cheer him on, and now they live in fear.

In *Shadowland* #1, the games comes to an end when Daredevil kills Bullseye (a scene that closely echoes Elektra's death at the hands of Bullseye). Here, Matt steps over a line he promised never to cross, as he finally takes a life. Surely the Hand wouldn't have sought him out as their leader if they didn't know he was capable of such an act, but he wouldn't have been weak enough to be possessed by Snakeroot if his soul hadn't been so damaged over the years.

At its core, *Shadowland* is the story of how good can be corrupted and turned to evil. Daredevil is the perfect candidate. He's already broken so many moral boundaries by this point that all he needs is a push. The power the Hand offers is the final temptation; worn down by the cumulative effect of all the sorrow he's endured, Matt all too willingly embraces it. By the end of *Shadowland*, he's almost indistinguishable from the villains he fights. He's a murderer and a tyrant. He's lost sight of everything that once made him a hero. He's betrayed his ideals, friends, and even the people he swore to protect. He now strikes preemptively, directly causing violence rather than reacting to it. While vigilante heroes break the law every day, they have to live by their own rigid self-imposed rules in an effort to differentiate themselves from the villains they encounter. Matt breaks the one rule that has kept him sane ("thou shalt not kill") and finds himself lost as a result. In the end, it's not the other heroes who rise up to oppose him (including Spider-Man, Luke Cage, Iron Fist, Wolverine, even the Punisher) who defeat him, so much as the sudden realization of what he has become.

Conclusion

It's impossible to ignore the fact Daredevil has violent tendencies. At the root of it all, the Fixer threw the first punch. He started the battle that has continued ever since. Matt was a coiled spring waiting to explode until the Fixer gave him the focus to direct his aggression. Fortunately, his father, while deeply flawed, instilled a strong sense of right and wrong in the young Matt Murdock, and fighting crime became the perfect excuse to let go and give in to this inner rage. To quote Miller from *The Man Without Fear* again: "There's something strong inside him, passed from unknown mother and doomed father to son. Something tested by tragedy. Tempered by conscience. Honed by discipline. Something that holds the bloodthirsty beast within and forces it to serve the cause of justice." He can't kill the monster within but he can harness it, give it a purpose, and turn it into a tool to serve his own agenda.

The simple act of setting himself up as protector of Hell's Kitchen invites conflict. Criminals didn't need to resort to such measures until the likes of Daredevil started patrolling the streets. Being prepared to use extreme violence became a prerequisite to be a crook in NYC. Part of the reason Daredevil is so quick to resort to violence is because he is only equipped to deal with villains he can defeat with quick fists and martial arts. It's the only resource he has to fall back on. It offers a stark contrast to his day job, which relies on brains and a strict adherence to the law; it's as if he has compartmentalized aspects of his personality (the caring attorney / the violent vigilante) as a coping mechanism. As time has passed, Daredevil has sunk deeper and deeper into a world ruled by aggression, until it's the only response he understands.

This hardline stance means only the most brutal villains in the Marvel Universe risk facing Daredevil, and that is exactly what makes the title so readable. You know the characters are in real danger. This adds an edge and gives writers the chance to explore powerful emotions (anger, guilt, grief, etc.). Matt *is* a hero, and the fact that he contends with his own internal struggles on a daily basis just makes him all the more heroic.

Science Fact!

by *Stéphane Guéret, Marie-Laure Saulnier, Manuella Hyvard, and Nicolas Labarre*

Ostensibly, Daredevil is a "realistic" super-hero. He's no god, he cannot fly, and he cannot shoot rays with his eyes, nor is he invulnerable or able to teleport. Mostly, he's a super-hero in the Batman mold: highly trained, driven by vengeance, and using fear as his main weapon. Even his super-human abilities were conceived as balancing a serious handicap, his blindness. However, realism is a word that takes on a singular meaning, in the context of a super-hero narrative: Daredevil may be easier to accept than Spider-Man or most of the X-Men, but does that mean his abilities are plausible? How would he fare if the laws of physics applied to him?

Child of the Atom

Daredevil's origin has not changed much since *Daredevil* #1 (Apr 1964). After being exposed to radioactive material when hit by a truck carrying a dangerous load unsafely across New York City, young Matt Murdock becomes blind but witnesses a notable increase in the efficiency of his other senses, even thinking to himself in a manner indicatively expositional of the time: "*Everything* seems easy for me now! All my senses are razor sharp!" Daredevil is thus another child of radiation, the default origin story for Marvel heroes of the Sixties.

The main flaw with that story, of course, is that radiation is unlikely to give anyone superpowers. Radiation had been known by scientists to cause genetic mutations since the late Twenties,[1] but the popular image of the radioactive mutant has little basis. Radiation cannot generate mutations that would not occur naturally, and even more problematically, they only affect the *descendants* of the exposed individuals. The more likely outcome of exposure to radiation is cancer, or in cases of direct and severe exposure, "acute radiation syndrome,"[2] with dramatic, spectacular, and ultimately deadly effects. After the creation of a regulatory body, the Federal Radiation Council, in 1959, and after Congressional enquiries on the subject in 1960, information about these adverse effects was widely available, and what may have been a sustainable explanation for the powers of Marvel's earlier heroes was therefore a lot less convincing in 1964. Is it plausible that a regular truck would carry radioactive material with no safety device in New York in 1964, even leaving aside the idea that this material may be contained in easily opened cylinders? Depending on the type of material, it is not entirely unimaginable. Among the three types of radiations, alpha radiation can cause mutations or cancer in cases of direct contact, yet this type of radiation can be stopped by even a single sheet of paper.

The implausibility of this origin story should not be overemphasized, however, since radioactivity is not what *Daredevil* is about. Its presence in the narrative reads like an afterthought; were it not for a panel on the truck and three mentions in speech balloons later on, it would be utterly absent from his origin story. As early as the first issue, Daredevil finds himself in a criminal, urban setting, which has remained the default environment and mood for the

---

[1] Hermann Joseph Mueller, an American geneticist, published the first article on the subject, "The Problem of Genetic Modification," in 1927, in which he detailed his work on the effects of X-rays on the genome. He received the Nobel Prize for his work in 1946.

[2] Acute Radiation Syndrome, also known as radiation sickness, occurs after a severe irradiation of the bone marrow, the gastrointestinal tract, or the brain. It rapidly causes nausea, vomiting, and then, depending on the level of irradiation and on the affected parts of the body, it may become lethal in a few hours to a few weeks. A. C. Upton, John M. Last. "Radiation, ionizing". *The Oxford Companion to Medicine*. Stephen Lock, John M. Last, and George Dunea. Oxford University Press, 2001. Oxford Reference Online.
www.oxfordreference.com/views/ENTRY.html?subview=Main&entry=t185.e419

character. Radioactivity works as a simple excuse, an added thrill rather than a thematic component.

"This is DD's Greatest Secret"

Among the things that radioactivity did not alter is Murdock's physical strength. In stories such as *Daredevil: The Man Without Fear* (1994), writers have consistently emphasized rigorous training as the source of Daredevil's impressive feats, although Miller himself noted that he appears "nearly super-human" (*Daredevil* #167, Nov 1980). To consider the physical feats Murdock has been shown to master with ease through a prism of pragmatic consideration and applied mathematics, we can scientifically discuss how realistic, and thus exactly how amazing, his body and its abilities are.

In *Daredevil* Vol. 2 #86 (Aug 2006), in the climactic conclusion to the storyline during which Murdock is imprisoned on Rykers island, Daredevil is restored, morally and physically, through a show of strength and skills. Michael Lark's realistic and photo-referenced environments allow us to evaluate just how extraordinary these strengths and skills are. At one point, Daredevil jumps from the prison floor to catch a guardrail, four meters above him, without a run-up. Since the measurement of one's vertical high jump is routinely used to evaluate athletes, points of comparison abound. If we subtract Daredevil's size (1.83 meter) plus the length of his arm from our four-meter estimate, he needs to accomplish a vertical jump of roughly 1.64 meters in order to catch the rail above him. The average person has a vertical high jump of about 0.5 meters,[3] but the height of the jump is proportional to the expanded energy, which makes substantial improvements possible. Trained athletes can go three times as high as regular people, and the world record, held by basketball player Kadour Ziani, stands at 1.52 meters. This is close to the figure we inferred from that issue, and specific training combined with an exceptional physiology could explain that 8% difference. Since Murdock is shown displaying exceptional predispositions (he blows a punching bag off its hook before his accident in issue #1) in all the versions of Daredevil's origin stories, to accomplish this jump may be an extraordinary feat, but it can hardly be described as super-strength. All of Daredevil's powers are on display in this issue (including super-human

---

[3] See David D. Patterson and D. Fred Peterson, "Vertical Jump and Leg Power Norms for Young Adults," in *Measurement in Physical Education and Exercise Science* 8(1), 2004, pages 33-41.

stamina), as he resurrects his super-heroic persona, but his strength is still depicted as falling within conceivably human parameters.

The same sense of measure does not apply to all of Daredevil's acrobatics, however. His journey over city rooftops typically involves spectacular jumps and catches, but we rarely get to gauge exactly how impressive they are. In *Daredevil* #7 (Apr 1965), however, the man without fear lets go from a plane flying over the city and breaks his fall by catching the horizontal bar of a traffic light. The plane is an unusual feature, but it appears to fly as high as a six-story building; a very similar fall, from a comparable height, is pictured by Frank Miller 17 years later, in issue #178 (Jan 1982). How likely is Murdock, in either of these cases, to fall without dislocating his shoulders or spraining his wrists?

Six floors mean around 18 meters, and the traffic light must be around six meters high, so as not to hamper the passage of tall vehicles. This is thus about a 12-meter fall, and we can safely ignore air friction, thanks to Daredevil's aerodynamic position. Daredevil's vertical speed when he catches the bar is thus about 15.5 meters per second.[4] However, after his first half-revolution around the bar, his vertical speed reaches 0 m/s, since he is no longer moving downward. To reduce his speed this much, he must first have pushed on the bar, when he was above it, and then have pulled on it, while under it.

It takes approximately 0.26 seconds for his center of gravity to complete the semi-circular movement around the bar and for the deceleration to be over. Daredevil's body, muscles, bones, and sinews have to furnish the force necessary to absorb this speed, 5000 N[5]. The first part of the effort is tantamount to lifting 500 kilograms, while the second part is equivalent to holding the same weight at arm's length. This is enormous: professional weight lifters, depending on the sport and the category, lift weights between 200 and 265 kg. Although the bench press record stands at 500 kg, it seems too far from Daredevil's acrobatics – in the athlete's postures, as well as in their morphology – for the comparison to be relevant.

The lack of emphasis put on Daredevil's agility, which he shares with other non-super-powered characters such as the Black Widow, makes it easy to forget that much of what he accomplishes relies not only on speed and coordination

---

[4] Newton's laws provide us with a relationship between the height of the fall (h) and its vertical speed (v): $v = \sqrt{2gh}$ where $g \approx 10 m/s^2$.

[5] Newton's second law ($F = m \times \Delta v / \Delta t$) allows to us estimate this force at $F = 83 \times (15.5-0)/0.26 \approx 5000$ N.

Daredevil performs acrobatic feats which ought to be impossible. From *Daredevil* #7 (Apr 1965). Art by Wally Wood. Copyright © Marvel Comics.

but also on superlative physical strength. Thus unbeknownst to all, Daredevil must have received super-strength from his exposure to radiations, though perhaps it is only available to him when moving through the city.

"I Can Hear Them Two Floors Away"

Without his sight, Daredevil becomes blessed with hyper-acuity in his other remaining senses. Considering the personal nature of many of these senses, some are easier to run through the scientific grinder than others.

Of the side effects that were supposedly induced by radiation, the improvements in the way Daredevil smells and tastes can hardly be tested, since they rarely, if ever, feature in the narrative. The principle in both cases is clear, implying a multiplication and an improvement of the dedicated receivers. Expertise and focus significantly improve one's capacity to discern subtle variations in taste and smell, as any oenologist will demonstrate. It appears therefore non-problematic for Daredevil to display super-human uses of these two senses, as long as it remains impossible to quantify.

Touch, however, is used more often and is integral to the character. In most cases it functions as a useful narrative shortcut that gives Daredevil access to printed matters, since he is able to read the content of a printed page by running his fingers over it: "His super-sensitive fingers could 'read' ordinary print if he wished, merely by feeling the impression of the *ink* on the page!" (issue #4, Oct 1964). Blind people generally see the efficiency of their other senses improve, simply because these senses then receive more attention. This could account for an increase in the sensitivity of Daredevil's fingertips, but it would not be sufficient to read a newspaper article. An increase in the number of appropriate receptors may bridge the gap from braille to regular print, to the point where even the tiny volume of ink dots on paper may be detectable. Additionally, trained readers can usually reconstruct the meaning of a text through very incomplete information: the top half of the characters will usually suffice; vowels can often be inferred, etc. The ability can therefore be explained by a combination of specific physiological aptitudes and by Daredevil's oft mentioned capacity to process information.

This does not account, however, for Daredevil's ability to perceive colors by touch. It would be a marginally extravagant use of the character's powers if it were not mentioned to explain how he conceived his costumes: "Each colored fabric has a different *feel* to me!", remarks young Murdock in the first issue. A possible explanation was given nearly 10 years later (in issue #106, Dec 1973) and used a couple of times afterwards: Daredevil is able to sense minute differences in the heat absorbed by different types of materials. There is a scientific basis for this claim, as objects placed in the light will become hotter at a different rate depending on their color: dark objects rise in temperature faster than light ones. However, while this would allow Daredevil to distinguish between different tones, different colors may absorb heat at the same rate, making it impossible to distinguish between them. Thus, he may sense the difference between dark and light material to a certain extent (Differences in heat are minute, so this would not work in the dark. Different materials conduce heat differently which makes comparisons even more complex.) but would still be color-blind. This also implies that any text printed on a colored background would probably be illegible to Murdock, since he would not be able to distinguish between the various types of inkblots, such as what is seen with offset printing and similar techniques.

However, of all his super-human senses, Daredevil's heightened hearing is unquestionably the most defining feature of the character. When Mark Waid and Marcos Martin reintroduced him in "Here Comes Daredevil" (the back-up story to *Daredevil* Vol. 3 #1, Sept 2011), it is through the pairing of blindness ("Sometimes, in my dreams... / ...just sometimes... / ...I can see") and super-hearing. In the opening scene, Murdock is disturbed by the sound of Foggy Nelson eating crisps a corridor away, represented in gigantic letters. Super-hearing is easily imagined: there are a variety of sounds the normal human ear will not discern because they are pitched too low, too deep, or because they are too weak. These limitations are interconnected, since at the extremes of the hearing spectrum (sound deeper or higher than the human voice, basically), a sound has to be louder to be heard by a normal human being. In the scene from "Here Comes Daredevil," volume is an issue but frequency is not: normal ears tend to perceive the sound of crisps.

If we estimate this sound to be at a level comprised between a normal conversation and a whisper, a normal human being would be unable to hear the sound in the described situation: a closed door and a 10-meter long corridor lie between the sound and the listener. The threshold for audibility by the human ear is 0 decibel (dB), and in this configuration the sound would have a level of -15 dB. If that threshold is lowered by super-hearing, the scene works. On the other hand, we have a plausibility issue if the doors were closed at both ends of the corridor, a possibility left open in the sequence. A closed door muffles a sound and reduces it by approximately 25 dB. A sound at -40 dB does not exist. Sound is a wave carried by molecules, and below a certain volume the natural movement of these molecules becomes an obstacle: if a sound is weaker than -23 dB, the signal is utterly lost in the noise. In other words, beyond this threshold, even super-hearing becomes useless, because there is no "sound" to be heard, just a continuous hissing sound with no informational value. If the second door was closed then Nelson could eat his crisps without disturbing anyone.

In the open, however, a normal human being can hear a conversation a hundred meters away, while Daredevil could do so at 1.4 kilometers. Standing in the exact center of Hell's Kitchen, he could theoretically notice a conversation anywhere in the streets within the area, as he does in Vol. 2 #98 (Aug 2007), for example. On the other hand, the muffling effect of walls and ceilings is such that to have Murdock overhear a conversation two floors away in Rykers (Vol. 2 #86, Aug 2006) appears strictly impossible. This also applies to him hearing the gates of the prison being locked, while being taken back to his cell in the same issue, which goes far beyond any physical property of sound.

For all its limitations, super-hearing can yield unexpected results. In *Daredevil* #7 (Apr 1965), Daredevil fights Namor, and at one point makes a remark about Namor's pulse indicating that the Sub-Mariner is still angry, while in the same panel a gigantic "BA-ROOM" signals that a wall is being battered down by a wrecking ball. Super-hearing would indeed allow Daredevil to make that distinction. Hearing a pulse from a distance is difficult, since its frequency makes it hard to distinguish for a normal ear, but once one can do that, sounds with different frequencies (the pulse and the BA-ROOM) do not affect each other. There may be a slight masking effect, but the louder sound does not cancel the weaker one.

That example also explains why Daredevil can be neutralized by sounds that allow normal human beings to function. Since he perceives frequencies the human ear cannot process, all one has to do is blast him with extremely loud sounds within these frequencies. Of course, they may be disagreeable to normal humans as well, because sounds are not pure and tend to be heard over several frequencies. This is exactly what happens in Garth Ennis's "The Devil by the Horns," in *The Punisher* Vol. 5 #3 (Jun 2000), a story which includes judicious remarks about the Punisher's choice of frequencies and the possible side effects.

Thus, super-hearing is not a ludicrous notion. If one improves the threshold of sensitivity and the range of frequency, through a physical transformation of the ear itself, one does get impressive results. The only factor that does not seem to exist in Marvel physics is the dissolution of sound into random air movement under a certain level.

"His Pulsebeat is Steady, He's Telling the Truth"

What of Daredevil's lie detector ability, then? In its most straightforward appearance, it seems to rely on a very simple test, derived from his super-hearing: "His pulsebeat is steady, he's telling the truth" reads a thought balloon in *Daredevil* #194 (May 1983), echoing the explanation given as early as issue #1, when Daredevil thinks, "I can hear his *pulse rate*! It's speeding up, indicating he's *lying*!" There is, however, no reason to suppose that Daredevil ignores the other signs that may indicate someone is lying, primarily body language. He was even famously fooled once by a man with a pacemaker, first in *Daredevil* #184 (Jul 1982) and then in the 2003 movie. If lying is tied to an intense emotional reaction, it is likely to cause an increase in breathing frequency, of body heat, of blood pressure, and dilatation of the pupils. In addition to the heartbeats, Daredevil's super-hearing and his training as a lawyer should also help him spot variations in the pitch of the suspect's voice, caused by the shaking of his larynx: "I *wanted* to believe him, but I heard it in his voice" (*Daredevil* Vol. 2 #96, Jun 2007). His sensibility to minute variations in heat may also allow him to spot the increase in temperature around the eyes and on the cheeks commonly caused by a state of unrest, or to know someone is sweating without a direct contact, as the evaporation of water lowers the temperature of the skin.

Having access to all these parameters enables Daredevil to function as a human polygraph: he has the necessary tools to spot any sign of nervousness. What he often does not have, though, is a frame of reference, since all these tests work through a comparison with the person's normal physiological pattern. To pass judgment on the state of nervousness of an old acquaintance, such as the Gladiator in *Daredevil* Vol. 2 #95-96 (May-Jun 2007) is quite different from reaching any conclusion from a short discussion with a stranger. Furthermore, what is detected is not a lie as such, but tension. This is acknowledged at times – "I still think you're lying... but your heart is beating *so fast*, I can't tell if I'm *wrong* or not," Daredevil notes after beating down Leland Owlsley, the Owl, in Vol. 2 #83 (May 2005) – but conveniently ignored when Daredevil's intimidating presence is by itself likely to disrupt the test.

Again, science seems mostly on Daredevil's side in this case. The difference between actual physics and Marvel physics lies in the transformation of high probabilities into certainties, of long procedures into instantaneous tests. In extreme cases, it also means that Murdock is also able to interpret the state of mind of an entire people just by listening to pulses from a car – "All through the countryside is that feeling of hatred... overshadowed only by an even stronger feeling of stark *fear!!*" (issue #9, Aug 1965) – but that was uncommon, even early in the character's existence.

Bouncing off History

Marvel physics, however, raises some thorny questions when it comes to Daredevil's final and most efficient power, his "radar" sense, which allows him to scan his entire environment. While Daredevil's senses are merely improvement on existing human capacities, his radar offers a very different challenge, starting with its definition. Radar emits electromagnetic waves – radio waves – at regular intervals, and the time it takes for these waves to bounce back to their point of origin serves to establish a map of the environment: the longer the delay, the further away the object. The problem of course is that there is nothing in the human body to emit or receive radio waves.

An alternative representation, the bat's "echolocation," provides a different explanation that fits more neatly with Daredevil's other abilities. Echolocation works the same way a radar does, with one important difference: it relies on sound at extremely high frequencies rather than on electro-magnetism. Since Daredevil can hear frequencies much beyond the normal human ear, echolocation resolves at least half of the problem. This explanation has the further advantage of being used by actual blind people, though with sounds at a lower frequency and hence with a lower definition: using brief clicks of their tongues to send the necessary signal, they can nevertheless spot objects as narrow as a flagpole from five meters away.[6] As the echoes reach the right and

---

[6] Lore Thaler, Stephen R. Arnott SR, Melvyn A. Goodale. "Neural Correlates of Natural Human Echolocation in Early and Late Blind Echolocation Experts". *PLoS*

left ears at slightly different intervals, the technique permits one to reconstruct a three-dimensional environment. The alterations affecting the echoed sound also provide information about the type of material, as the sound will not bounce the same way off a carpeted wall or off a wood panel. Minor mutations could even serve to generate ultrasonics, in ways similar to the aforementioned tongue clicking, though this is left unexplained in the comic book. Unsurprisingly, *Daredevil* Vol. 3 #1 mentions the character's "radar-like" sense and offers echolocation as a possible analogy, but as early as Vol. 1 #1, the new ability merely works *like* a radar. Although the word is most often used without quotation marks, the "radar" is not meant to be one.

Well, it sometimes is. In issue #10 (Oct 1965), Murdock's "radar hearing" enables him to pick up a radio message, while a few issues earlier, he needed special antennas in his costume's ear to do this. This was, again, a short-lived variation. By contrast, David Michelinie explicitly linked the radar to sound waves, as in issue #167 (Nov 1980): "Daredevil has an uncanny *radar-sense*. Like a bat, he emits probing, high-frequency waves… waves which break against any solid object, and breaking, send back signals audible only to Daredevil."

As with super-hearing, echolocation has interesting applications. For instance, Daredevil would indeed be able to see through some walls. If he emits a burst of ultrasonics at 50 kHz, it would travel at the speed of sound until it encountered an obstacle, whereupon only part of it would be reflected back, depending on the nature of the material. Since Daredevil has apparently learned to process information optimally (he was disrupted by objects moving too fast early on, but as noted in Vol. 3 #1, "it really seems to have gotten sharper over the years"), he could deduce the nature and the depth of the object, but also "see" through some material, from clothes to plaster walls. Glass is problematic, though. For obvious narrative reasons, Daredevil's perception mostly coincides with what the reader is shown: he perceives his immediate environment with no difficulty and he "sees" through windows. The problem is that glass will reflect 99,999% of the sound coming through, and since the signal has to cross it not once, but twice, it will be reduced by around 80 db, making it utterly opaque to Daredevil from a distance. This also means that the representation used in Vol. 3, of a colorless, texture-less three-dimensional environment, does not fit with Daredevil's penetrating perception.

Does the radar-sense work then? To a certain extent, it does. It simply improves on an existing, efficient technique, and this improvement is mostly a direct consequence of Daredevil's super-hearing, combined with his intensive training. Nevertheless, a serious limitation lies in the fact that to form a coherent picture of his environment, Daredevil needs to emit bursts at regular intervals to refresh his perception. However, a new burst of ultrasonics cannot be emitted before the previous one has been processed, otherwise the two signals would interfere. Since the range of the radar-sense is approximately 25 meters – at least according to *The Official Handbook to the Marvel Universe Master Edition* Vol. 3 #7 (Jun 1991, more recent Handbooks do not give a figure) – it means there needs to be 0.2 seconds between each burst.[7] Daredevil would therefore be able to update his perception roughly five times per second, which is fine when it comes to locating fixed or slow-moving objects but may be a lot more problematic in combat. If a walking man moves within the range of the radar sense, by the time the information gets to Daredevil, the man will have moved by about 12 centimeters, an acceptable margin of error. However, a vehicle going at 100 km/h will have moved by 2.4 meters by the time it is detected. In order to appreciate its trajectory, Daredevil will have to wait for a second ping, 0.2 seconds later. Similarly, it takes a tenth of a second for him to perceive movement taking place 25 meters away from him, but also to hear the sound of gunshot, for example. It is possible that in Marvel physics, the speed of sound is different from ours, but that would be a major, world-altering difference. Barring that, however, Daredevil has a serious handicap to overcome when fighting from a distance people who can see, rather than hear.

Fortunately, the radar-sense is complemented by super hearing. At a very simple level, this means that he will be aware of the car long before it enters the 25-meter range. In a more sophisticated fashion, the Doppler effect means that sound also carries information about trajectory and speed: the sound of an object moving towards us will be pitched higher than if it were moving away from us. If a knife is thrown in Daredevil's direction at 20m/s, and assuming as we did that he emits sounds at a frequency of 50kHz, the reflected signal will have a frequency of 53.1 kHz, a semitone and a very noticeable difference. Therefore, he would not have to wait for his fairly slow radar-sense and can act accordingly. This would explain how Murdock is able to save Milla from the

---

[7] $t=2\times30/340=0.18s$, with 340 m/s being the speed of sound.

Gladiator's spinning blade thrown across a restaurant, in Vol. 2 #97 (Jun 2007). Generally, the radar-sense is only efficient in conjunction with Daredevil's other heightened perceptions. A specifically outrageous example is to be found in the same issue. Daredevil walks into a bathroom, finds a body in a bathtub, and with "radar" circles filling the panel, states: "The crime scene doesn't feel staged. / It's clear to me that no one *else* has been in here for weeks." That can only make sense if we take into account his heightened smell.

All of this points to the fact that the radar sense is an extremely useful scouting device, since it performs a 360° scan and can penetrate certain objects. It is, however, a very unreliable way to apprehend fast-moving objects, which should put Daredevil at a notable disadvantage in direct confrontations. In particular, bullets go much faster than sound. Extremely fast reflexes may theoretically allow someone to dodge one, but in Daredevil's cases, the bullet would hit him before he could notice it, either through his radar or through his other senses. Having him deflect a bullet with his cane in *Daredevil: The Man Without Fear* #5 (Feb 1994) makes no sense in a world bound by physical laws.

Marvel Physics

When we started thinking about Daredevil's powers and physical feats, we were expecting them to contradict every single known fact about physics and the human body. In a way, they do, since particularly egregious examples of misuse can be found for each of his abilities. If we consider, however, their depiction in the long run, they generally make sense. As noted above, there is a tendency to turn high probabilities into certainties and to go to the limit of what physics and physiology allow, and sometimes above that. However, these simplifications and exaggerations apply as well to all the other aspects of Daredevil's life, from his nigh-instantaneous love affairs to his bafflingly simple legal cases. The point is to be realistic enough not to shock the reader out of his willing suspension of disbelief, and the use of science in *Daredevil* accomplishes that. The origin story is, of course, the most problematic aspect of the character, but radioactivity should really be seen in this context as a mere excuse, rarely discussed, and even more rarely used in the narrative afterwards. Daredevil may live in a world where Marvel physics apply – with nearly instantaneous sound travel and mutation-generating radioactive material as its salient features – but this world never devolves into a pure fantasy.

Daredevil: Not Ready for Primetime?

by M. S. Wilson

Daredevil has always been an effective and successful super-hero, and yet he is usually at his best when operating alone. Many other super-heroes *consider* themselves to be loners (Spider-Man, Punisher, Ghost Rider, Wolverine) yet all of those heroes seem to have *more* team-ups (and are more comfortable with them) than Daredevil. Daredevil truly *is* a loner. Why is this? Is Daredevil anti-social, incapable of working with others? Is there some fundamental difference between him and other "street-level" super-heroes like Spider-Man? Is it possible Daredevil just isn't good enough to play in the big leagues? Or is there another explanation?

Maybe the problem isn't with Daredevil, but with the *stories* themselves. It can be posited that Daredevil simply fits better in a certain type of story, and doesn't fit as well in others.

Daredevil is not what we would call anti-social. He's had plenty of successful team-ups over the years. Yet we still think of him as a lone wolf – someone who is not a team player. Daredevil seems to fit better in his own corner of the Marvel Universe. In contrast to a team like the Avengers, who are constantly saving the galaxy or surrounded by dozens of other super-heroes in gigantic crossover events, Daredevil is at his best when he's on his own, in more familiar surroundings. Why should this be? What makes Daredevil fit better in stories with a smaller scale?

We know Daredevil is capable of teaming up effectively with other superheroes, especially one-on-one. He's certainly had his share of successful team-ups, the most obvious being with the Black Widow. That's a special case, though, as the two were romantically involved when they began their partnership. Sharing a bed obviously changes the dynamic of their relationship, making it different from the usual super-hero team-up. Moreover, Daredevil and Black Widow's partnership wasn't without its rough spots. They certainly had plenty of arguments over the years. Even in his most successful team-up, Daredevil still shows he would be better off working alone.

Over the years, Daredevil has also teamed up one-on-one with many other super-heroes, though he often seems uncomfortable with it. Even his long friendship with Spider-Man has had its share of disagreements (and even fights). While Spider-Man is often thought of as a loner too, he certainly seems to team up much more readily (and more comfortably) than Daredevil does. Although they like and respect each other enough to reveal their secret identities to one other (multiple times), Daredevil and Spider-Man still don't find their team ups so special as to make them a full-time arrangement. It's hard to imagine them having a permanent team-up – we *know* it couldn't last very long without some kind of acrimony growing between the two. They seem to be better off as occasional allies; perhaps this gives them some distance and allows them to maintain their own worldviews while still respecting each other's perspectives.

Daredevil has had numerous other team-ups and friendships with super-heroes – Moon Knight, Captain America, Black Panther, Luke Cage, and Iron Fist, to name a few. These friendships are built on mutual trust and respect, but none lends itself to a permanent arrangement. Daredevil has even managed to work in conjunction with established teams, like the Fantastic Four, the Avengers, and the Defenders. In fact, all of those teams have asked Daredevil to join them at some point (and he *did* finally join the New Avengers, but more on that later). It's not like Daredevil *can't* work well with others – he just seems to *prefer* working alone. His heightened senses are less effective when someone else is around to interfere with them, and his fighting style doesn't mesh easily with other heroes' styles. Daredevil was trained to fight alone and he is most effective as a fighter when he's not hampered by a partner.

If Daredevil doesn't team up readily with other super-heroes one-on-one, he definitely doesn't fit into the gigantic, cosmic storylines major team-ups often entail. Nor does he fit well with some of the weirder aspects of the Marvel Universe. This is not to say Daredevil has *never* been involved in these storylines, but on the few occasions he has, he's always seemed out of place. More likely, it's just us, as readers, who are uncomfortable with it. Daredevil can handle himself when he's out of his depth but it isn't what we regularly tune in to see.

One of the earliest sustained eras of "strangeness" in Daredevil was when Steve Gerber took over as writer, which lasted from *Daredevil* #97 (Mar 1973) through #116 (Dec 1974). Gerber was famous for weird characters and even weirder situations in Marvel books like *Howard the Duck* and *Omega the Unknown*, and he made no exception with *Daredevil*. In the course of Gerber's run, Daredevil faced such offbeat foes as Dark Messiah, Angar the Screamer, Ramrod, Mandrill, Nekra, and Death Stalker. He also met Man-Thing, worked with the Avengers, and told his origin to *Rolling Stone*'s Jann Wenner. There was even time for a team-up with Uri Geller.

Daredevil's clashes with Dark Messiah, Ramrod, and Angar were part of a larger storyline, which included memorable meetings with Moondragon and Captain Mar-Vell. This storyline illustrates Daredevil's discomfort in dealing with otherworldly menaces. In *Daredevil* #106 (Dec 1973), he says to himself while on Moondragon's spaceship: "I sound like a country boy who's just seen his first *skyscraper*...! / But I can't *help* it! I'm just not *used* to thinking in cosmic terms. / ...It's *way* out of my *league*." In *Daredevil* #107 (Jan 1974) even Black Widow is overwhelmed by the scope of the adventure, and Daredevil is noticeably out of his depth throughout this entire issue. While fighting Terrex (a creature with the power to affect any organic material with which it makes contact), Daredevil is paralyzed from the waist down; this soon wears off, but Daredevil's usual stoicism is shaken by the encounter. He shows his helplessness when he shouts: "What *I* want to know is – how can a glorified *acrobat* fight a *god* gone *mad*?" The hero himself is aware of his inherent limitations. Eventually, Terrex is defeated, but Daredevil's role is confined to distracting the creature while Moondragon, Captain Mar-Vell, and Angar the Screamer do the heavy lifting.

A few years later, in *Daredevil* #275-276 (mid-Dec 1989 and Jan 1990), Daredevil ran into an incarnation of Ultron, which he defeated with the help of

Karnak and Gorgon, two Inhumans from the moon. Again he managed to overcome his almost indestructible foe (by smashing Ultron's head with a tree branch!), but this storyline was clearly a bad fit for Daredevil. He was out of his depth fighting an enemy that had once held the entire team of Avengers at bay. A blind lawyer and a vengeance-filled robot aren't equal partners in a super-struggle.

Immediately following that story was one in which Mephisto and his son Blackheart try to corrupt Daredevil. This story ran from *Daredevil* #278 (Mar 1990) to #282 (July 1990). Mephisto and his son Blackheart argue about corrupting human souls. Blackheart decides it's easy to make an evil person sin and it would be even sweeter to make a good person (like Daredevil) abandon his principles and commit a sin that would forever stain his soul. Gorgon and Karnak are also involved in this story, and there are many esoteric digressions, which only serve to dilute the overall story.

In spite of the exaggerated scope of the story, Daredevil's basic humanity still shows through, notably in issue #281 when Daredevil literally and symbolically kindles a flame in the heart of Mephisto's frozen wasteland and vows: "Okay Mephisto. / I'm coming for you. / You made a mistake. / You believe your evil breaks a man. Sometimes it does. / But when it doesn't break a man – / it makes him even *stronger*." Daredevil ultimately triumphs over Blackheart and Mephisto (with some help from the Silver Surfer – an "opposites attract" team-up of the highest magnitude) and reaffirms his own humanity by choosing to stop fighting and simply walk away. He even forgives Mephisto before leaving.

In spite of Daredevil using his own humanity to defeat a most inhuman foe, he again is out of his depth in this storyline. Daredevil could easily be snuffed out by these titans, were the constraints of the narrative not stopping such action. In fact, when Silver Surfer shows up and engages Mephisto in battle, Daredevil yells for his companions to run, saying: "This is no fight for human eyes!" The resolution comes from Daredevil engaging this monumental threat on a more personal level, which is where Daredevil is most effective.

These mystical stories seem out of place for Daredevil, who works best when he has a solid grounding in reality. There have been mystical aspects to Daredevil's career at other times, such as his encounters with the Hand and Elektra returning from the dead. In these instances, the higher-level mystical elements are brought down to Daredevil, rather than the reverse. Looking at

Even in the most wild plots, Daredevil's best moments tend to be isolated, human, and even existential in focus. From *Daredevil* #280 (May 1990). Art by John Romita, Jr. and Al Williamson. Copyright © Marvel Comics.

Elektra's resurrection, it ultimately had more to do with love and faith than *actual* mysticism, which only makes Daredevil seem *more* grounded and realistic, since love and faith are things anyone can achieve, or at the very least aspire to.

Unlike his friend Spider-Man, Daredevil has traditionally been left out of the major crossover events. While some of that may have to do with real-world politics and sales figures, it also seems like the writers of the big events know Daredevil doesn't fit with such storylines. Daredevil was completely absent from the first *Secret Wars* mini-series and his role in *Secret Wars II* was little more than a random encounter with the Beyonder in a tangential tie-in story. In the first *Contest of Champions* mini-series (June-Aug 1982), Daredevil was chosen as a representative for one of the teams vying for the mystic artifacts. He did well, finding one of the artifacts for his side, but he still wasn't a great fit with the *de facto* team-up. He complained about his radar-sense being affected when there were others around and showed his preference for working alone.

Years later, Thanos became a menace and an uneasy champion for the universe in general in a handful of mini-series (*Infinity Gauntlet, Infinity War, Infinity Crusade*). However, Daredevil was left out of *Infinity Gauntlet* completely. He did participate in *Infinity War*, but was relegated to the team that stayed on Earth instead of the primary team that went to confront the Magus. In *Infinity Crusade*, Daredevil was included with the heroes gathered by the Goddess, though his actual participation was limited to appearing in a few background scenes, and when the confrontation came between the two sets of super-heroes, Daredevil was defeated rather abruptly by a power blast from Guardian. Daredevil was left out of other major crossovers, such as *Secret Invasion* and most of *Civil War*.

One crossover where Daredevil *was* a major player was *Shadowland*, in which Daredevil was possessed by a demon and began acting very out of character. One reason *Shadowland* was such a good story (regardless of how we feel about the whole "demon possession" aspect of the tale) was because it had most of Marvel's "street-level" heroes in one place. They were all relatively on a par with each other. *Shadowland* had more than its share of mystical mumbo-jumbo too, but Daredevil ultimately proves himself through his willingness to sacrifice himself to save others, which serves to emphasize his down-to-earth qualities and makes it easier for us to relate to him.

In fact, our ability to relate to Daredevil is what really sets him apart from the rest of the Marvel Universe. Marvel is *known* for having super-heroes that are relatable (Spider-Man, Captain America, the Fantastic Four, etc.), but Daredevil is a special case. His best adventures are the most down-to-earth ones, in which he wrestles with moral dilemmas and emotional issues. These stories speak to us because we can all relate to them in some way. We all have problems that force us to make moral or ethical choices every day – the stakes may not be as high for us as they are for Daredevil, but that doesn't mean our choices are any less important to us. This is why Daredevil seems out of place when he's involved in massive, cosmic storylines or multi-part crossovers – we simply can't relate to those stories as readily as we do the ones that are more grounded in reality. Another reason we can easily identify with Daredevil is that he seems *vulnerable*; he's not perfect. In fact, he has many of the same flaws we see in ourselves: he can be impulsive, short-tempered, arrogant, and sometimes cavalier with other people's feelings.

Even more compellingly, Daredevil *knows* he isn't perfect. He's made enough bad choices (and owned up to them) that he no longer assumes every decision will automatically work out for the best. The fact he can recognize his fallibility lets him acknowledge that his choices may be wrong. In fact, Daredevil has occasionally questioned his entire belief system, which is something many of us do from time to time (though none of us likes to dwell on it). Daredevil's crises of faith serves to reaffirm his humanity, to make him seem more like one of us: flawed, imperfect, but trying his best to navigate through uncertainty and doubt in order to better himself – in other words, it makes him seem more *human*.

Daredevil has carved out a niche for himself in the Marvel Universe – one where he stays grounded. The reason Daredevil never seems quite comfortable in outer space or other dimensions is because he needs to stay on Earth in order to be at his most human. In fact, the best Daredevil stories are those that are set in New York City, specifically the ones set in Hell's Kitchen. This is where Matt Murdock grew up, where he faced the trials and tribulations that helped mold him into the man he is today, and where he learned the basic lessons of humanity that have served him over his long career as both a lawyer and a super-hero. We could almost say Hell's Kitchen itself has served as a "character" in Daredevil. If he had been born and raised somewhere else, he wouldn't be the same person we know so well. He would still be a hero, though he may not have the same drive, the same compassion, or the same vulnerability he has now. Hell's Kitchen and all it entails is a large part of what *keeps* Daredevil grounded, what makes him fit better into street-level stories than cosmic crossovers. That's why so many writers keep bringing him back to his roots there, both literally and emotionally. This could also explain why Daredevil has never fit well with super-hero teams – it's hard to stay relatable and keep your feet firmly planted on the ground when you're living in a mansion with a butler and a dozen other super-heroes.

Of course, Daredevil *did* end up joining the New Avengers in *New Avengers* #16 (Nov 2011). It's interesting to note that the team that finally recruits Daredevil (or the one he chose to join, given his past refusals) wasn't one of the "official" Avengers teams headed by Iron Man or Captain America, but the *New Avengers* – a more unofficial, independent, street-wise team – led by Luke Cage, an old friend. Daredevil also teamed up with the Defenders years ago and seemed to work rather well with them. This is hardly surprising, since the Defenders were always considered a "non-team" team and Daredevil has always been a non-"team player."

Why does Daredevil prefer to operate alone and why do we feel more comfortable when he does? Is he simply not on the same level as the heavy hitters in the Marvel Universe? Or does he just fit better when he stays within his comfort zone? The latter seems to be the more likely case. It's certainly not some defect in Daredevil's character, considering all the risks he's taken and the sacrifices he's made to help others over the years. (That Marvel's other super-heroes universally respect and admire him speaks for itself.)

Nonetheless, when Daredevil confronts cosmic menaces or teams up with a bunch of other heroes, his basic humanity seems somehow... *diluted*. Something essential about the character is lost or overshadowed when the scope of the story is broadened too much. It just *feels* wrong, somehow. Conversely, when the scope is narrowed, when the stories focus in on the essential qualities possessed (in some measure) by every human being, Daredevil shines. His nobility, compassion, and strength of spirit are brought to the forefront. If this sometimes allows his negative qualities – vulnerability, self-doubt, arrogance – to show through as well, it only serves to make him *more* human and as such far more relatable. In the end, it's not that Daredevil isn't *big* enough for those grand cosmic and crossover stories, it's that those stories are too *limited* by their scope to showcase Daredevil's best qualities.

The Life and Times of Foggy Nelson

by Christine Hanefalk

In the very first issue of *Daredevil*, we are not only introduced to Matt Murdock, but also to his most loyal friend and law partner Franklin "Foggy" Nelson, the only other character from the early years to still be around for readers to enjoy today. What kind of impression he made on this first generation of *Daredevil* readers is hard to say, but judging by the text on the cover of the origin issue, it seems that Marvel was aiming for "fun-loving."

With the benefit of hindsight, the early Foggy might strike readers as comically self-effacing. Halfway through the first issue, after Foggy has gone to the trouble of securing a new office – and the beginnings of a staff in the form of the lovely Karen Page – he says to his new partner, "We're in *business* Matt! With your brains and my dad's money, *nothing'll* stop us!" With this simple statement, it is made clear that whatever his other traits may be, Foggy Nelson is clearly not quite Matt Murdock's intellectual equal, at least not from his own perspective.

Fast forward to the present day, and a very different picture emerges. In *Daredevil* Vol. 3 #5 (Dec 2011), the usually unlucky-in-love lawyer is seen chasing his stray shoe around the apartment of a beautiful new lover and her equally fetching roommate. And in *Daredevil* Vol. 3 #1 (Sep 2011), Matt explains: "Foggy Nelson is the other half of *Nelson & Murdock*, the one man who knows *everything* about me. / He's my partner because he's a brilliant litigator with an encyclopedic knowledge of case law. / I'm his partner because of people's characteristic hesitation to hire a lawyer named *'Foggy.'*"

Clearly, the Foggy Nelson of the 21st century has moved far beyond his modest beginnings. This change did not happen overnight, however, nor did it happen in any kind of linear fashion. Rather, Foggy Nelson's evolution into the character we know today has been an interesting journey in its own right – and often a reflection of Matt Murdock's journey as well. Just as the pendulum between the light and the darkness has swung back and forth for Daredevil, so it has for his most loyal ally.

Adventurous Beginnings

Foggy started out, first and foremost, as a supporting character. Daredevil – and his civilian alter ego Matt Murdock – has always been the main protagonist and focal point of the book. In this context, it is easier to study Foggy Nelson, as he appeared in the very first issues, from the perspective of what he tells us about Matt. Because in essence, Foggy Nelson exists due the need on behalf of his creators Stan Lee and Bill Everett to populate Daredevil's world with characters for our hero to interact with.

One thing to keep in mind when looking at early Daredevil is just what a novel concept a blind super-hero and lawyer must have been in the mid-1960s. The creators may have sensed a risk that readers of the newly launched *Daredevil* would feel more pity than awe for the blind hero, in spite of his amazingly heightened remaining senses. However, by immediately showing off Matt's academic and legal intellect as well as his physical prowess, Stan Lee makes sure that readers come to respect all of his abilities. In this context, Foggy Nelson plays an important role as the first person to be in perpetual awe of his best friend. Before casually referring to himself as the guy whose biggest contribution to their new business is having a father who can pay rent, Foggy can be seen admiring Matt's scholastic achievements: "Matt, you ol' hound dog! How do you do it? I study like a demon but *you* just breeze through the courses with all the top grades!"

With the addition of the lovely young secretary Karen Page, Stan Lee also sets the stage for the love triangle that would provide most of the soap opera elements for the first half of his run. As Matt and Foggy both pine for her attention, it's clear that charming the opposite sex is yet another arena in which Foggy is cast in the role of second-stringer. Matt may be blind and of modest means, but he is also portrayed as the better lawyer and clearly the more attractive of the two.

Foggy, in his earliest incarnation, is not, however, without a certain amount of guts and initiative. Decades later, in *Daredevil* Vol. 2 #88 (Oct 2006), Foggy says, in an internal monologue aimed at his absent friend: "But you know me, Matt... / You know I've never been like you. / I'm not a coward. / But I'm not very brave." Given this dominant view of Foggy, as the average guy who constantly – and reluctantly – finds himself dealing with high crime and super-villains who are clearly out of his league, it's interesting to note that Foggy regularly showed a remarkable amount of courage during his early days.

In *Daredevil* #6 (Feb 1965), Foggy sees a man he thinks might be the Ox, a villain wanted by the police, during a visit to a wax museum. Not wanting to frighten Matt or Karen, Foggy says nothing, but vows to return later, alone, to confirm his suspicions. Unfortunately for Foggy, his hunch proves to be spot on, and he finds himself in more trouble than he can handle. Daredevil steps in to save the day, though not quite in time to prevent the head trauma that sends his friend straight to the hospital.

Suffering such bitter consequences does not stop Foggy from putting himself in harm's way yet again. In *Daredevil* #34 (Nov 1967), Foggy actually jumps in to try to save Daredevil from the Beetle – an act of bravery made even more honorable by the fact that the man he believed to be Daredevil at the time was none other than Matt's highly fictional twin brother Mike, a persona that kept rubbing Foggy the wrong way for most of that subplot's 18-issue stretch.

Driven more by love-sick foolishness than a sense of adventure, Foggy also tries to win Karen's heart by donning the Daredevil costume himself in *Daredevil* #18 (July 1966). The seeds for this crazy idea were planted when Spider-Man showed up at the law office two issues earlier, his Spider-sense giving him a clear indication of Daredevil's presence. With Karen and the blind Matt Murdock eliminated from the short list of suspects, Spider-Man targeted Foggy, giving Karen a reason to suspect that Foggy might in fact be Daredevil – and Foggy an idea for how he might make Karen fall in love with him. In *Daredevil* #17 (June 1966), the reader is given a glimpse of Foggy's thoughts on the matter, as well as his complicated feelings for his friend and law partner: "I feel like a *heel* for trying to give Karen the wrong impression! And yet... all my life I've *dreamed* of being a heroic figure! / Even in *college*, I remember how it was *Matt* who had all the glamour! Although blind, it was *he* who won top honors in every course, while *I* just plodded along! / I've always been nothing but... *Mr. Ordinary!*"

Foggy's Daredevil career proves to be a short one. By the time we get to *Daredevil* #19 (Aug 1966), the news that attorney Franklin Nelson is the man behind the mask has leaked to the press, and Foggy's life is immediately in jeopardy. When the real Daredevil swoops in to save him, the hoax is revealed. Karen, to her credit, does not hold the high-stakes game of masquerade against Foggy, and he goes back to his life as it was.

The earliest 20 or 30 issues of *Daredevil* have a bit of an anything-can-happen vibe to them. One highly plausible reason for this is that it takes time for any creator working on a recently created set of characters to truly define, for himself, who these characters are supposed to be. This is true of the entire Nelson & Murdock staff, as they navigate through a complex love triangle layered on top of Matt's struggles to combine his two lives as well as the previously established relationship between Matt and Foggy that Stan Lee is trying to convey. In Foggy's case, this means that it takes a while for his core personality to emerge and begin to stabilize. But when taken together, Foggy's early appearances give the impression of someone who is kind and supportive, albeit with a jealous streak, while at the same time being brave in spite of his own perceived shortcomings.

The Serious Side of Foggy Nelson

Anyone who is only familiar with Foggy Nelson from the Frank Miller run might be forgiven for seeing Foggy as a bit of a comic relief character. Looking only at early Foggy, however, a slightly different picture emerges. Aside from some of his early antics of trying to play Daredevil and single-handedly fight super-villains, Foggy is able to come across as a fairly levelheaded guy, especially for a supporting character in a Silver Age comic title, with all that entails. Moreover, it does not take long before Matt, initially described as "mild-mannered" and portrayed as a rather boring fellow, starts adopting the erratic behavior that seems to go hand-in-hand with being a costumed crime-fighter on the side. This gradual shift in Matt's behavior starts to put Foggy in the position of the "straight man" of the title.

The most glaring example of the extremes Matt has to go to, in order to hide his life as a super-hero, is when he decides to come up with an imaginary twin brother, in *Daredevil* #25 (Feb 1967). Rather than simply go along with this story, Foggy immediately calls shenanigans: "Come *off* it, fella! I *roomed* with you all thru college – / we were *buddies* – we confided about *everything* – and you never *mentioned* a brother!" Matt presses on, saying that his brother "Mike" was a loner and did not want people knowing about him and Foggy counters with, "We're both *lawyers*, Matt! You *know* how thin that story sounds!" Foggy comes across as the obvious voice of reason in this scene, a role he takes on repeatedly throughout the Mike Murdock era. In a sense, he is able to echo whatever objections the reader might have to what they see unfolding on the page. While the reader is fully aware of what is going on behind the scenes in ways that Foggy is not, it's easy to relate to Foggy's relative sanity when placed in situations that are anything but.

Though eventually convinced of Mike Murdock's existence, Foggy never completely warms to Matt's new alter ego – probably due in part to the latter repeatedly making fun of Foggy's weight – and maintains a reserved stance, while Karen seemingly cannot get enough of Matt's rather obnoxious twin.

By the time we get to *Daredevil* #36 (Jan 1968), Foggy has other things on his mind. He is approached by a couple of gentlemen asking him if he would be interested in running for District Attorney, an idea that he embraces immediately. Not a minute later, he receives a phone call from his old girlfriend Debbie Harris, who is out on parole and asking him out on a date.[1] Foggy has his doubts however. He is willing to forgive Debbie, but not sure what dating an ex-convict would do to his political campaign. In *Daredevil* #39 (Apr 1968), it's Matt who finally convinces Foggy to go ahead with the date, reminding him that the American public is more understanding than Foggy might imagine.

Before long, Foggy and Debbie start a relationship that is surprisingly long-lived, not ending definitively until nearly 20 years later in *Daredevil* #222 (Sep 1985), when Foggy learns that Debbie has met a new man during their separation. The stability that Foggy's relationship provides further cements his role as the ordinary man on the street, while Matt continues, as Daredevil, to climb buildings, fight villains, and have various love interests along the way.

---

[1] Deborah "Debbie" Harris was introduced – in *Daredevil* #10 (Oct 1965), by Wally Wood and Bob Powell, in a story that continues in issue #11 (Dec 1965), by Stan Lee and Bob Powell – as a former sweetheart of Foggy's. However, she was sent to jail after being convicted of working with the villain the Organizer, who was trying to set Foggy up to run for D.A. on the ticket of the Reform Party.

During this time, Foggy makes big strides in his professional career. By *Daredevil* #48 (Jan 1969), he wins the election and becomes District Attorney, a position he would hold until losing his re-election in *Daredevil* #131 (Mar 1976). These are not carefree times, however, and just before his win, Matt and Foggy have their first major falling out. When Foggy needs Matt's support with his campaign, Matt's Daredevil "career" interferes, forcing Matt to kick Foggy out of their office in an effort to protect his friends. By the time the election finally rolls around, Foggy has not spoken to Matt in days.

Foggy approaches his new career, in *Daredevil* #50 (Mar 1969), with a sharp mind and enough passion to do the job, but in characteristic Foggy fashion he's plagued by self-doubt: "It's *Matt* who should have this job – not *me*! / He was the real *brains* of 'Nelson and Murdock'! / *I* was just – the *work horse*! / But they say a man can sometimes *grow* into a job – / maybe *this* will be my chance to *prove* myself! / My chance to finally get *out* – from under the shadow of *Matt Murdock*!" This deep-seated motivation for our character to grow and change stems directly from his placement as the second-string man of the title. Matt continues to provide the contrast for Foggy's character, and the latter's feelings of inferiority are frequently touched on in different ways.

Soon enough, Foggy at least gets the chance to be Matt's boss when Matt becomes Foggy's special assistant in *Daredevil* #58 (Nov 1969), following the former's return from having faked his own death (for the first time). This arrangement lasts until Matt moves to San Francisco with Natasha Romanoff, a.k.a. the Black Widow, in *Daredevil* #87 (May 1972). Matt's relationship with Natasha puts a strain on his working relationship with Foggy, which becomes quite dramatic. When Natasha is on trial for murdering the Scorpion, Foggy shows little compassion. He talks about the heroes having gone too far and says it's time to start cracking down on irresponsible vigilantes. Matt leaves Foggy's office, slamming the door shut, and in the following issue he even refers to Foggy as an "ex-friend." Without even knowing it, Foggy is working against his hero's lifestyle in order to promote strength within his own.

There are other problems in Foggy's life as well. In a subplot that runs from *Daredevil* #77 (June 1971) until issue #85 (Mar 1972), Foggy is blackmailed by the mysterious Mr Kline, who knows of a mistake Foggy made in his role as District Attorney. It's eventually revealed that the mistake in question was signing incriminating documents presented to him by his former assistant Hollis, later identified as the villain Crimewave. The situation with Mr. Kline gets serious enough that Foggy first contemplates killing him(!) and later decides to resign as District Attorney, before finally changing his mind.

In more recent decades, it's Matt who has frequently been portrayed as a man with the weight of the world on his shoulders. What we learn from Foggy's history, however, is that the burdens of a life spent fighting crime is not reserved exclusively for the title's main character. In fact, while Matt has always had a safety valve of sorts, the ability to act out his frustrations in the guise of another, Foggy has no other life to turn to and shows no escapist tendencies. Being forced at every juncture to deal with the here and now puts Foggy in the role of the responsible adult.

After Matt leaves town in *Daredevil* #87 (May 1972), Foggy does not appear again until issue #108 (Mar 1974). When he does, it's clear that being District Attorney has come very close to costing him his life. Having come too close to a mystery involving the Black Spectre, Foggy has been shot and is in critical condition. This prompts Matt to immediately return to New York to be by his friend's side. Giving a fairly mixed review of Foggy's personal strengths and weaknesses, Matt thinks to himself, "If Foggy *dies*, I really *will* be alone – no one to turn to – nowhere to *go* –! / [...] / For all of Foggy's many *faults* – his proud *stubbornness* – his occasional thick-headedness – / – he's a *good* man, trying his best to do an important job – and do it *well*. / A man like him shouldn't have to die *this* way."

The shooting has lasting effects on Foggy as he tries his best to recover, frustrated by the slow progress. In *Daredevil* #118 (Feb 1975), Matt and Foggy have a conversation, and Matt points out that Foggy sounds bitter. Foggy replies, "You spend a chunk of your life trying to *help* this city – trying to make it *safer*, a decent place for people to *live* – / – You put up with the *crackpots*, the bad cops, the *crooks* – / and then *wham*, you get the city's *thanks* – a crummy bullet from a third-hand *Saturday night special*. / So sure – I'm bitter, Matt, this has been building up in me since it *happened*. I'm bitter as *hell*." In a scene that seems almost like a 180-degree reversal of Matt and Foggy's respective roles in later years, it's Matt who has to help Foggy regain his purpose, by reminding him that there are still good people in the world and that he just has to have a little faith. It appears both men have been striving for the same goal, but the fact that it has crushed Foggy, in this particular moment, helps us see how very similar and yet different our two friends can be.

Comic Relief

Mention Frank Miller's run on *Daredevil* to a fan of the book and you are likely to get a reaction that mentions one or several of the words "noir," "gritty," "dark," or "character-defining." Miller's work on *Daredevil* took the title and its main character in new and interesting directions and left a legacy that later writers have felt compelled to emulate or to relate to in various ways. He brought a freshness to the book that made *Daredevil* relevant to a whole new generation of readers.

However, some readers who have not actually read Miller's *Daredevil* in a while might be surprised to find the majority of his work is not as dark as they remember. The story arc "Born Again" (*Daredevil* #227-233, Feb-Aug 1986), with its gut-wrenching destruction of Matt Murdock's life, is a good example of the kind of Shakespearian tragedy Miller is capable of, but it's not necessarily representative of his earlier, longer run on the book (*Daredevil* #168-191, Jan 1981 - Feb 1983).[2] Miller's *Daredevil* was often funny, with plenty of room for comic relief to go with the action and high drama, and much of that comic relief came courtesy of none other than Foggy Nelson.

While the Miller run does not represent a substantial overhaul of Foggy as a character, it could be argued that it represents a shift from Foggy as more of a serious character to someone who (while still a respectable professional) comes across as a bit of a goof. It is, however, difficult to determine conclusively when this subtle shift occurs and whether the responsibility for this change can be placed entirely on the shoulders of Frank Miller. Roger McKenzie, who wrote Daredevil when Frank Miller came on as penciler (with *Daredevil* #158, May 1979), may have been influential in this change as well.

McKenzie's first issue was *Daredevil* #152 (May 1978), where we meet Foggy at a real low point in his life. His fiancée Deborah Harris has recently broken off their engagement due to being badly traumatized after her kidnapping by someone connected to Maxwell Glenn, the father of Matt's then-girlfriend, Heather. Matt, through his Daredevil activities, is convinced that Maxwell Glenn has been under the influence of the Purple Man for some time and is innocent of the criminal charges brought against him. Their

---

[2] Frank Miller joined *Daredevil* as penciller with issue #158 (May 1979), and he co-wrote a couple of issues with Roger McKenzie. However, he did not take on full writing duties until *Daredevil* #168.

disagreement on Maxwell Glenn creates a severe rift between the partners, and Foggy has turned to drinking.

At the beginning of *Daredevil* #152, we find Matt and Foggy at Maxwell Glenn's funeral, following the latter's suicide. After snapping at Matt and punching a reporter, Foggy goes to his office and grabs a bottle of whiskey, hoping to drown his sorrows. Fortunately, he stops himself just in time, saying, "*No*! I don't *need* this stuff! / Not now... Not *ever* again! I *promised* myself that this stuff won't *solve* my problems!" In the end, Matt – in his Daredevil guise – manages to save the day by forcing Debbie out of her seclusion and setting up the two estranged lovers' reunion. The issue ends on a high note, but the way Foggy is portrayed here is very different from his portrayal in *Daredevil* #165 (July 1980), the first issue in which Roger McKenzie and Frank Miller are unambiguously listed as co-writers.

Daredevil #165 paves the way for the wedding between Debbie and Foggy in *Daredevil* #166 (Sep 1980) and sees Foggy arrive at the office singing, happy to show off his new – and very bright – wedding tuxedo for the first time, saying, "Matt, you ol' hound dog, I wish you could see what I'm holding in my hot little hands! / Got it just for my wedding next week. / The latest in tuxedoes. / ...She's a real beaut!" The Foggy we see here is not just happy and carefree; both his personality and his new outfit are vibrant enough to come across as a bit over the top.

In *Daredevil* #166, Foggy's story continues with his wedding to Debbie, an event not without complications. Things start well, with Foggy's family flying in from Akron, and his reunion with his old fraternity brother Porkchop Peterson, a man who clearly shares Foggy's questionable fashion sense. Later, however, Foggy realizes he's dropped the wedding ring. After sending Matt and Porkchop to search for it (and Daredevil finding his usual brand of distraction), everyone is reunited in time to catch Foggy finding it on his own finger. Whether the reader finds the scene charming and endearing or a cause for concern regarding Foggy Nelson's intelligence, it's clearly a departure from the man we saw 15 issues earlier. It's clear the roles between the two lawyers have shifted: Matt comes across as an older and wiser "big brother," while it's become Foggy's turn to play and let loose.

Daredevil #168 (Jan 1981) marks Miller's first solo effort on *Daredevil* as both writer and penciler. This is where the reader is first introduced to Matt's college girlfriend turned ninja assassin, Elektra, and taken on a journey back to the lawyers' early days of college. In the scenes depicted, Matt is portrayed as suave and confident, and it's Foggy, rather than his new blind friend, who trips and drops his books all over the library steps. To be fair, this might be perceived as just a slight exaggeration of the scenes from Matt and Foggy's college days in the very first issue of *Daredevil* from 1964, but there's now some awkwardness to Foggy's demeanor that wasn't a dominant character trait during his long stint as District Attorney.

"Guts"

In *Daredevil* #185 (Aug 1982), Foggy takes center stage in the story "Guts." The issue in question is a great example of how Miller's take on the character can be viewed through two very different lenses. On the one hand, it shows Foggy taking charge and displaying an impressive amount of courage, cunning, and legal expertise. On the other hand, as much as Foggy is clearly the hero of this story, there are scenes in which he might also be perceived as somewhat child-like and naïve. In a sense, "Guts" is almost like two stories told simultaneously – or rather, the same story told from two different vantage points. The reader is "told" Foggy's side of the story, with his thoughts and words written on the page, while shown a slightly different take on things through the artwork. It's a technique that would be difficult to pull off quite so successfully in any medium other than comic books.

Daredevil #185 opens with Matt addressing the reader in a one-page panel sequence, a fourth wall-breaking move that tells the reader right from the start that this issue is different. He finishes the introduction: "Bet you're wondering why I'm telling you all this. / Well, it's because the *narrator* of this month's adventure is *Foggy Nelson* – Matt Murdock's *partner*... / ...and he doesn't *know* I'm Daredevil."

When we shift our focus to Foggy, we find Matt's girlfriend Heather Glenn in Foggy's office. She says she's in deep trouble and Foggy is the only one who can help her. Heather has discovered that Glenn Industries, the business she inherited from her father, is involved in criminal activity. The two head over to Glenn Industries, where Heather is shown a purchase order she signed, making her as involved as the rest of the company. Foggy encourages Heather to go home while he keeps exploring their options, going to the commissions and government agencies that might have the information they're looking for.

Everywhere he goes, Foggy's met with red tape, and it's at this point that the story takes an interesting twist.

Having thus far stayed within his own area of expertise, Foggy now ventures into the domains normally reserved for Daredevil. He thinks to himself, "As night enshrouds Manhattan like a *pup tent*, I stalk the darkest corners of the New York underworld. / I am a *hunter*. / The city is my *jungle*. My quarry will *not* elude me." This is where Daredevil, who has been stalking Foggy from a distance for much of the issue, becomes more directly involved and where Foggy's internal dialogue starts to deviate from actual events depicted in the panels. Foggy's commentary keeps running along the same lines as in the quote above, while the actual situations, as Foggy seeks out seedy bars and meets with the mobster Mr. Slaughter and even the Kingpin himself, are conveyed more truthfully through the artwork and word balloons. As the story progresses, by observing the differences in the two perspectives, we see Foggy's inner monologue transform mistakes, misjudgments, and narrow escapes into successes. Foggy is clearly in over his head, but there's quite a bit of doubt as to whether he's aware of his own ineptitude in dealing with these situations.

In a fight scene against Slaughter's men, Daredevil who comes to the rescue – after killing the lights, of course – while Foggy walks away thinking he did it all on his own. The skilled attorney, a mature professional all the way, turns into a kid playing dress up when he enters Daredevil's world. Granted, he acts with more courage and presence of mind than most people would, but it's difficult to determine whether one should laugh *with* him or *at* him, and in one instance we even find Daredevil himself doing a full face-palm while observing the trouble Foggy is getting into. Fortunately for all, Foggy emerges triumphant at the end, when he's able to trick Turk into getting on a plane bound for Chicago before sneaking off and leaving the hapless thug behind.

"Guts" highlights many aspects of Miller's portrayal of Foggy as a character. Foggy is smart yet naïve, brave yet insecure. To be fair, there are many instances during Miller's run in which we get to see Foggy excel as a professional – in *Daredevil* #177 (Dec 1981), Foggy cleverly gets new client J. Jonah Jameson to pay for their new office by insisting on a retainer, and in *Daredevil* #175 (Oct 1981), he turns a case in their favor by remembering an obscure legal precedent. However, we are also treated to many other instances in which Foggy is used mainly as a way of introducing humor, sometimes of the slapstick variety. In *Daredevil* #178 (Jan 1982), Foggy approaches the Heroes for Hire to see if they would be interested in working as Matt's bodyguard. The most memorable part of the scene, however, is when Foggy – who is being kept on a diet by his wife – eats their last slice of pizza and lets out a loud belch.

To complicate things even further, we also get to see Foggy act in ways that can only be described as morally questionable. After watching Matt try to sabotage Heather's career and take away her confidence, making neither party happy in the process, Foggy decides to solicit the help of Natasha (the Black Widow) in bringing the relationship to a close. In *Daredevil* #189 (Dec 1982), Natasha forges a separate note for both Matt and Heather, making it appear to each as if the other wished to end the relationship. This is perhaps one of the cruelest things Foggy has ever done, but he clearly feels he is sparing both Heather and Matt a lot of pain. This creates an interesting new twist on Foggy's character and makes him more complex and less one-dimensional.

During "Born Again," Miller's second run on the book, the tone has shifted to become a few shades darker. This applies to Foggy as well. He continues along the same trajectory laid out during the very end of the first Miller run. He hasn't become dark *per se*, just a more well-rounded character. In fact, his life seems to be going in the right direction – despite having to worry about the increasingly distant and delusional Matt. He has started dating Glorianna O'Breen – his now ex wife's niece and Matt's former girlfriend – and the scenes of Foggy and Glorianna enjoying life together stand in stark contrast to the torment Matt goes through. During one of his talks with Glorianna, in *Daredevil* #226 (Jan 1986), the issue leading up to "Born Again," we also see Foggy eloquently sum up his and Matt's relative strengths and weaknesses in a way that is both poignant and a good reflection of their years of working together: "Matt was the *whiz*, no doubt about it. You read him *four words* and Matt, he'd do you a *speech* on it that'd make *Jefferson* crawl up out of his grave and take notice. / [...] The only thing Matt *wasn't* much good at was the *details*, never had the *patience*. That's where *I* came in, with my steel-trap mind. / Way I always put it, Matt was *inspiration*, and me, I was *perspiration*..." Any reader who has followed the work of Nelson & Murdock for any real amount of time would likely agree with Foggy's assessment: Matt is the creative genius with a natural talent for his chosen career, and Foggy is the ever-dutiful workhorse as well as the more disciplined of the two.

As the story in "Born Again" progresses, we see yet another shift take place in the lives and respective roles of Matt and Foggy. Matt gradually emerges from the darkness into the light – at the end of *Daredevil* #233, he's seen happily reunited with Karen Page – while Foggy's life takes a wrong turn when he agrees to take a job for a corporation connected to the Kingpin. This direction for Foggy is explored by writer Ann Nocenti in her subsequent run on the title, in which the charming Foggy Nelson becomes more and more corrupted by his new environment. In a story arc that begins in *Daredevil* #248 (Nov 1987) and that marks Foggy's first appearance during the Nocenti run, we see Foggy brag about his office to Glorianna as he's getting ready to defend Kelco, a company whose dumped waste has blinded a little boy named Tyrone. In *Daredevil* #255 (June 1988), Foggy faces off against the lawyer Matt has trained to represent Tyrone's family, and his conscience catches up with him: "It shouldn't matter. Law is *indifferent*, law defends the *laws*. / A lawyer is not supposed to question who's right or wrong, but rather to represent his client, and therefore the *system*. / Then why do I feel like I'm sitting on the *'wrong'* side of the courtroom?"

Being reminded of his old friend, and the ideals they used to fight for together, has a big impact on Foggy. Realizing the extent of his own corruption, Foggy eventually leaves his new flashy job, and by *Daredevil* #291 (Apr 1991), Nocenti's final issue, the old partners are reunited. In the next few issues, they begin setting up a new practice together. Nelson & Murdock is back, but we don't see anything close to the silly Foggy we met in the early Miller run until Karl Kesel comes along to usher in a new era.

And so, the pendulum swings yet again.

My Best Friend is a Super-Hero

In terms of the relationship between Matt and Foggy, the most pivotal event in *Daredevil* history is the moment in which Foggy finally learns the truth about Matt's secret life as Daredevil. Karen Page finds out as early as *Daredevil* #57 (Oct 1969), but it takes more than three decades and well over 300 issues for Foggy to discover that his closest friend and law partner is actually a well-known super-hero. Things are made even more complicated by the fact that, by the time the truth is revealed, Matt had been presumed dead ever since he faked his death to protect his identity in *Daredevil* #325 (Feb 1994). Since then, and until Karen and Foggy find Matt in his apartment at the very end of

Daredevil #347 (Dec 1995), Matt had been living under the assumed name Jack Battlin.

When Foggy and Karen find Matt, he's in a state of complete apathy following the unraveling of his sense of identity, as portrayed in the story arc "Inferno" (*Daredevil* #345-347, Oct-Dec 1995), written by J. M. DeMatteis. Because of Matt's failure to communicate, Karen is the first to take the brunt of the rage Foggy experiences after the initial shock of discovering his friend has been lying to him for years starts to subside. In *Daredevil* #348 (Jan 1996), when Karen suggests that the two of them try to find Matt some help, Foggy lashes out at her:

> *"We"?!* / When did it suddenly become *"we"?!* / All these years you kept me out of it... kept your little secrets... you and Matt *both*! / *You knew*, Karen! / You knew he was *Daredevil*, and you never trusted me with the truth... me, his best friend / You didn't tell me – even when we thought he was *dead*! / Or did you know that was a lie, too? Sure, I'll bet you *did*!

At the end of the issue, the ever-dependable Foggy – likely a better friend than Matt deserves – goes to patch things up with Karen and tell her she is not alone. When Karen says she thought Foggy hated her, he replies, "You need me now. *Matt* needs me. I'll hate you *later*." As a reader, it's natural to feel relieved that Foggy is finally truly in a position to join Matt's inner circle. At the same time, no one can fault him for feeling resentful even as he's able to temporarily set aside these feelings out of the sense of loyalty that has become such a hallmark of his character.

This doesn't mean all is well, however. Foggy, to his credit, given the scale of Matt's many years deception, is not quick to let his old friend back into his life. When the two estranged friends meet again, in *Daredevil* #352 (May 1996), it is a strained encounter. In his Daredevil guise, Matt rescues Foggy from the villain Mastermind (Martinique Jason). Before they go their separate ways, Matt offers Foggy his outstretched hand, saying, "Foggy, I want to be here for *you* – for my *friends*. *Today*. / What do you say, *partner*?" Foggy says nothing and does not shake Matt's hand. It would have been easy for the various writers of the issues to come forward in the wake of "Inferno" to get Matt and Foggy's relationship patched up quickly and move on. To their credit, they give this shift in the two friends' relationship the time it needs to happen in a way that feels more natural. By not having Foggy dismiss Matt's betrayal so easily, he comes across as a more realistic character. He may be loyal, but he also has a breaking point and will not allow Matt to take his friendship for granted. If Matt wants him back, he is going to have to work for it.

Fortunately for Nelson & Murdock, the story does not end here. In *Daredevil* #353 (June 1996), Matt simply walks into court in the middle of Foggy's case and takes a seat next to him. After the trial ends, they are met by an army of reporters and Foggy keeps up appearances, holding the front door to their office for Matt, until the two make it inside. In reference to a comment Matt makes about remembering the number of steps to their office, Foggy finally speaks out: "Okay, Matt – you can stop *pretending*, now. / This whole 'blind' thing. I know you're really *Daredevil*! / Some 'best friend' – lying to me all these years... playing me for a *fool*..." At this point, Matt sets him straight and tells him the accident that blinded him also heightened his remaining senses. At long last, Foggy finally knows everything there is to know about the man he thought he had known for years. Learning the details of the special gifts that allow Matt to be Daredevil, despite his blindness, makes it easier for Foggy to move forward because it saves him from feeling like a complete fool for never realizing the truth on his own. It also makes Matt's deceit into more of a case of lying by omission than the full-scale betrayal that Foggy had initially suspected. During their conversation, Matt adds that he never even told his own father, which further underscores what a rare privilege it is for Foggy to now be among the few who know the truth. This too makes forgiveness easier.

Daredevil #353 also marks the first appearance of tough-as-nails lawyer Rosalind Sharpe, who approaches Matt and Foggy to ask them to join her practice. It's clear who she's really after – it's Matt's skills she wants, not Foggy's – but it's Foggy who's yearning for a step up in his career. As we are about to find out, Rosalind Sharpe and Foggy Nelson have a very special relationship. In *Daredevil* #360 (Jan 1997), we learn that Rosalind is Foggy's biological mother and was once married to Foggy's father. The woman Foggy refers to as "mom," Anna Nelson, is the one who raised him.[3]

---

[3] Foggy's family was first introduced in *Daredevil* #108 (Mar 1978), when they arrive at the hospital after Foggy, then District Attorney, has been shot. His parents are introduced as Mr. and Mrs. Edward Nelson, and with them are Foggy's sister Candace, the only other member of the Nelson clan who would go on to make recurring appearances in the book. In a later issue, *Daredevil* #122 (June 1975), a TV reporter refers to Foggy's father as Franklin Nelson, Sr. – rather than Edward Nelson – while reporting on Foggy's kidnapping by HYDRA. Oddly enough, there has also been mention of an older, unnamed brother, in *Daredevil* #347 (Dec 1995),

With the news of Matt's secret and his biological mother back in his life, the remainder of *Daredevil* Vol. 1 proves an interesting time for Foggy. In terms of his relationship with Matt, the two quickly mend their friendship, even though Foggy keeps bringing up the topic of Matt's deception every now and then. However, the two of them are now free to be a team in ways they never could be in the past. With Matt being able to talk openly about his activities as Daredevil around Foggy, the need for lies and smokescreens is eliminated, which makes for a much healthier relationship between the two lawyers.

Foggy learning about Matt's other life is a pivotal point in their relationship, to the extent that it's difficult to imagine the stories that have come later playing out as they did had Foggy not been in on Matt's secret. The reveal shows that Foggy should be taken seriously as a member of Daredevil's supporting cast. No longer is he the buffoon outsider; Foggy Nelson can finally stand up and be counted as a man to be trusted and a man who knows completely the world he inhabits. The Daredevil identity becomes a central aspect of Matt and Foggy's personal and professional relationship.

When Matt's secret is leaked to the press in the arc "Out" (*Daredevil* Vol. 2 #32-37, Jun-Nov 2002), Foggy immediately makes the decision to support his friend, even though lying to protect him makes Foggy an accomplice. In *Daredevil* Vol. 2 #33 (July 2002), when Matt talks about the outing as his cross to bear, Foggy says, "I've been waiting my entire life for this. For the *one* time that you needed me more than I needed you. / To *be* there when you *really* needed me. / I am *so* in this." Clearly, Matt really does need Foggy, because when Matt starts contemplating coming clean, it's his best friend who needs to start doling out the legal advice:

> Oh Matt – / "Come clean"? / What are you talking about? / Matt Murdock tries cases as a lawyer... / ...and as Daredevil, he's a vigilante? / Working either side of the law? / This means Matt Murdock defrauded the American justice system by faking a trial against Daredevil. And that's just the most recent example. Matt – you can't. / You can't come clean.

Foggy has always been the voice of reason to the thrill of action that Matt represents. Matt is known to fly off the handle, and it's now Foggy who must steer the ship and right the course.

Foggy stays by Matt's side every step of the way. What is so compelling about this time in Matt and Foggy's life is that Foggy really is able to deliver on

---

but the brother in question has never been featured or mentioned since.

his promise to be there for Matt, who needs him in a way he never has before, because the troubles Matt is facing are not the kind you can alleviate through fisticuffs. Not this time. Foggy is with him when he faces a sea of reporters and lies to the entire world (*Daredevil* Vol. 2 #36, Oct 2002), and he is with him when they go on to sue a newspaper for printing what both he and Matt know to be the truth (*Daredevil* Vol. 2 #37, Nov 2002). He's the one who goes to help Matt out, bringing him coffee and waiting to give him a ride home when he's brought in for questioning by the police (*Daredevil* Vol. 2 #44, Apr 2003), and he finds Matt a safe place to live after the Yakuza have nearly killed him (*Daredevil* Vol. 2 #59, Jun 2004). When Matt is all but defeated, Foggy becomes the strong one, for once coming across as the "big brother," if you will.

The Bendis run also contains a fair amount of humor and paints a very convincing portrait of why Matt and Foggy are such good friends. In the past, their differences in terms of temperament and overall personality have been big enough to make the two seem like something of an odd pair, but in these issues Matt and Foggy are completely believable as the kind of longtime friends who actually would enjoy hanging out together and just talking. In *Daredevil* Vol. 2 #43 (Apr 2003), when Matt meets Milla, the first woman he has ever married, he asks Foggy what she looks like. Foggy jokingly comes back with an "I'm not telling you," before teasing him with, "How is it that, blind as you are, every one of your girlfriends ends up looking like a European supermodel?" On a different occasion in *Daredevil* Vol. 2 #62 (Sept 2004), when Matt calls him Franklin, Foggy replies, "I love it when you call me Franklin; it's so Irish Catholic of you." Bendis writes Foggy and Matt on an even playing field. Though the world has clearly gifted Matt many times over what Foggy has, they only know each other as friends. After 40 years, these men finally feel like equals.

Conclusion

In the early days of *Daredevil*, the big question seemed to be what poor Foggy would do without Matt. These days, the question everyone should be asking is what Matt would do without Foggy. Just as Matt has evolved as a character, becoming at once more resilient and vulnerable, Foggy has changed with the times as well, and grown into the complex character he is today.

While Foggy has developed a sense of independence and confidence, particularly over the last decade, he still harbors aspects of all the different iterations on the character we have seen to date. He is brave in spite of himself, a serious professional with a sharp mind, and a charming character who, when used to that effect, can put both humor and heart into any scene. He also continues to be the mirror in which we are able to see Matt Murdock's reflection more clearly, in good times as well as bad. In terms of supporting characters, it doesn't get much better than Foggy Nelson. I am sure Matt Murdock would agree.

Brian Michael Bendis makes the relationship between Matt Murdock and Foggy Nelson feel more like true partners than ever before. From *Daredevil* Vol. 2 #46 (June 2003). Art by Alex Maleev. Copyright © Marvel Comics.

Blind Dates and Broken Hearts: The Tragic Loves of Matthew Murdock

by Ryan K. Lindsay

Does how we love define us as people?

Matthew Michael Murdock is a man who seems only to know how to love completely. He has never let go of the perfect image of his parents, even though they both failed him in many ways. Every woman he has ever been serious about has resulted in tragedy. He still expects to find a peace in Hell's Kitchen that doesn't want to be found. Matt sees everything in the world as pure until proven tainted – except for himself. Matt doubts and berates himself constantly, so finding acceptance and love in the arms of another person is a quest for which he will always battle. For this hero, it may be the ultimate battle, even more important than saving innocent lives or stopping deranged maniacs. Filling the gap in his soul is Matt's true pursuit.

There have been five major women in Matt's life. Each partner represents a different love: true love, first love, convenient love, nasty love, and self love. There have also been other ladies but they're of lesser concern and were certainly banal in comparison to the main five. Heather Glenn and Glorianna O'Breen might have been interesting, but they aren't stellar. And while Echo had potential, it was left sorely untapped. You can't say Murdock hasn't tried. But you have to wonder, is Matt Murdock searching for true love or does he float through a haze of sex and intimacy without believing in its existence?

Matt is also a character who has been active for five decades. His relationship with relationships is often a product, in any given story, is a product of the time as well as his major creators. Since love is a social construct rather than a concrete commodity, this means Matt is a great indicator of how love has been viewed over the years. What does it then say that he predominantly peddles in tragedy? Does it take the Devil to prove that "there is no evil angel but love?"

Karen Page

It all begins with Karen Page, Matt Murdock's true love. How interesting that we don't save the true love for the end. Stan Lee, huckster and mastermind that he was, did not bury the lead. From the very first issue, we are delivered the woman to whom Matt would always compare all others. After a handful of obligatory pages filled with text-dense, expository narrative, Lee instructs his artist to drop a blonde onto the page. Karen Page gives herself away with her first line spoken to Matt Murdock in *Daredevil* Vol. 1 #1 (Apr 1964): "I hope you'll be pleased with me!"

This bombshell of coy pomp and big hair is initially a token for the hero to collect. This working girl shows no hint of being independent in thought or action; she is merely the prize. She waits for her chosen man to make his move. While he idles, she keeps a photo of him in her desk drawer. She obviously cannot bear to be far from him. In retrospect, Karen can come off as a female stereotype, and she receives not a whiff of characterisation that doesn't involve fawning or yearning.

Karen is a stranger to New York, further allowing Matt can swoop in and play the gilded saviour. Today, it's hard to understand why Matt would be interested in such a paper-thin construct as Karen. For this to make sense, you must take into account the fact that Matt isn't a modern man. He's an alpha male from the '60s, via the ego and hype of Stan Lee, and a romantic conquest is exactly what it sounds like. This is not a union on equal ground but a passionate climb with Matt at the pinnacle for both parties.

Whenever Matt and Karen inhabit a panel together, the soap opera drama is cloying. There is no trope too sickening or turgid to be exploited in Lee's run.

The main dynamic between Matt and Karen during this period is that she wants only to care for this poor blind man. She does not see the capable man who looks like a movie star, has the body of an athlete, graduated with a top degree, and now practises successfully in his chosen field. None of that is as important to Karen as his ability to see. Her motivation to care for him could not be more superficial, yet it works perfectly within the drama. Every time Karen wants to help Matt, to cradle his gentle soul in her arms, he shuns her because he does not believe someone like her would ever want to shoulder the burden of him and his many, many problems.

Blindness is such a factor between the two that Karen spends a good deal of her time and effort trying to prompt Matt towards cures for his affliction. It's as if she believes that, with this barrier removed, there would be nothing to stand in their way; happiness and eternity could roll out before them. She wants to care for Matt in every conceivable way, yet for all her studying of him, she does not see that he loves her too. It's as if caring for him would actually itself be the bond between them, and she does not actually want a cure because she prefers the Florence Nightingale effect too much. It's as much about how much the *situation* makes her feel as it is about how *he* makes her feel.

With neither lover willing to actually love, we are thrust into the dramatically ironic waters of the unrequited. Lee clearly knew that a hero in love is nowhere near as interesting as a hero forever in lust. The latter can be played off indefinitely in a variety of ways, but the former can only lead down a predictable and formulaic path (a principle still believed by the establishment at the House of Ideas). Lee obviously knew the chase is the most important part of any love, and what better medium to show this endless courtship than the perennial second act of comics, in which firm conclusions are not always the norm.

The use of thought balloons during this era offers us great insight into the ensuing dramatic irony, in which we see parallel trains of thought that never meet because the interpretation of events is skewed on both sides. Matt hears Karen's heart escalate, something no man other would have the ability to do, yet he misreads it as her being in love with Foggy Nelson, Matt's best friend and law partner. She sees Matt covering his tracks as Daredevil and wrongly assumes he is acting strange because he does not like her. It's a train wreck of emotion and miscommunication – and is also exactly what makes the book interesting. Nothing is easy for this hero.

The final problem between Matt and Karen is that Daredevil is a man who can put Karen into danger's path, and he often does, causing Matt to feel guilty. He knows if she were to become more intimate with him, the target on her head would grow exponentially. For those of us who know Karen's future, we can see how wise a choice this is, but at the time it is just Matt making yet another excuse. He'll find any way to sabotage his own happiness because that's what a hero does: he sacrifices all for the greater good.

If Karen Page is Matt's true love, he certainly isn't ready for her under Lee's tenure. To prove how ludicrous his feelings for her are, he sets about throwing the ultimate spanner into the works of their budding romance. In doing so, he creates one of the greatest Daredevil players to ever exist: Mike Murdock (*Daredevil* #25, Feb 1967).

Matt Murdock was an only child, and his college friend Foggy Nelson surely knew that. Yet when Mike Murdock is introduced as Matt's twin brother, everyone seems to buy into this thin tale. It's mildly believable in that, if you had a twin as embarrassing, dated, annoying, jingoistic, and psychologically anachronistic as this, you'd probably have hidden him from sunlight all your life too. Mike Murdock explodes onto the scene and shocks and appalls everyone so quickly, you can't help but see Matt's plan work instantly. The focus is taken away from Matt, and that's all he needed. The heat was getting too close to identifying him as the Scarlet Swashbuckler of Hell's Kitchen. This is sparked by a letter from Spider-Man – a plot point so contrived, you know Lee assumed the majesty of his new creation would take all attention off the plot hole, the same way it takes the spotlight off the blind lawyer.

For a much longer interval than you might imagine, Mike Murdock wears loud shirts, talks jive, and leeches over Karen Page. He clogs up the pages and obfuscates the truth to the point where you worry if Matt might have lost all concept of reality. In truth, Mike is just a construct to show how far Matt will go to avoid love or commitment. He uses Mike to create a love triangle (or possible square, with Daredevil involved) in which only two people actually exist. How this is preferable to the situation Matt previously found himself in is debatable. Matt goes from being one confused man to being three very conflicted individuals, all vying for one lady's attention and love. It's as if he wants it to be as difficult as possible.

Only Matt and Karen are real, yet Matt worries Karen is more attracted to Mike. He thinks she likes his extroverted confidence, and if she buys that he's Daredevil, it's another reason to like the loud, sighted twin. But does Karen like Mike because he's Daredevil, Daredevil because he's the hero to be idolised, Matt because he's the one she can rescue, or none of the above because they represent a man with a completely fractured psyche and far too many convoluted avenues to go down in order to avoid any real feelings?

In the end, when Mike and Karen are getting too close and Matt doesn't know which persona is more fun to be, Mike has to die. Matt must realize that coordinating one repressed love life was hard enough; doing it for a bunch of different guys just is not satisfying. Matt fakes the death of his fake twin, and he's once more left alone with Karen. It's hard to tell if Matt is happy with this resolution or if it's merely another corner he's painted himself into, one where Karen is always present with him and he just doesn't know what to do.

Rather than go back to the old status quo, Roy Thomas and Gene Colan finally got Matt to move a little bit forward and reveal his identity to Karen. The moment itself is delivered in some gorgeous pages. The flashback page in issue #58 (Nov 1969) is a fractured moment of quiet beauty, but it's not what Matt does that interests the reader so much as it is his reasons why. Daredevil had just gone through a serious battle, one he almost didn't survive, and then he decides revealing all to Karen is the best move. Is it his own mortality and selfishness that propel this move, or are his intentions pure? You can only wonder if this is a man invigorated and seizing the day, or if he's simply a drowning soul struggling to hold onto the one solid piece of debris in his sphere of murky waters.

How is it possible that Karen has not run screaming from this mess of a man or is she simply blind to his faults?

The comic spent years developing these characters as the perfect bookends for one other, but once they come together you instantly wonder if all the hype was anywhere near reality. It's the Comics Code-approved version of finally waking up next to that dream girl, suddenly seeing every flaw, and knowing you have to get out of Dodge, stat. The shine is off the apple and you cannot unring that bell.

If drama is the currency of the series (and most entertaining narratives), once Matt and Karen come together there's no motivation to make their ride suddenly even out to a smooth run. The creators simply had to find new twists, and they drop a great one. Karen and Matt have found each other, and we finally get the answer to whom Karen loves more: the blind lawyer or the lithe super-hero. Karen asks Matt to stop being Daredevil because she fears for his safety. For such a thing to actually take place would rob the book of its lead, so you don't expect Matt to acquiesce at all – which means guaranteed drama.

But while this adds another dramatic layer to the book, it also serves to further split this couple apart – you would think higher forces wanted happiness to only be an illusion. For a love painted to be true and pure, the first five years or more of *Daredevil* work very hard to constantly place obstacles and barriers between these two characters. It makes you wonder why people look back on this connection as being the sort of love that's best for Matt. Is it nostalgic myopia or a retroactive force of will?

When the baton was passed from Stan Lee to Roy Thomas, Karen Page's days were numbered. She's a drag, a ball and chain, and Thomas was stewarding Daredevil into a new time and age – the '70s. You don't step into this decade with the girl you had in the '60s; you move on, you explore the world and other nationalities. You have a little fun, and when it comes to women Daredevil at the time certainly could have used a bit of this.

The love between Matt Murdock and Karen Page is more an indication of the verve and drama Lee wanted woven through every panel of his books. It's hard to assess the purity of their adoration, or why Lee found it so necessary. Sometimes you just have to sit back and enjoy the ride, even if the characters cannot.

If Karen Page was Matt Murdock's true love (when she returns much later, we see she might just have seemed that through the fog of Matt's mind, not her actual relationship with him), it soon becomes apparent that his next girlfriend, Natasha Romanoff, a.k.a. the Black Widow, is a femme clearly selected to match up better with Daredevil. Karen couldn't handle Matt going out and risking his life as Daredevil, but Natasha encourages it through her own actions as a spy and superhero. She brings out the dormant love tiger within Matt, and he would never be the same again.

Although Karen leaves Matt and the title, she's rarely far away. Matt attempts to move on, but his thoughts often wander back to Karen, and on the occasions she appears, he again feels conflicted by her presence or aroused by her touch. There's no way for Karen not to stir an engaging response within Matt.

In the years following their break up, Karen manages to sashay into Matt's peripherals enough to steal the odd kiss and cloud his mind once more. They are like a binary planet broken out of orbit but eventually crossing orbits in the dark. Their movements always seemed defined by the other, or some intangible connection that exists between them.

Karen was the girl Matt pined for, the pinnacle of his idealistic love. She was retroactively perfect, and Frank Miller had the idea to have her brought so very low. "Born Again" (*Daredevil* #227-233, Feb-Aug 1986) opens with Karen sweating about a lot of things. She's stuck in a seedy world on an endless loop of drugs and worse. Instead of finding solace in the memory of her old life, she sells it because it's worth something. She knows the truth about Daredevil and that's knowledge worth tangible cash to some people. She needs a hit badly, and there are only so many ways she knows to pay for it. She's betraying her love, and a man who deeply loves her, but the next dose of mind-altering medicine might just wash away the memory of her terrible act.

This is the moment Karen breaks Matt's heart. He doesn't see it coming and doesn't know it's her. This is also the moment Karen becomes the ex we hate, the one who uses our confidential knowledge against us. A lover is someone in whom you confide, in whom you trust, but it's harder to trust that same person when they've changed, the world has changed, and they're suddenly no longer beholden to you.

Miller uses one page to show Karen's destructive moment. It's a hard moment to redeem. It would have been easy to leave Karen down the river, but Miller takes the time to return to her later, and build audience empathy, because that's exactly what Matt feels.

Most men would hate Karen for her actions, and be justified in most feelings, and yet Matt can't do it. He's too good, inside, and his love for her is too pure. It only looks like Miller is ruining and crushing Karen; instead, he's actually making her relevant again. He's tangibly showcasing Matt's love for her and what it can overcome. The hero is being run through a gauntlet and so is his love. There's a romantic story behind all the porn, drugs, guns, and utter destruction.

It doesn't matter that Karen's sold information ends up in the hands of Wilson Fisk and that he uses it to ruin everything Matt holds dear. It doesn't matter what Karen has done with her time away from Matt. It doesn't matter how long it has been. Karen Page and Matt Murdock are in love. Karen has her crosses to bear, and her journey is long, but when she ends up in Matt's arms in the snow, it feels right. It's a perfect moment where the head might not understand the information, but the heart processes everything instantly.

Fisk tore Matt's life apart, but upon Karen's reappearance, Matt realises he's lost nothing – nothing that was important to him, anyway. It's when Nuke, the pill-popping and delusional veteran, attacks and harms Karen that Matt springs back into action as Daredevil. For everything that's been done to him, this is the line he will not accept being crossed. Karen is his muse, his inspiration, his everything. She might have done him wrong, but it led him to a new place in his life and he's able to see the positive in that change. Matt doesn't stand injustice, yet overlooks Karen's ultimate transgression of his moral code. That is his love.

The final splash page of Matt and Karen, by David Mazzucchelli in issue #233, looks remarkably like Bob Dylan's cover for *The Freewheelin' Bob Dylan* (1963). It's visual shorthand for that perfect connection and one hell of a way to close such a dark and violent arc. Despite it all, everything is okay again. Matt is happy; he's got Karen. This is how Miller and Mazzucchelli leave Matt. This is how they thank him for all the good times. He's forgiven, and extremely forgiving.

Karen then enters another period of being in and out of Matt's life. Ann Nocenti uses her, and makes her excessively supportive, but eventually washes her away with the spicy rinse that is Typhoid Mary. Matt betrays Karen (*Daredevil* #255 Jun 1988), which can't come as a surprise considering his wandering ways over many years, and they enter an uncertain future, possibly on the rocks. Matt works to get her back but his heart never seems in it. He isn't the driven, motivated, and passionate Matt we know. He's just keeping up appearances, and by forcing the connection between them to remain open, he's hurting her more than he's helping them.

Eventually, though, as is inevitable, Karen and Matt reconnect. It's just too easy for them to backslide into a relationship that satisfies and offers completion but never delivers. Things look good for a brief time, and then Matt lets Karen believe he is dead. She suffers the ultimate grief, only for him to return soon after. Their rollercoaster doesn't just include break-ups but now transcends the mortal plane. With a fresh commitment, Matt lands Karen yet again. This is all within a few dozen issues, and the soap operatic element is apparent and in full force. The good times are only as interesting as their

The final page of "Born Again" echoes the classic cover of *The Freewheelin' Bob Dylan*. From *Daredevil* #233 (Aug 1986). Art by David Mazzucchelli. Copyright © Marvel Comics.

moment of breaking up, which can only be topped by the inevitable reconciliation. It's formulaic, rote, and relatively uninspired. The story might be good (and is in parts), but the relationship within it doesn't hold much merit at all. Even the murder charge Karen faces don't hold much interest because they are only more things to overcome in a long line of things to overcome. The drama and scandal become overkill.

Daredevil was cancelled in 1998 and relaunched one month later. To help bring in new readers, filmmaker Kevin Smith was put on writing duties. He decided to kick the hornet's nest by bringing back Karen Page. He then gave her AIDS. Realistically, she lived a dangerous lifestyle for far too long, and this is the sort of real-life risk that many worried about. The only surprise is that Matt doesn't seem too concerned about himself. If she contracted the disease during her porn star / drug addict days, he had definitely knocked boots with her after that. This *should* be addressed, but isn't. The fact it took so long to finally show in Karen's system is discussed, but Matt's safety isn't a concern.

It's hard to tell if Smith is being socially prescient, scandalously salacious, or just conforming to a trend in comics where a new writer stamps his feet by killing off something precious and established. Plenty of writers have removed something from the communal sandbox because they didn't know how to add anything, and Smith's plot has this familiar feel. He sets Karen up with AIDS, and this drives a strong wedge into the rift that already is her tortured past. It's another opportunity for Matt to judge her, or hate her, or blame her, yet he does none of those things. He snaps at her once, more out of frustration than true disgust, then stands by her. He is still the best man he can be. But is this a reflection of Matt's love for Karen, or just his usual moral code?

The final moment comes courtesy of Bullseye. He was the one to kill Elektra, so it's fitting that he get to end Karen's life as well. A monstrous massacre in a church culminates with Bullseye hurling Daredevil's billy club back at him and having it lodge in Karen's chest (*Daredevil* Vol. 2 #5, Mar 1999). She dies in Matt's arms – also echoing Elektra's death. The repetition forces Matt to assess how toxic he is to the women he loves.

Matt reflects, after Karen is gone, about the good times. He doesn't dwell in the many terrible times they had shared; he looks to the light. It only causes him more anguish. There's a sad aspect to Karen's death, in that the ways it was a carbon copy of Elektra's death make it mean less. Any emotional resonance only reminds you of the far more effective death of Elektra at the hands of Frank Miller. Smith played with most of Miller's toys: the terse captions, Bullseye, a death of a loved one, and Maggie Murdock. His arc is good, but ultimately it's a Valentine to Miller's superior work, and Karen Page becomes collateral damage, committed to the history books. Her tragedy is a headstone in the landscape of Matt Murdock's life.

At least it's been over a decade, and no one has resurrected her.

The Black Widow

Matt spent years being an unsure and almost coy lover. He played games not only with Karen but with his own heart. If he constantly misled anyone, it was himself. As he progresses in his relationship with Natasha Romanoff, the Black Widow, he becomes more dominant. She unleashes his inner fire, then acts surprised when she gets burned.

By the time Matt Murdock gets to the Widow, Lee and Thomas had made way for Gerry Conway, and our Scarlet Swashbuckler is no longer simply a blind lawyer but something more than human. He doesn't only date his secretary; he makes love to another hero. He conquerors that which all men seek to tame: the independent woman. The Black Widow is a Russian agent, trained in many martial arts, and she is a smart operative. She holds her own against any opponent and on any battlefield. This is the next conquest on Matt's list, and it's a complete change from what he had with Karen.

A massive difference between Matt and Karen was the fact she wanted him to settle down – no more Daredevil, simply a nice blind lawyer husband in the suburbs. Matt did not want to acquiesce to these conditions and so moved on. His next femme is someone who *herself* goes about town dodging bullets and wearing skintight leather. The odds she'll want Matt to stop doing the same are pretty slim. Is this Matt trying to have the best of both worlds – a bit of love, without having to actually change his life?

At the very start of the relationship, you can already see Matt and Natasha are not going to be together forever. Matt is merely stretching his wings and enjoying the life of a super-hero. Natasha is Matt's rebound girl, everything Karen could not and would not give him. He's with her more because of the juxtaposition to Karen than the actual merit of Natasha herself.

But none of that means the two of them can't have any fun along the way.

In some ways, Matt becomes a more distinctive and stronger character; in other ways, he can be interpreted as a chauvinist. He morphs to reflect the swinging '70s; it's not 1964 anymore. Continuity follows the present, and the present of the '70s didn't want the stuffy Matt who doubted himself constantly and couldn't score with a girl so clearly in love with him. The '70s demanded that Matt to take charge and finally enjoy himself. Conway does his best to wrest Daredevil from the shadows of the past (and flagging sales) by drastically altering the love life aspect of this book.

The Black Widow oozes more sex appeal than any secretary could ever manage, and the title certainly capitalized upon this. The sexy spy Black Widow is eye candy for the book – and quite a welcome addition. She has curves and a suit that shows them off. She has the outgoing nature, and the profession, that put her in a position to look appealing. Beyond that, she's constantly put into positions of various undress, during her early appearances. It's as if we aren't even supposed to take her seriously. She's barely a character on her own. Instead, she's relegated to being more a representation of Matt's new ability to control his own life.

The Widow is a snack of a girlfriend, and Matt was never going to be full afterwards. It's a fun ride but not a wholly satisfying one. Matt doesn't even over-think it; he barely knows how to function without agonising internally, but four issues after introductions, he's having Natasha visit for sleepovers. He plunges into the waters with both feet, and the only options are to drown or get back out of the water; he's not going to live down there. Matt is not Namor.

Everyone is on the same page. They can see "You take caring where you find it... when you live as [Matt] does" (*Daredevil* #87 May 1972). No one goes into this relationship unsure of what they'll get, but it apparently seems worth the inevitable heartbreak. Two captions later the epigraph of this relationship is written over a scene of its beginning: "But even the good things don't last."

Before Natasha and Matt can even get off the ground, they are grounded by a very cruel act. Matt is graced with the presence of his original love, and in a hot minute he drops Natasha like a bad habit and embraces Karen Page in a kiss that can only be described as passionate and full of meaning. Neither Karen nor Matt, both in front of their respective new flames, make any effort to hide this moment. It's only a true love you cannot hide. How sad for Natasha. The captions from Conway spell it all out: "For in his *memory*, nothing ever changes -- / -- *nothing* is ever *past*" (*Daredevil* #85, Apr 1972).

Matt isn't moving on any time soon, and everyone knows it. However, his return to Karen is played out in this issue as more of a "you can't go home again" scenario. And directly afterwards, Natasha is waiting for Matt. She even gets a wave and a "your turn" from Karen. It's awkward. It's unbelievable. And yet we're sold on it completely, because the cause for such lust is Matt Murdock – and who could ever resist?

The great San Franciscan Experiment for Daredevil failed on many levels. Sales didn't pick up, he still didn't solve crime, and his love life became a hot mess.

It's a shame the San Franciscan move didn't lead to greater success, because it really should have worked. When a hero dates a hero, they ought to understand each other; they should save *each other*, yet it does not work that way. Perhaps it's a matter of timing, or a matter of drama, but Matt and the Widow are disastrous together. They don't become a team through their lusty union; they don't become *more* because of each other and their shared love. Instead, Matt becomes more aloof, and Natasha becomes more dependent. They ruin each other as they progress through their relationship. They aren't what Matt truly wants, and most of the time he can barely work to hide it.

Eventually, Matt pushes Natasha away. There was never going to be any other option. The longer it went on, the more each would fall further into their new negative role. The move to San Francisco only exacerbates the issue; it isolates both of them, especially Matt, from their usual safety networks. This wasn't a flirty love getaway, but rather a destructive withdrawal from the real world and a slide into the sludge of a harmful relationship.

The fascinating thing is that Matt obviously wants out of the relationship, yet he's not the one to pull the pin. Natasha starts to feel assimilated, like she's the sexy sidekick in Daredevil's life. How funny, because that's exactly what she becomes in the book. Even with a shared title on the cover, Natasha is relegated to a damsel-in-distress role *far* too often. She is another shiny element in the background of Matt's tale. She removes herself from the relationship with some internal self-respect intact – though she doesn't move on to headline another title. The character might win on the page, but she doesn't taste victory within the business of comics. If she's not going to reflect a transition for Matt, then she's not going to be seen at all.

Dating a Russian superspy proved to be no problem for Matt. She should have been his physical, intellectual, and emotional equal, but instead melted to butter in his hands. The Widow wasn't presented as a match for Matt, and that's a real shame. In years to come, she would be shown as a woman more in control of herself around Matt, but their initial pairing proved to miss the point that Matt was dating a hero, and thus an equal.

Natasha is perhaps the most appealing woman Matt has ever dated, but beneath the surface none of the right connections lined up. It even lasts longer than it should, purely because of external factors, but it was never meant to be. Kevin Smith writes an excellent coda to their relationship in his run. In *Daredevil* Vol. 2 #2 (Dec 1998), Natasha appears in Matt's house and slowly unzips her suit. "Couch or roof?" she asks him. There will always be a connection here, but it will also always be surface thin.

I doubt anyone would complain about that.

Elektra

Frank Miller created Elektra because he felt super-heroes should date other superheroes. Black Widow should have fit this criteria, but the way she was portrayed with Matt didn't make her seem very "super." There was barely enough strength left in her to end the relationship. She – or the times – didn't have enough vigor to sustain it. Elektra was a strong lead who could not only hold her own with Matt but could potentially subjugate him.

Miller wondered, in the stellar documentary *The Men Without Fear: Creating Daredevil* (2003), "Why wouldn't [super-heroes] be operatic in their romance, the way there are in their combat?" He felt they should "bring down buildings with their passion." Nothing should be pedestrian; you either go epic or you go home. Miller certainly brought a heightened sense of drama and emotion to the relationship of Matt Murdock and Elektra Natchios. The melodrama is present, as much as it was in Lee's day, but the violent edge to this love is something that Matt had never truly dealt with before.

Miller doesn't just make Elektra Matt's equal but in many ways his superior – or at least so it would appear. She can match him in battle but also brings with her enough issues to match Matt's torrid past. Her name is a giveaway, and the cover of her debut appearance delivers all you need to know: Elektra appears violently out of the shadows, a woman of weapons and death. Poised to strike, her backdrop is a fierce bolt of lightning. She's quick and amorally precise in the delivery of her power. She's so confident and amazing that, looking at that first cover, not even the misspelling of her name on the cover seems to hold her back; she surely knows the entire issue will be given over to her, and it'll get the correct treatment there.

Matt, however, is left stunned and unsure of his next step. He is interrupted and seemingly caught unawares. He's the ultimate fool whose love returns to cripple him and hold his world upside down. Nothing is ever the same after Elektra re-enters his life. She's the storm of his world – sudden, bright, and somewhat scary.

It's then a slight shame that the actual contents of Elektra's initial appearance do not completely live up to this promise. It feels like Miller is going to introduce a true feminine power within the pages of *Daredevil*. But upon closer inspection, both of these characters are equally crushed, not empowered, by the power of their love for each other. In the process, Elektra's tough-as-nails demeanour is shattered as quickly as it's revealed.

Miller shows us a younger Matt Murdock, studying law at Columbia State University. He catches a mere glimpse of Elektra and he's in love. He's prepared to do anything to catch her attention, and he's willing to risk his secrets. It's a bold statement about Matt's initial feelings for this girl that he'll do just about anything for her. He's never been anywhere near as committed to another female that we've seen, and now perhaps that makes sense. He rolled all his dice on Elektra, and it didn't work out. He's been gun-shy ever since the series started because of what happened with her in the past. It's a retcon you can actually use to make sense of the craziness of the Lee era. The flashback is of a young Matt, a man eager to love. This is the unfettered youth of innocence, and Matt's heart is tabula rasa.

The entire sequence – meet, fall in love, enjoy the spectacular perfection of being together, finding adversity, succumbing to adversity, and weeping over the bleeding gap that will never diminish between the two – is played out at a fever pitch. The pages are jam-packed with raw emotion. And while current writers would have decompressed this over a few issues, the brevity of it all makes it play out as it must have felt for the duo, and the characters' connection and separation both feel more visceral for it.

The pairing of Matt and Karen was always sold as pure, but it never felt like a true love. Elektra is explicitly portrayed as a true love, and that adds plenty of inherent qualities to their relationship. It's a younger Matt who loves Elektra, and thus she, and his lingering love of her, will always drop him back to an earlier state of mind. The skills Matt learns, in love and battle, become dulled and transparent by Elektra's mere presence.

She is the first girl to truly instill a set of flaws in Matt. He's usually been pretty cool, or sabotaged himself, but Elektra affects him on a more personal level unlike any other femme did or could. Finally, Matt does not have the upper hand.

In the present, Elektra returns to Matt's life as a villain, and we're made to understand that Matt is himself responsible for the shift in the heart of the one he loved. Without Matt's nascent vigilante actions, Elektra's father would not have died the way he did. In essence, he killed her father – and while the smoking gun wasn't in his hand, it was certainly between their hearts. They might have been perfect for one another, but they'd only ever return to a fractured fable in the future.

In flashback, the way these two young lovers react to the death of Elektra's father is a defining statement for their futures. Elektra cannot see her love for Matt through the haze of her hatred at the world for letting her father die. Surprisingly, she doesn't blame Matt directly, but she knows he stands for a justice system that will never seem just in her eyes. For his part, Matt resiliently tries to bounce back and keep the romantic status quo. He believes they can work through it all, and he's wrong. Elektra gets to be Matt's first love – and the first woman to shatter his heart.

During their great divide, Matt elected to bury Elektra in his mind. She might as well have perished with her father, for all the thought Matt gave her, and their love, over the years afterward. He doesn't want to be hurt, by new girls or by the specter of the old one, so he forgot about Elektra and systematically ignored the others in various ways. That's his short-sighted coping strategy, and it shouldn't shock by this stage. When Elektra emerges, his first romantic wound is torn open, and Matt isn't ready to deal with such pain. Elektra is a little colder toward the entire situation. She's a trained soldier, a mercenary of blood, and so her actions come before her feelings.

By the end of the issue, Matt has saved Elektra, and they share a kiss. It's unclear if they're re-enacting their first kiss, enacting their final kiss, or starting the first kiss of this new era. The answer comes quickly, as Matt leaves Elektra wallowing in the tears of an emotion she hasn't felt in years, while he carries the villain of the story off to face the consequences of his actions. Matt stands for justice and the system, and Elektra's heart will always be crushed within the cogs of that system. Nothing has changed, and no reconciliation is possible.

It's probably a good thing Elektra relearns this lesson so quickly, because she can then get on with being Miller's best Marvel creation – and the ultimate female to temper Matt Murdock's masculine ways. If she returned and there were any doubt or hope about redemption, then Elektra's actions would be tempered. She needs to remain pure in order to completely challenge Matt's concepts of love. Who knows what motives Elektra hid in her heart upon return? Maybe she thought things would be different. She gets one kiss, and then Matt shows he hasn't changed at all. She has to understand that if she follows him it will lead to the same pattern, and who is there left in her life to die but herself?

The next time these two estranged lovers meet, Elektra can't help herself and saves Matt's life. Love isn't a choice; it's barely a reaction. It's just an element of yourself you can no more deny than you can the beating of your heart – or the breaking of it. Elektra is a trained warrior, yet within her lives a human being, with human desires and wants. To be good at her chosen profession of assassin, she feels that she needs to be more than human – or less, depending on your point of view – so she tries to shut down this aspect of herself. It's a brave front she presents.

In issue #175 (Oct 1981), Elektra states her case plainly to the costumed Daredevil: "In college, we were lovers. Now we are enemies. It is that simple." If only it were. Like an orphan trying to tell himself he's not sad, or a soldier about to go "over the top" telling himself he's not scared, Elektra is barely fooling herself, much less anyone else. Daredevil certainly isn't buying it, as he slinks around for another kiss. What endgame is he after? He had her lips on the docks, and he purposefully left them to haul in his criminal prey. What's to say he won't repeat the cycle within a minute, if his hypersensitive ears pick up a distress signal elsewhere in his city?

Elektra responds with a physical statement that she isn't going to be his masturbatory puppet any longer. Glass shatters upon the street below as Elektra kicks Daredevil out the window of this high apartment. Of course, he manages to grapple a hold on a ledge and save himself, but the statement rings true and clear: she's not playing this game again. She might not be fooling herself, or even all of us, but she certainly has Matt on the ropes. This one-page sequence of a near kiss and a closer kick, ending with Elektra sailing off through the air into a smoggy New York sunset, represents the reclamation of Elektra's independence and her determination not to be a victim again. This is her display of strength, both physically and emotionally.

Her resolve doesn't last the entire issue, however; she teams up with Matt to tackle some ninja enemies. The fight concludes, and Matt states his intentions to take Elektra in; she's going to face the justice he champions. He's a single-minded character, and Lady Justice is always going to be his one true love because it's the only femme to which he can stay true. But Matt collapses from injuries sustained defending himself and aiding Elektra. This is Elektra's chance to end their cycle of pain, to "finally be free of him." All she has to do is let him bleed out. It's not her killing him; it's her letting him die. Failure to act makes her less complicit than acting in anger. Yet she cannot do it. True love doesn't die; it just grows old enough for you to start hating its naïve and youthful beginning.

The same page jump cuts to Matt in court with his actual girlfriend, Heather Glenn. We don't need to see Elektra's actions, nor her proof of caring for Matt. The mere sight of him alive tells us everything we need to know. She did the right thing, and it's an admission that she cannot, and will not, live without this man. She is bound to him, and that's probably what she hates the most. She spends just as much time declaring him her enemy as she does wandering the streets around him to protect him and watch from afar. To her, Matt is, as the narrator says in the 1999 film *Fight Club*, "the little scratch on the roof of your mouth that would heal if only you could stop tonguing it, but you can't."

There is a conundrum at the heart of Matt and Elektra's new situation. Life is no longer as simple as being college lovers. They are now people of the world, adults with responsibilities, and their responsibilities are both grave and conflicting.

At the end of issue #176 (Nov 1981), Miller shows his hand in wanting to bring this relationship to a head. A storm brews over Elektra, and the captions ask, "Will she be strong enough when the time comes? / Will she be able to kill the only man she has ever loved?"

The endgame is inevitable, and neither side is able to choose any other alternative. How fortuitous, then, that the resolution is taken out of their hands. It certainly appeared as if neither soldier was prepared to stand aside from their cause. One of Elektra's final acts of independence is to accept a contract killing for the Kingpin, Matt's sworn enemy. For a first love, she becomes a destructive force, steeled in her effort not to be the one broken from this union.

Elektra has gone down in Daredevil history as an object of love, first and foremost. People sometimes seem to forget Elektra was an assassin, a contract killer. They remember she was loved by Matt, and they remember how Miller closes her tale, but they forget that in between she was a murderer. She might have started by helping Matt, against her better judgment, but she also walks into a cinema and kills the informant sitting next to Daily Bugle journalist (and all-around great guy) Ben Urich. Without compunction, she punctures this poor talkative sap and threatens that Ben will be next – a threat she very nearly makes good on by the end of issue #179 (Feb 1982).

Elektra's sai may be read as a phallic symbol that she brings into Matt's world and uses to slowly penetrates and destroy that which he holds dear. This is Elektra taking masculine control, a destructive role, and not a passive stance in the slightest. She doesn't hesitate. She pierces the bodies of men with her steel, which protrudes freely on the other side. It's a role reversal that subtly plays under the radar. The sexually destructive element of Elektra's weapon won't become overtly apparent until a few issues later.

In almost every way, Miller created Elektra to be something Matt had never come across. You might even say she was an anomaly in the super-hero genre at large. Batman might have loved Catwoman, but she was rarely this deadly. Superman always went for the easy and alliterative marks, and Spider-Man hopped from one comely co-ed to the next. With Elektra, Matt found himself drawn to the equivalent of molten lava, rather than the muddied waters of old. It was time for Hell's Kitchen's most eligible bachelor to finally be burned – even if he did have a girlfriend all the way through the Elektra Saga.

Elektra and Matt punch and grapple more than they ever kiss. These are their sex scenes, each blow and magnified sound effect a moment of ecstasy. Perhaps Miller doesn't think these immortals of the rooftops know how to just lie down and express themselves. Perhaps once you've fought aliens and cheated death, you need a little more to get you off. You start off rough and see where it takes you, while your heart pounds in your ears and your words are forever lost.

A hidden bear trap on a rooftop holds Daredevil in one place, and Elektra has won the fight. She doesn't want to kill Matt, nor sever his foot; she wants him helpless. She wants him to know how she felt, all the way back on that fateful night in college when her father was taken from her. She wants to bring Matt's own world down around him and show him how crushing and destroying such an experience can be. One kick sends a wall of bricks over her former love. Revenge is exacted. Then one quick throw takes out the single witness, the ever-present and unfortunate Ben Urich.

It's an interesting to note that Elektra so rarely appears in consecutive issues. She has an impact on the narrative, and Matt's life, and then she disappears again for a little while. It's like Matt can only take her in small doses, or she has to retreat and regroup to steel herself for her next assault on Matt's world. There's no sight of her in issue #180 (Mar 1982) until she appears at the end. The Kingpin gives her the assignment to kill Foggy Nelson. This is the ultimate test to see if Elektra can truly pull the trigger on that which she's so far only knocked around a bit. Foggy is Matt's actual true love, in many ways, and to take that away would be going too far. Asking Elektra to do it is a smart move by the Kingpin.

It's frightening how close Elektra comes to completing the mission. She only stops and lets Foggy escape when he remembers her as Matt's old college flame. This startles Elektra; it almost offends her and certainly angers her. She quickly tells him to leave, almost as if she wants to break Matt but doesn't want the world to know what a terrible ex-girlfriend she's being. Not that Foggy would know – he was just about to be executed. Perhaps it's simply the simple mention of Matt's name – not Daredevil but Matt – that makes her reconsider. Ultimately, she can't do it. That's the last thing we learn about her, before Bullseye enters the scene.

Bullseye is worse than a crazy ex; he's the warped doppelganger who wants to be inside the man he hates. Or perhaps loves. It's complicated with this guy. He gets out of jail and is instantly on the trail of Daredevil. He finds out Elektra has become the Kingpin's new chief assassin, and thus Bullseye's competition for main Daredevil foil, so he sets out to eliminate the competition. He quickly finds her and probably isn't aware that every punch to her face or knee to her chin is another blow he takes at Daredevil's world. He's performing surgically brutal foreplay against the true love of his greatest enemy. And then he ends the fight with his next trick.

Miller states it plainly that Bullseye shoving a sai through Elektra was a rape / murder in the funny books. It was a horrendous sex crime in spandex, and it got past the Comics Code Authority, even with the blood Elektra spills onto the sidewalk as she slowly slinks back to the doorstep of Matt Murdock. These are her final moments, her truest thoughts, and in them her animosity drops completely. There's no point making a last ditch effort to destroy this man, when it will be so much easier to revert back to love. His name is her last words.

Matt is indeed so distraught by her death that he does something most super-heroes never do: he lets his emotion get the better of him, and he takes the villain off the board in a brutal manner. Daredevil and Bullseye perform a ballet of violence across the city, with Bullseye using Elektra's weapons. Bullseye wants to penetrate Daredevil; he wants to be intimate. Daredevil causes Bullseye to fall off a high wire over the street. He does the hero thing and catches the falling villain, but when Bullseye tries to lash out at the hand that is the only thing saving him, Matt has no choice but to drop the sociopathic murderer to his own demise. Sometimes all you need is a simple excuse, and Matt certainly has that.

How interesting that Matt's strongest love is one we don't actually experience on the page. Elektra isn't Matt's girlfriend when Miller depicts her; she's his enemy, and that's how they remain. It takes until her final breathing moments for anything close to care or adoration to appear between the two.

The ultimate act of love, and care, isn't truly become expressed until it's too late, in issue #182 (May 1982). If you ever doubted the effect Elektra had on him, or how much he missed her once she was gone, then you need to slowly read this issue. There's a large element in it of the Punisher, which sets up the next issue, but at the heart of the issue is a man rendered immobile by the dread that he has completely missed his chance with his one true love. He doesn't want to believe she's dead, even though he was there and his extra senses gave him very clear and definite signs that she died in his arms.

Amid the swirling mess of emotions and confusion, Matt does the only thing he feels will help him: he searches for confirmation. He goes to the source. Watching Matt tear apart the Kingpin's goons in a vain attempt to get closer to Elektra is just sad, but it all leads to a creepy graveyard scene in which Matt opens her coffin and smells the dead atoms trapped in with the corpse and does what any blind man does: he touches her face. She's still fresh and looks the same, but there's no life in the skin. Elektra is dead.

It is as if Miller understands the comic-book habit of resurrecting characters, or doing away with the previous month's danger through an easy

Matt initially cannot accept that Elektra is gone. From *Daredevil* #181 (Apr 1982). Art by Frank Miller and Klaus Janson. Copyright © Marvel Comics.

out. There's no easy out for this scenario. There's no mystical ability to save Elektra. Bullseye shoved her own sai through her body, her lungs filled with blood, and she died. Miller effectively closes the book on her, and Matt Murdock is irrevocably changed.

This became a double-tied knot when Miller ended his run by playing through a resurrection scenario for Elektra. The Hand need a vessel, and she fits the bill perfectly. The ninja prepare for her return, and it's only mid-ceremony that Daredevil, with the Black Widow and Stone (a ninja ally), arrive on the scene. The Hand are working hard to bring this lady back to life as their instrument of destruction, but doing so will make her theirs forever. Matt doesn't want this to happen, but after he works his way through the Hand soldiers, he tries his best to finish the ceremony himself. He is certain he has heard a heartbeat, but his skills are nowhere near enough to bring life to a body formerly occupied by death. The only change he affects is purifying her soul, which is a selfless act, and one he neither knows of nor benefits from.

The heartbeat he hears could have been an apparition of his hope, but it's just as likely that the Hand nearly completed their task. Instead of letting her go completely to the side of evil, Matt lets her slip through his fingers. The latter only makes things sadder, in that Matt's sense of worldly justice still trumps his love.

Elektra is gone, her has truly disappeared, and Miller closes the book on her with a coda, in which we're shown her finally ascending the unscaleable wall and receiving the peace she sought for all along – the peace she would only ever find in death. A white-clad Elektra stands triumphant, and the scene is one Matt will never share.

It makes sense to remove Matt's perfect love from the table, because to leave her dangling would be a heartbreakingly mean thing to do to the man. The way Miller constructs the couple, it's apparent they occupy different planes of existence. The only way they could ever meet on common ground would be for one to change. That didn't seem to be likely to happen, and seeing Elektra soften, or Matt change his stance on crime, would feel like a cop out.

Elektra finally reveals her love for Matt, and it only takes her dying for it to happen. That was the necessary change, but sadly it's also irreparable and dooms the love it saves. This meeting with Matt in the middle is brief and fleeting – which also makes it all the more poignant, because Matt gets a glimpse of what could have been. He gets that one moment to appreciate her love, and then it's gone. She's gone.

It seems true that the irresistible force and the unmoveable object can only each yield. And then no one wins.

Years later, Miller returned to his creation in a graphic novel for Epic Comics (a Marvel imprint) titled *Elektra Lives Again* (1990). The book is a deconstruction of how much Matt is affected by her death from many years prior. Time doesn't heal all wounds, it seems, and he spends his nights dreaming about her and feeling the torment of lost love.

The ultimate message of *Elektra Lives Again* is that she's not alive and they'll never be in love again. In fact, were she to return, the whole dynamic would shift right back to the violence and the death neither of them want. There's a cycle to Matt and Elektra, and a cycle is repetitive. This is exactly why Marvel should not use Elektra anymore. This was Miller's hope, and he spelled it out on and off the page, but future writers wanted to see Matt suffer. They wanted Elektra back.

Bastards.

Can't you just let a man grieve and remember the good times?

Typhoid Mary

Perhaps it took a female creator (writer Ann Nocenti) to finally twist love back on Matt Murdock. Or perhaps it was finally Matt's turn to writhe on the barbed hook that is love. Either way, Typhoid Mary entered the scene in issue #254 (May 1988), and Daredevil's love life would suddenly start to look as bleak and barren as his overall life had become since Frank Miller stormed through, twice, to destroy his world.

Typhoid Mary falls into a similar category with Elektra, in that she's a personality larger than life. She's a villainess out to burn the world, yet the heat of her flame draws in Daredevil with both lust and intrigue. She's possibly worse than Elektra ever was, because although Elektra killed and certainly acted the part of the bad girl, underneath it all she doubted herself. There was good at Elektra's core, whereas Typhoid is cold and calculating and has no pretentions of innocence or actual sweetness. She leaves those character traits to her alter ego, Mary.

Sadly, Typhoid suffers from dissociative identity disorder. She's the nasty villain, and Mary is the sweet and timid girl who only wants to love and be loved. It's an honest tenderness within the same being, which becomes even more poignant when you discover the major obstacle to her happiness comes from within her own body.

At the time, Matt Murdock was happy with Karen Page and his life was on track. He upheld justice, and did it honourably through his street firm; the terrible days should have been behind him. Happiness was finally his, yet it could not last. The Kingpin offers Typhoid a million dollars to make Daredevil fall in love with her so he can be crushed, and she jumps at the chance – using Mary as the sweet bait. Given an option, a path he knows is wrong, Matt still finds himself tempted.

Mary fits into the Karen Page mold of a girl Matt likes to dabble with. She's sweet, pleasant, and representative of a simpler and happier life – or so it would appear. Matt professes to be happy with Karen, yet he ignores her to hold and kiss Mary. While this betrayal occurs, Karen calls and, though her voice rings past the unholy union, Matt still persists. If he cared, then the voice of his true beloved would pause his hands and his lips, but they do not. This is yet another example, in a long string of them, of Matt not seeing his wandering lips in a relationship as any cause for alarm. He doesn't think he's done anything wrong – he just thinks he came close.

Matt is a man possessed by the allure of this new girl, and it feels like he's simply enamoured with the allure of the new. Karen is a conquest he's used to, and he's had more than one ride around the carousel with her. Mary feels like a chance to recapture what he initially loved most about Karen: the chase of something pure. Karen might be his love, but he can admit she is far from pure after her travels.

To add further confusion to Matt's poor brain, he is then presented with the visage of Typhoid, who is more up-front with her sexual self-representation. She seems to have the perfect two-pronged attack on Matt's heart, as she sends the sweet girl after the lawyer and temptress after the devil. Matt is a man torn. Justice in the courts and on the streets are certainly two different concepts. If you look at his two greatest loves, you'll notice Karen seems much more suited to Matt, while Elektra was the perfect partner for Daredevil. Typhoid and Mary seemingly complement each other to give the whole man the complete package he needs.

However, instead of uniting Matt in a way no one else ever truly could, Typhoid and Mary only serve to split his concept of self further. He can't see how Daredevil and Matt actually fit together in the world, as a man acting outside the law also trying to enforce it. It's the sort of contradiction someone wishes he could make work, while every fiber in them knows such a triumph is impossible. At least, in absolutes it is. You can't break the law to rectify a broken law; the cycle won't ever end until someone gives in and lets it go.

This dichotomy within both the hero and the new lover could be indicative of Ann Nocenti working out how to write this character and his title. By the time she takes up the reins, there have been decades of Daredevil stories, and they seem to wildly veer between sweet and saccharine swashbuckling and grim-'n'-gritty grimacing, then back again. If you laid out Daredevil's stories in a linear fashion, including his loves, there's such variation that you could almost think you were looking at different people. Daredevil is a comic-book character who has experienced extremely dramatic change over the years, so it's no surprise he keeps taking new lovers too. What one woman could keep up with such an ever-changing man?

Typhoid and Mary could.

Matt Murdock is indeed a man for all seasons, and so needs a lady for each occasion. Society does not deem it prudent to hold multiple dates with multiple ladies, so instead Nocenti offers him a lady with multiple skill sets and personalities. Either it's the best thing for the character or it's a statement that the character needs to change. Matt needs to find a center and have all his personalities, and all his actions, stay true to that.

Mary falls in love with Matt, but Typhoid detests such weakness and consequently yearns even more to kill Matt. It's a twist on the love triangles of old, but instead of Matt and his imaginary brother duking it out for a girl, it's a girl and her imaginary evil half battling for the rights to their red-headed prize. However, Typhoid can't kill him because Mary's love is somewhere inside her. It's a messy relationship – and that's before you even look at the fact that Karen Page is sitting at home waiting for Matt to arrive.

The more this deception continues, the more you must hate Matt Murdock. He's doing a terrible thing to Karen, and he knows it, and he doesn't even realise what he's doing to Mary. Matt has a a decidedly low level of thought about his own actions. It's as if he's living in the moment, and whoever is in front of him at any given time will get his lips, his attention, and maybe even his heart. It's a loose way to play at the game of romance, and while it isn't evil it certainly *is* selfish – and harsher than what either lady deserves. It's also worrying to Matt, because he does seem to care about both partners and, while he's with them, seems concentrated and devoted. He appears to be a loving partner, but it's his actions that really define him as a man.

This is the last great love of Matt's for some time. This is the relationship that tears down his gender-focused interpersonal barriers and hopefully makes him realize he needs some time to look inside himself. Either Typhoid Mary ruins Matt for women, or she fixes his approach to them. In every relationship prior, Matt was so quick to fall, so quick to trust, so quick to reveal. He's a passionate man and one who always commits instantly, then translates his rashness into the ability to just as quickly distance himself from the same love interests. Typhoid Mary seems to finally make it clear to Matt that needs to slow down and reassess his romantic pattern.

The more you examine Nocenti's run as a study of the dual nature of Daredevil, the more flip sides you see in all aspects of the story. Apart from the binary relationship of Typhoid, there's the homoerotic mirroring of Daredevil and Bullseye. Then there's Matt's time as Jack Murdock, his own father, and the replay of throwing the final fight. There's the concept of Daredevil asking others to lower their weapons, while he constantly raises his. Nocenti might well be commenting on the nature of super-hero comics and their heroes' "might makes right" actions. She takes Daredevil from the city and puts him on the roads of America. She removes him from the comfort of street-level team ups and makes the Inhumans supporting cast members. Nocenti is very interested in showing the absurd duality of super-heroism.

Daredevil is a dual natured man afloat in a world of binary relationships. He wants everything to conform to his own ideas, but he must learn that his actions inspire reactions. His dalliance with Typhoid Mary certainly confirms this by showing him the worst in the world. It brings out the very worst in him, but it must all be done to create the closest thing to a positive outcome. Daredevil finally understands that sometimes he'll have to compromise – to do the wrong thing to get the right outcome. That's the sort of world he lives in, and those are the sorts of people he loves and fights. Typhoid Mary comes close to killing Matt, she ruins his relationship with Karen, and she exposes his world view as fraudulent. She operates as a human agent of chaos, like Daredevil's version of the Joker. She's capable of ruination while remaining untouched herself.

So when Matt next comes across her, he acts in an excessively harsh manner. Is he dealing with her as an ex or a villain? It's hard to say when he uses his personal connection to bring Typhoid Mary down low. "The Termination of Typhoid Mary," in issue #297 (Oct 1991), is one of the most brutal issues of *Daredevil*. It shows Matt Murdock as a man who holds a grudge. He's also a changed man who understands he's crossing a line he built, but he sees the realistic outcome he can achieve on the other side of it.

Matt keeps his distance from Typhoid. He clears his mind a little and then formulates a plan. Typhoid spends her time being the dirty plaything of the Kingpin. The toxic relationship between Wilson Fisk and Matt Murdock is a union both men try to terminate, yet seemingly cannot. Their hate is greater and more enduring than the love either can muster. Matt is finally going to crush his foe, as Wilson did to Matt in "Born Again," and the first piece to take off the board is Typhoid.

Matt might argue that he's crushing her because of her connection to the Kingpin, but there's certainly some angry ex-boyfriend gristle to his actions. When last they met, he was the plaything for her desires, both for love and hate. She made him feel out of control and useless, and he desperately wants to take back that control and show her what this was like. He wants to confuse and discombobulate Typhoid Mary, so he can manipulate her feelings into a victory for himself.

Mary was a girl Matt felt like he could love. He wanted to look after her; he wanted to be the "man" in her life. With Typhoid, he was emasculated; she could equal him in battle and frequently mocked him. She knew the allure she held over him and flaunted it while abusing it. Matt was powerless with her, and it took him time to realize how he could take that power back. When a force is constantly pulling at you, if you suddenly run forward, you'll topple it.

So he jumps into Typhoid's arms, confuses her, and they kiss in the rain. Anyone could be forgiven for seeing it as a sweet moment, a victory in which Matt is going to save the innocent girl captive within. The sequence cuts to Matt wearing only the Daredevil suit's red pants; Mary is seemingly naked in bed.

It would appear that Matt has won, in at least the crudest, virile sense. The reconciliation with Karen that Matt is working towards must be a thought buried deeply – or "Daredevil" sleeping with someone doesn't count in the world of Matt Murdock. His psyche might be as divided as that of the woman

Daredevil is reunited with Typhoid. From *Daredevil* #297 (Oct 1991). Art by Lee Weeks and Al Williamson. Copyright © Marvel Comics.

he has rendered comatose with his affection. From the serene nature of her sleeping face, it would appear that only Mary is in the room. And this is the person Matt will take advantage of.

He departs, his solemn goodbye falling on sleeping ears, and he leaves forged paperwork committing her to a mental health facility with the innocent woman. The authorities arrive in the morning and finalise Matt's plan. Mary has no clue what's going on. She's collateral damage in a war she never entered. And this is the last we see of Typhoid or Mary in Daredevil's world for some time.

Matt isn't emotionless; he feels terrible about what he's done. But that didn't stop him from doing it. He lured an opponent to drop her guard, share a motel bed with him, and then sent her up the river.

It feels too close to revenge for a failed relationship, and it might represent Matt exorcising demons from all of his past dalliances. Karen comes and goes, and he can never consciously hurt her, though unconsciously he does plenty that certainly wounds her deeply. She's committed the worst act by selling him out during "Born Again," yet he'll still never punish her for this. Heather killed herself, leaving him guilty and unable to gain closure with her. Glorianna ran into the arms of his best friend, so Matt thoroughly lost on that count. Elektra was taken too soon, reopening a deep wound he thought was healed. Matt's never ended a relationship with a victory of any sort, so perhaps his treatment of Mary is his opportunity to feel that he's won. Typhoid won the last battle but Matt wants to win the war. Super-heroes so often defeat the villain, but it's a toothless grip. Though he only sends Mary to the nuthouse, something Batman's been doing to his rogues for years to no avail, it feels more final for Matt because no matter her future, the relationship is irrevocably crushed. Typhoid might end up back on the streets but she'll never again grace the long and lonely lanes of Matt's heart.

Every Murdock girl eventually returns to the title – even some of the ones who died – but Typhoid Mary isn't seen again for the entirety of the original series. When Brian Michael Bendis reintroduces her, it's definitely as a villain and not a lover.

It's hard to imagine that any girl could forgive being seduced under false pretences and then committed under even more false pretences. Not even the suave Matt Murdock can get past that. So Typhoid Mary goes down in history as Matt Murdock's most destructive relationship. Through his actions, Matt admits as much. It's a shame that she has to be the scapegoat for all his female woes. None of what happened to Matt, even what Typhoid did, was Mary's fault. She simply provided Matt with an excuse to work through his problems under the guise of helping with hers.

Typhoid Mary bashes Matt into a strange spiral from which it takes years to break free. She acted as an agent of entropy and finally made Matt see *himself* as part of the problem. She created more change in Matt than all the other doting women ever could.

Typhoid Mary both disgusted and enticed Daredevil. She might well have been his perfect match.

Milla Donovan

Milla Donovan is a girl custom made to fit into the jagged interlocking structure that is Matt's beaten and scarred heart. Despite her lack of sight, or the hypersense ability Matt Murdock employs, Milla leads a strong and meaningful life. She's yet another example of how people overcome adversity every day, an example anyone can aspire to. She's a real character who stars as the lead in her own story. She's enough of a woman to stand next to Matt Murdock and hold her own.

Introduced on the first page of Vol. 2 #41 (Mar 2003), Milla walks the street with her friend, Lori. Their discussion revolves around Milla's quest to make a building useful for the community, instead of having it stay the way it was, as a shrine to the past without functional utility for the future. This is a subtextual statement of intent for Brian Michael Bendis's entire run on the title. He doesn't want to simply shine the boots of the glorious runs of the past; he wants to forge ahead and give readers something new they can use. His insertion of Milla is but one step on this quest.

There is one quote Milla drops, from a book she is "listening to": "Nostalgia is a state of inarticulate contempt to the present and a fear of the future."[1] She talks about how everyone puts a pedestal beneath the glory days, but not everything old is good. Milla is a soul who looks to the future, and she encapsulates Bendis's ideals as a *Daredevil* writer. Or at least, she embodies Bendis's plans, if not actually his final product.

---

[1] This quote comes from Luc Sante's book *Low Life: Lures and Snares of Old New York* (1992). Coincidentally, this arc by Bendis is also titled *"Lowlife."*

When looking to Daredevil's golden days, we think of names like Stan Lee, Karen Page, Frank Miller, and Elektra Natchios. These are the best moments, as decided by consensus. Bendis refuses to yield to any of them. He wants to create two new names to this echelon of scarlet swashbuckling: Brian Michael Bendis and Milla Donovan.

Bendis makes another reference to the past, arguably to the first moment of Daredevil as we know him, to connect this fresh woman to this very storied man. While crossing the road, Milla is nearly hit by a truck. The rampaging titan of steel would have taken her life, were it not for Daredevil swinging through like an ersatz Spider-Man and removing her from danger. Bendis is overwriting one of the most famous moments in Matt's history, associated with Lee, and he's doing it with a woman named Milla. Does her name sound familiar, almost like the surname of the other most famous Daredevil scribe? It probably should.

Bendis uses the past to create the future, and that's his real legacy. He takes what was and does it better, does it with finality, and makes himself the new and dominant name on *Daredevil*. And in the process he creates one of the strongest relationships Matt Murdock has ever known.

One should also look at how Milla handles herself, even in this scene. There's confidence in the way she carries herself; she's no one's handicapped fool. She can't see, but still interacts with the world, daily and safely. It then makes no sense that she should find herself on the street in front of a truck, with its brakes screeching, and not have enough time to get to safety. In fact, over the course of the page, she looks over her shoulder (a useless gesture), yet makes no move to get out of the way. Was she baiting herself for Daredevil? His secret identity as Matt Murdock had been outed by the press; did Milla need to meet the one blind superhero in her city? Her actions later on indicate she didn't exactly know what was going on after being saved, during which the couple smashed through a Vintage Thrift Shop storefront. It's hard to completely understand her situation, and such a nebulous start makes for a good jumping-on point.

Milla ends her first issue by pining softly at a window, with the city watching her and she sightlessly observing back. She shared only a few moments with Daredevil, and most of them obscured by the pain of a shard of glass wedged in her shoulder, but it was more than enough time with Matt Murdock for the infection to spread. Milla is infatuated. She needs more. But is her infatuation based on needing a man to look after her, wanting to tame the man she's heard so much about, or simply thinking she might be able to connect with this man on a level no one else ever could?

Matt has dated coy femmes, zany broads, deadly assassins, and mentally unstable villains; he's been around a few times. Then along comes Milla, and she represents something new. She's a modern woman, or at least the approximation of one at the turn of the millennium. After only one encounter, Milla tracks Matt down and doesn't pull any punches. She knows Daredevil is Matt Murdock, knows it from his voice, from the touch of his face, and she doesn't want to play games about it. Matt's past is full of games, especially in his love life, but Milla cuts through it all. It stuns Matt into a page of silence – and rightly so. She asks Matt to dinner. Daredevil might have saved her life, but she wants the connection to be with Matt.

Their first date, in Daredevil Vol. 2 #44 (May 2003), is more than Matt could hope for. He had just been outed through the press as being Daredevil, he's battling a war on drugs that doesn't feel like it has a victory in it, and he wasn't that far from the death of Karen Page at this time. Matt Murdock needed a win, and he gets it – for a few hours. Upon returning home, federal agents are there to question Matt about the death of a press member involved in said outing. As far as first dates go, it's a terrible end. The interesting part comes as Matt's mind scrambles, during the seconds where he knows what's coming but Milla still doesn't. He instantly falls into a dark place, thinking "I don't deserve her. / I don't deserve to be happy." The armor is already up, and Milla has her work cut out for her.

Milla does take some time to digest their first date. She doesn't go into any of this blind. She understands the threats and the consequences. She believes it's all worth it and puts her faith in Matt Murdock. She's only known him a collective handful of hours, but he's a man who knows how to make an impression. She wants to make an honest go of it all – and then Typhoid Mary, both villain and ex, sets him on fire. That's the second date.

Before a third date even gets off the ground, Matt and Milla run into trouble. The largest factor in all of Matt's relationships has been the one man ending them repeatedly – Bullseye. He's killed Elektra and Karen and left both to die in Matt's arms. In issue #49 (Sept 2003), he arrives to complete the trifecta with Milla. Bullseye is a sick man, and one linked to Matt in more intimate ways than he'd ever care to analyse, so when he finds a blind and defenceless girl in Matt's bed, he knows what he has to do. He also knows he'll take his time doing it. He wants to ruin Matt's life, to get under his skin, and to enjoy the process. Poor Milla has survived some police inquiry, and an attack from Typhoid Mary, but here she's presented with the most dangerous force to ever cross the bleak landscape of Matt's lovers. If she doesn't learn her lesson, eventually she'll learn it fatally at Bullseye's hands.

Matt has failed twice before to stop Bullseye killing the woman he loved. Was this because Bullseye was just too good or because Matt didn't care enough? The true reason doesn't matter, compared to the doubts Matt holds against himself on the inside. Matt honestly feels as if he's to blame for those deaths, and if *once* was a calamitous occurrence, *twice* was surely his fault and a third time cannot be allowed. To place Milla against Matt's other love interests, it's quite telling that he couldn't save Elektra or Karen, his two greatest loves, but he instantly doubles back and removes Bullseye from Milla's presence. Is this because he loves Milla more or because this instance has better timing? The true reason doesn't matter half as much as its future implications will. Matt does save Milla, and they can continue. He's being given the chance to do with Milla what he never got to do with Elektra or Karen. He can finally right previous wrongs and move forward with his life.

Matt finds the resolve with Milla to intercept Bullseye and hand him the beating he's so richly deserved for far too long. In the past, Matt has erred on the side of justice, but Bullseye messing with Milla is more than he can withstand and he dispenses justice brutally and swiftly. Is Matt doing so to protect Milla, or to avenge Elektra and Karen? If Milla wasn't constantly placed in dangerous situations, from their very first date, would this union have formed as strongly as it does? There are so many tenuous variables to Milla's entrance into Matt's world that must factor into any analysis of their relationship.

Milla might just be the right girl at the right time, after an endless tide of wrong girls at very wrong times. But in the end, it doesn't matter how a relationship happens – only that it does. Milla is a product of circumstance, and ultimately a victim of it as well.

After an interlude with Wilson Fisk, in which Matt enthrones himself the new Kingpin of Hell's Kitchen, Bendis and Maleev jump forward in time a full year. We skip the details of what Matt's regime, in his new self-declared role, was like. As the story continues, Daredevil has cleaned up the town, and Milla

Matt and Milla seem content together, in Daredevil's new order. From *Daredevil* Vol. 2 #56 (Mar 2004). Art by Alex Maleev. Copyright © Marvel Comics.

has her own place in this new order, working with the housing commission to determine how best help the community. Everything is apparently great, and we even get a splash of the couple's happiness that pays homage to Mazzucchelli's final image of Matt and Karen in "Born Again."

However, the most important development in this relationship is slipped into a conversation (in issue #57, Apr 2004) four months after the fact. In the present, Matt Murdock goes missing, after a Yakuza attack, and Milla follows protocols established by Matt to seek Ben Urich for aid. In the ensuing dialogue, she mentions that Matt is her husband.

It's fitting that no one knew Matt finally got married. While Peter Parker and Mary Jane got a special issue for their big day, as did Reed and Sue Richards, Daredevil isn't the kind of hero who gets the sparkly day, or issue, for his relationship union. Matt won't be the center of attention in the Marvel Universe, or on the racks of stores globally. Matt operates off the radar and getting married in his office, in a closed-door ceremony with no guests. It feels like exactly what he was always destined to get. Perhaps a wedding to Karen Page would have made a hell of a special issue, but otherwise it's not that sort of event. Daredevil might be a lot of things, but he's not a conformist.

It's never revealed whether or not Matt was a happy groom, or if anything funny happened on the day, or what the bride thought as she walked down the aisle. Matt always either put his relationships under such scrutiny that he never failed to find fault or seemed content to keep the relationship frozen in place. Here, he eliminates both by taking the plunge. He plunges so hard and fast the audience isn't even allowed to keep up. Milla gives up few details to Ben in the following issue (#58, May 2004), and one quote is particularly haunting: "He said I was like this whole city all pushed into one woman. / And – he *does* love this city." Matt might love Hell's Kitchen, but it hasn't always been great to him, as Milla explains. It took his eyesight, took his father, and has proceeded to take every true love of his forevermore. Matt sticks it out in the city through determination and a desire to prove something. That's not a great base upon which to build a marriage.

This sudden and shocking occurrence is revelatory about the relationship Matt and Milla share. Milla is the girl Matt's willing to settle for. The perfect ones, the blondes and the killers, are all long dead or gone. Matt has to find new love, and here he embraces it. Matt is moving on with his life and, more importantly, moving away from his past.

Matt and Milla are married, and we are left, rather than celebrating it, to deal with the aftermath when it goes wrong. How fitting.

Ben Urich is the man to figure it all out. When he goes looking for Matt, he finds a man who isn't like the Matt he knows. This man doesn't wear the Devil costume and has declared himself the Kingpin of his city. He's gotten married in solitude, and he's ignoring his old friends. It's as if a Bizarro Matt Murdock is now suddenly our lead. Urich posits the theory that Matt had a nervous breakdown after Karen Page died in his arms. It's a sound theory, and whether accurately true or not it is enough to place doubt into Matt's mind. It's enough to bring back the Matt of old. It's enough to drive a wedge between Matt and Milla.

It makes sense for this man, who has suffered so much, to finally crack. He's actually cracked before, taken on new personalities and wandered the country, so this new break in his psyche fits perfectly. It also explains why he would cling to Milla so strongly, when she's good for him but hasn't proven herself great. She's a great woman, no doubt, but not exactly matched to Matt, though he might like to think so. Regardless of whether she's right or not, Matt does love her. That's the kicker here, because it's a pairing that *should* work, and almost *could*. He wants it to, but it won't. Not for any overarching reason, not because of one single trait, but purely because it *won't*. This is love's final cosmic laugh at Matt. Just as some lovers seem fated to be together, many others are perennially forced apart with no more logic behind it.

Milla is a woman with extreme levels of perseverance, and that's something Matt needs in a lady. She puts up with so much because it comes from the life Matt leads; she understands that. When she finds out Ben's theory, via Foggy, and it hurts more than she thought being married would ever allow, she walks. It's the ultimate rejection because it wasn't a villain's attack or a suspicious public; this was purely about Matt and his feelings. This was about Matt not letting her completely in, making a fool of her, and betraying her trust and their vows to one another. A marriage should be between two people, but a spectral third hovered over and pulled strings and Milla would not stand for it.

Without a thought, Milla files for an annulment on their marriage. The legal retcon of love. She's smart and strong enough to know when to cut her losses. Milla loves Matt completely, but can tell when things aren't right. She won't stand for being someone's second best, or simply filling a hole left by another. It doesn't matter if it *should* be right, or it *feels* right; when it ceases to *be* right is the moment you walk.

Milla is replaced, within days, by the Widow, who reappears in Matt's life. Natasha is only trying to lay low for a while, and the place she thinks she'll be comfortable and have fun is in the world of Matt Murdock. He arrives home to find her mostly undressed in his bed – it's her statement of return. She's in it for the fun. She certainly enjoys the team up to take down Jigsaw, and afterwards enjoys a kiss on the rooftop. It's too easy to fall back into this because it's a familiar relationship, with plenty of passion. But this shows how Matt's view of love can so easily be skewed because it's been so constantly fractured. He hasn't signed his annulment papers, but here's a deadly hot super-spy throwing herself at him just for a good time. Matt skips from one woman to another, and that's only if the new lover has the decency to wait for the last one to leave before sliding into the frame.

It says something when Matt withdraws from the kiss – and from the rest of what the evening surely offered. He's still internally married to Milla, and certainly still loves her, and he's finally smart enough to know that you don't play around on those you love. He spent years doing it previously, and he still kisses the Widow. But now, finally, it actually serves to remind him how much he loves Milla. Matt is a good man, underneath, and he does understand the love he feels, but he's often at a loss due to his conflicted emotions. Perhaps there's often so much love around and within him that it can become confusing.

The Widow soon leaves Matt with parting words, addressed not to the Matt now married to Milla, the Matt tied down by love, but to the Matt of old. The Widow hugs Matt and whispers, "Next week you'll be lying in bed... / ...and all of a sudden it'll dawn on you... / ...You should have slept with me when you had the chance" (*Daredevil* Vol. 2 #64, Nov 2004). The old Matt definitely would have. Hell, for a time, the old Matt did. And in time, so the Widow believes, Matt will come to realize that love was going to have nothing to do with what they would have done. It was all about fun, about the moment, and Matt has finally stopped living in that instantly gratifying moment. Matt is trying to think about the long game; it might cost him now, but it should pay off in the long run. The problem is, it's a gamble. What happens when you knock back an opportunity now, only to find the other chance you waited for doesn't occur? You are left with nothing, and the Widow is never in that position. Matt now is.

Matt, clearly in a gambling mood, signs the annulment for Milla. It's almost a bluff from her that he calls, and only time will tell if his move will work. If it doesn't, he can be happy he did the right thing, but it's a hard thing to do. Matt signs permission for the woman he loves to slip further away from him.

The arc of Matt Murdock under Bendis is one of growth. This is not how Matt played the game of love with his former partners. This is Matt trying to do the right thing, and not just by himself. Matt cares so much about Milla that he can think about her in the situation as well. Given Milla's blindness, and the way he initially rescued her, and her headstrong manner, you can't help but see a lot of Matt in the woman he loves. This relationship might just be his chance to show how much he loves himself and has accepted his position in life. This is why it then becomes so painful when Milla turns from him. He can't even love himself without catastrophe.

Matt is gambling as he walks from Milla, and not even his senses can tell him if he's going to win this time. That's true love.

It takes some time, and Matt is luckily occupied elsewhere both physically and mentally, but Milla returns to Matt. She takes her own time to reflect, but in the end knows that she loves Matt too. She wants to be with him, and she was left in the position of power to make this happen. Matt respected her decision so much that he didn't chase after her and scare her away. He waits, and the gamble pays off.

In issue #77 (Nov 2005), as they lie in bed, happy once more, Elektra appears at the window. Karen Page's long shadow led to the annulment of Matt and Milla's marriage, but Karen Page never returned. What chance does the reconciled couple have, if their first night back together culminates with Matt's other true love arriving at their window? Fate clearly hates Matt Murdock.

In a frenetic set of events, Matt protects his new love by instinctually fighting his former lover. Milla runs from the room, and upon her return finds that both larger-than-life individuals are gone. If Milla learns anything by this, it's that nothing will change, and she has to make a decision. She can choose to come and go as she pleases, but she cannot control the perimeters of the world her lover lives in. His life in unpredictable, dangerous, and not easy to deal with, no matter how much she tries to isolate herself from it. Or she can choose to reconcile herself with the reality that this life would be too hard. No one would blame her.

Before a choice can be made, Milla, still in her underwear and frightened, is confronted by yet another ex. This time it's the Black Widow, and she's trying to help Milla. If only Heather Glenn and Glorianna O'Breen were still alive, they could join the party. It's clear that Milla is never going to escape Matt's past, and neither is he. At least, in this instance, the Widow is offering a helpful and much needed service. Milla gives in and pleads for help from her; if you can't beat them, join them.

If Matt's exes are finally helpful, with one (Elektra) getting Matt medical aid and the other (the Black Widow) taking Milla both to safety and to her husband, than seeing these separate exes meet can only show Milla that loving Matt Murdock is not something easily broken. The Widow and Elektra threaten each other; each wants to feel more important to Matt at that moment. It's a battle, and it won't ever end. These women will fight behind Milla's back for as long as she holds the top spot, and once Milla is dethroned she will simply join their ranks. Loving Matt isn't a privilege, it's a sentence. And the duration is life.

Bendis ends his run with one hell of an issue (#81, Mar 2006), but it's the first half of it that holds some of the sharpest insight into Matt's internal views on love. Standing in court, asked what his plea is for being the masked vigilante Daredevil, Matt concocts a fantasy in which he runs from the courthouse and straight into freedom. Sweet, heartbreaking, freedom. Matt clears the press and the cops and goes straight to the Widow. She's his lifeline, and while it seems innocent enough (she's his fence to get to Milla in France), the story shows that Matt's closest confidants are going to include his ex-lovers. Matt doesn't move on so well, and while he might not backslide he will have constant reminders around him.

In the fantasy, Matt meets up with Milla and all is well. His hair is now dark (he looks a lot like Laurent LeVassier),[2] and the couple even get another splash page with Milla's arm linked into Matt's as they walk off into happiness. If their previous splash was a modern take on the "Born Again" ending, this is the European variant. The image has now become shorthand for happily ever after.

Or at least until the turn of the next page. Matt wakes to find Milla dead with a playing card in her throat. This is Matt's fear, his burden to bear. He feels responsible for the deaths of Elektra and Karen. He holds that burden at

---

[2] In the "Flying Blind" arc, in *Daredevil* #376-379 (Jun-Sept 1998), S.H.I.E.L.D. brainwashes Matt Murdock into believing he is the sighted, dark-haired Laurent LeVassier.

all times and worries Milla will be next. This might indicate Milla is a love on the level of the two deceased ladies, but it also means Matt is always going to be hesitant. He thinks the happy moment is always going to be followed by the "death by Bullseye" moment, and this will force Matt away from Milla either physically or emotionally. His fantasy only gives three pages to Milla and one is full of panels of her dead body. Matt worries about love and always will.

The next leg of Matt's fantasy journey takes him to Elektra. After Milla's death, and after killing Bullseye finally in retribution, Matt wanders aimlessly and seeks out Elektra in Japan. Matt is always going to come back to Elektra, even if only internally. She is his first, his true north, and while she died in his arms, she also came back. She became a different person, someone who didn't feel she deserved Matt, but that couldn't stop their attraction and connection. Matt wants it to happen, yet is still realistic enough to know it wouldn't work. Even with this knowledge, the simpering hope of love is not pragmatic; it's enthusiastic and ever hopeful, and so Matt will always wonder, always think. He sleeps with Elektra one last time – which is something he almost deserves. Perhaps it would give him some closure.

In the end, Matt's fantasy shows him that he cannot escape his fate. Matt's worldview, and his future view, is entirely egocentric. So what point is there to him running, if his fate will will only follow him? He can take his lover elsewhere, but what will it change? Matt resigns himself to the fact he can't modify his future, he can't sculpt it exactly as he wants it, so he has to make do with what he's got. Matt will stop running, stop thinking of the many other nubile options he'll always have, and he'll instead do the best with what he has. Sadly, this means first going to jail for his criminal activity, but it's also a fresh start for his love life, one in which he seems newly empowered to change and to settle down.

Brian Michael Bendis and Alex Maleev's run, when dealing with love, is all about acceptance. Matt is given a new love, something most people are not lucky enough to be graced with, yet his dark and broken side cannot accept it. Matt constantly doubts the relationship, though he never quite quits on it, and it doesn't help how much of a victim of circumstance he is. If it isn't villains attacking, then it's ex-lovers turning up. Milla runs the gauntlet of Matt's past, and she holds strong for the most part. The one time she falters gives Matt an opportunity to stand up and do the right thing. He does. Despite his life still being a shambles of random violence and eternal connections with often violent exes, Matt holds true to Milla and chooses her in the end. It's sweet – and the sort of thing a long-term relationship is built upon. Bendis wanted to make an outstanding love for Matt Murdock, and he succeeded completely.

What a shame, then, that with all the notes he gave incumbent writer, Ed Brubaker, taking over for Bendis, didn't seem to follow his predecessor's lead when it came to Milla. Bendis wrote a gritty tale, some say a Valentine to Frank Miller's run, but it was still upbeat. Bendis' run is about accepting your life and persevering. Brubaker took the title down a darker path and wrote the series like true noir. His noir means things don't end well, and that was true for Matt and Milla.

Brubaker depicted Matt Murdock in jail. It was a hell of a move to adjust to, but he handles it more than ably. Yet it doesn't offer much room for the relationship, to which Matt just recommitted. Conjugal visits certainly have the opportunity to titillate, but there won't be much room for true growth. Brubaker keeps Milla off the page for most of the first arc, and when she does appear, it holds great importance.

The first glimpse of Matt's love is only a single panel. Foggy Nelson is apparently dead, and Matt's been allowed out for the funeral, under very strict guard. Between trained shotguns, Matt stands alone. No one is allowed to talk to him. After the proceedings, we see Milla standing off, away from the crowd. She is still, silent, solemn. She makes no move to approach her love, her husband. This rift between man and woman is wide and difficult to cross.

The next panel with Milla, issues later, feels very similar in tone and timbre. Matt looks through plexiglass at the same spot where he last spoke with Foggy before his demise, only this time it's Milla in front of him. This should be a moment of glorious reconciliation, yet all Matt can think about is the danger Milla has opened herself up to by presenting herself in the prison, where his enemies reside on both sides of the law. The feelings of love, of care, and of gratitude are washed out by the need to protect and shield this woman. This is how Matt always seems to feel about his relationships. Because he sees himself as a liability, he must take responsibility. The murderous tint inherent in his world must always come before selfish feelings of pleasure or relief.

To do what he feels is the right thing, Matt loses his cool with Milla. He yells, he demands, he orders. Milla must leave the prison, and Matt will then feel safe. This is how he expresses his love, but you could forgive Milla for not understanding what she is receiving. She has every reason to react in kind, yet she does not. She has a cool head on her shoulders, and she leaves Matt with words of wisdom. This is their dichotomy, under the new regime, and it's a repetition of the old one. Matt will always feel bad about the good he has, and Milla will try to justify why the good in both of them is okay, yet she will never truly succeed.

Matt acts to put Milla's safety first; he's being the caring partner, he's doing the right thing. Right? It would appear that way, until Matt reveals other tendencies upon his prison release. Once free, Matt collects a minimum of things and sets straight out for Morocco to track down the person he believes is responsible for the death of his lifelong partner, Foggy. He doesn't even take a moment to see Milla or contact her. He's focused, determined, and completely ignorant to the obvious needs and fears of his love. Matt doesn't appear to give her a second thought.

If he's negligent and absent, how can he say he loves her, when his actions speak the opposite?

While across the globe chasing answers, Matt finds himself in a situation of someone else's design. A major player in this drama is Lily Lucca, who has been given a special power of scent. She wears a perfume which reminds any man of his greatest feelings of love. It will then also drive them just a little wild. When presented with this scent, Matt smells Karen. Milla isn't even a thought in his mind behind Karen's presence, Foggy's death, and justice's elusive trail. Matt smells Karen, and deep within himself he still loves her. He always will.

The truth of this ruse breaks Matt's heart. It's not his fault; it's not a conscious choice. But Matt still loves and misses Karen. The stark reality of this places a fair amount of doubt and guilt into Matt's heart and mind. He can't understand how natural or normal this is. He's been working so hard to be a one-woman man, yet his body is telling him that won't ever actually be possible. Smelling Karen only tells Matt how hard he will fail in moving forward with Milla.

Matt's feelings for Karen have not yet disappeared, and the odds are they won't ever. He feels like he should be a clean slate for Milla, but it's normal to still hold some level of flame for a past love. You don't need to forget the old to embrace the new. You simply need to be willing to move on to make that change. The new will slowly but surely eclipse the old, and with time Milla will become his everything and he'll be confident about that. It's a leap of faith, and Matt's faith has been slowly depleted over years of fights, deaths, sorrow, and constant backsliding into despair. He finds it hard to look forward, when the future has only ever brought him more sadness. Especially where women are concerned.

It's interesting to note that Matt is tied up with Lily because he sees parallels in her to some old loves. Lily is a damsel in distress, by her own design, and Matt likes the chase because he wants to save her at the end of it. She might smell like Karen, but she also acts like many of his old loves; she's delicate and requires saving, and that appeals to the part of Matt that wants to feel needed and strong. Most of Matt's strength and independence was stripped from him in jail, so to be free in Europe opens up new possibilities for him. Lily is just another reminder to Matt that he's incredibly fallible and might very well be so forever.

Brubaker returns the book to a status quo, in which Matt's secret identity might not exactly be back in the bottle but certainly can't be used against him for legal reasons. Milla is once more in his arms, Foggy is alive and walking the streets of Hell's Kitchen (after not actually being dead), the legal firm is going to get back on the straight and narrow, and it's a fresh new page for Matt Murdock. Except that, though this page might be new, it certainly isn't fresh.

"Blind Love" is a one-shot tale in issue #94 (Apr 2007), centered around Milla Donovan and her love for Matt. The John Romita, Sr. cover is a pitch-perfect romance comic image that evokes the weepy "books for girls" of the past (especially the 1950s). Milla weeps as Daredevil exits out the window. There's even a thought balloon giving voice to her internal woes. The rest of the issue does this cover justice, as we delve into Milla's mind while Matt patrols the darkness of his city.

The rain cascades across the windowpanes, and Milla hugs her leg. It's the same old song: Milla loves Matt, but she's not sure if she can handle the constant danger and division between them. You get the feeling that one more attack could knock Milla off her sunny perch. For all her concerns and worry, it's interesting to note that Milla knows she could never ask Matt to stop being Daredevil. She's very realistic about her situation and always has been.

The "Born Again" final splash page is once again echoed, here to show the fault in looking back on the good times. The panel looks happy, as it always has, but Milla says, "And for a year, it was perfect. / At least... I think it was. I remember it being perfect." Misleading memories, and only focusing on the good times, are a danger for any relationship, and Milla has far too much time on her hands to either take stock and starkly assess her relationship or to simply wallow in the falsities of the best moments she and Matt have shared.

In the end, Matt has left Milla a lot. He leaves her because he's Daredevil, and no matter how strong his lover is, this will hurt her eventually. Milla tries to look at it as Matt going off into the world and upholding the greater good, as many men do every day in their lives while away from their loved ones. Milla tries to feel understanding for Matt's altruistic pursuit, but eventually, when the night is cold and the thoughts turn dark, and when things just don't feel right, all the understanding and compassion go out the window and Milla is only left with two things: herself and Matt. When she lines up the facts against her feelings, it's hard not to take his actions personally. Matt is either consciously ignoring her to be Daredevil, which is not going to feel nice, or he is not even thinking about her as he shoots off into danger and darkness, which is absolutely heartbreaking. There's no real win when the man you love chooses to spend his nights punching people when he could instead be lying in your arms, enjoying the love for which he fought so hard. Milla envisions two options for Matt's night as she asks, "Are you saving lives? / Or just putting my heart in danger?"

Milla seemed to think, once upon a time, that there would be a "happily ever after." She thought there would be respite from the storm for more than a momentary breath. She thought if they both worked hard enough, they would get their just reward. She thought wrong. The only question is, how long will it take before she sees this error and corrects it completely? Or could she even do that, if the love in her heart won't ever actually diminish?

To eradicate this rift, Milla could ask Matt to stop being Daredevil, but she won't even see this as an option. She knows Karen told him to never stop, and she also knows because of that he never will. Milla knows this and more importantly respects it. That's how deep her love runs. She is in this for the long haul, but she understands that her situation must end in some form of heartbreak, "Either a sudden shock, or a long slow path…"

In "Blind Love," Brubaker shows us that Matt and Milla are doomed. He follows this up by showing us how this doom is executed. It might follow a long slow path, but it starts with a sudden shock.

Reunion always feels good, but it never takes long for the old rut to rear its painful head. Matt is missing meals and generally absent from Milla's world. When he finally takes her to dinner, they're attacked by the Gladiator. Nothing has changed, not a damn thing. When Lily Lucca turns up in Hell's Kitchen, Matt can't help but lend her a hand. It's bad enough that Matt is always with others, instead of with his wife. But he doesn't have to be with a hot lady who happens to smell like his true love. Milla cannot catch a break, and she's finally starting to sense that.

She becomes a damsel in distress for Matt, literally held off a building and made to scream his name as a lure. "Blind Love" might have been her story, but now she's relegated to the role of a plot device – and that's exactly what the villain behind all this is planning. Milla is to be crushed, turned into a woman in the refrigerator, all in the hope of angering Matt Murdock. Milla has become a pawn, and Matt has let it happen due to his inattention and lifestyle choices. Milla constantly questioned the situation she was in, but never took the time to properly assess it and leave. Her payment is an induced state of madness, caused by Mr. Fear's new toxin. In her rage, she causes the death of an innocent man in a train station. She's now on her way down the long slow path, and it hurts more because she basically saw it all coming.

Mr. Fear has crushed Matt completely. Matt feels it and knows he's a major part of that problem. While in a fear gas-induced stupor, Matt sees visions of all his loves. Each woman comes into focus, and then he loses her. He always loses his girls. Nothing is sacred; everything is one vicious cycle condemned to end in doom, and so rarely Matt's. How often can he do it before he accepts the responsibility? How often can it happen before he decides to finally stop? The internal representation of Milla in #100 (Oct 2007) wisely states, "It's okay, Matt. Don't be scared... Just admit it. You *know* it can never work. / That mask you wear *always* comes first... The mask and why you *wear it*." This level of honesty is so rarely expressed externally, but Matt is finally seeing it on the inside. Daredevil and love will always find it hard to mix.

In #101 (Nov 2007), Milla is locked in a cell, charged with murder, snapping in and out of fits of nonsensical rage, and Matt doesn't know what he's going to do about it all. He kisses her on the head and tells her, "I'm going to save you." But Mr. Fear has already won. There is no way to save Milla. There is no antidote, and Matt's sense of guilt and grief and responsibility is going to eternally weigh him down. He doesn't forget his defeats, nor does he forget his loves, and Milla will forever be both of these things for him. Fear has struck at Matt's weak point and delivered a devastating blow.

Matt has to commit Milla for constant care and supervision. She is never going to get better. She is never going to be able to love Matt back, not properly. Matt reflects on his fearful nature. It's never been about fighting villains; there was never anything there for Matt to fear. The greatest fear Matt ever conquered was love. He has consistently shown himself to be willing to dive into the murky waters of the heart and give himself to another, but Matt lives in constant fear that those he loved would go away. This started with his parents (one at a time), and then it slowly worked its way through the women in his life. Love is fear, and Matt Murdock conquers it constantly, but he also sees why it's such a worthy foe. Love doesn't last forever; it's doomed to end eventually, and Matt often finds himself the reason for this termination. Love cannot reign supreme, yet Matt chooses to take what he can, while he can, rather than give up.

Milla connects to Matt like no one else ever managed to do. She links to him in a pure way that cannot last. Milla suffered the same old fate, no matter what she tried. The problem, most clearly, is Matt.

Matt Murdock is a man without fear and a man full of hope. All choices are made out of fear or hope, and your path is decided by which you have and which you ignore. Matt certainly hasn't got it yet, but he might take comfort in the fact that what he can't quite wrangle is a universally elusive prize.

Matt Murdock and Daredevil are both victims of love.

Coda: Dakota North

Just because Matt isn't good at love doesn't mean it never affects him. Matt moves on, and he romances others. He always doubts, but he also drops like a lead zeppelin for girl after girl. If Milla was one of the heavyweight loves in his life, then he shows this in the aftermath of her being locked up for treatment.

Daredevil takes to the streets in a newly violent campaign against crime. It's nothing organized this time, simply a matter of whoever gets in Daredevil's way getting that night's beating. Matt's angry, and he doesn't have a cause to direct this fury toward. Mr. Fear has been locked up, the case has run its course, and Matt has to move forward – but there is no clear hook for him to grab. To make matters worse, Matt is soon advised to not visit his wife for a few weeks because he's negatively affecting her recovery process. Finally, a doctor actually acknowledges that Matt is a bad influence on these women.

This confirms Matt's darkest thoughts at just the worst time. This new status quo leaves Matt adrift in a bleak sea without many beacons guiding him.

Foggy, Becky Blake, and Dakota North light up a signal for Matt about a new case, in which he can bury his head. It's something to occupy his time, to take his mind off the worst and hopefully make him connect with those around him who still love him. It works, but too well. Matt's love of justice is rekindled, his sense of self-worth is reset, and the allure that follows him everywhere snags another victim: Dakota North.

It's not something Matt plans. There is no monumental build up or period of batted eyes and flirting hands brushing in passing. Matt has worked with Dakota North for some time; he likes her and respects her. After she is shot, he steps even closer into her life. She needs to heal, and Matt has connections and techniques that can help. He's just doing what he always does, helping others.

At the end of #111 (Nov 2008), Matt wakes next to Dakota the morning after. It's only here, after the passion, the naked skin, the open and honest contact, that Matt reflects on what he's actually done. He's still a married man, but he's also still the same old Matt Murdock. He succumbed to what might be his biggest weakness, and he knows it is wrong. Yet he asks himself, "Why doesn't it feel more wrong?"

Matt Murdock is a man who lives in the moment. He knows the difference between right and wrong, but he also recognizes that black-and-white morality cannot lead you through a grey world. Sleeping with Dakota is an act that is wrong, yet it made him feel right, at least for one night. Perhaps such reckless behavior is worth it in the end, at least for Matt, because you only live once and can beg forgiveness for transgressions, while you cannot retrieve lost moments.

There is no argument that Matt isn't a perfect man. He's hard to love, his world is violent, and his past is littered with mistakes that have cost women their lives and himself his sanity many times over. Matt lives hard, more so than perhaps any other denizen of the Marvel Universe. Perhaps, if he catches the warmth of a moment, he should bask in it for as long as it will have him. The world can hate him later. Such judgement will forever pale in comparison to what he puts himself through.

Matt believes in love, but it is a belief in a fleeting concept. Love is the glint of a sunset from a passing vehicle's windscreen. Love is the laugh of a stranger boarding a train going the opposite direction from you. Love is something you cannot trap, nor predict, nor take for granted. Matt loves the only way he knows how: at that very moment. This doesn't make Matt a bad person. It just separates him from the rest. Sometimes, this gives him something others would eternally miss. Other times, this can only break Matt's heart. The danger lies in never knowing. There's already too much of the world Matt does not know; he won't miss an opportunity again.

Matt's sense of love defines him as a person, but it seems more important that he as a person defines his sense of love.

Daredevil and Spider-Man: Dark Alleys and Bright Lights

by Vinny Murphy

When Daredevil debuted in 1963, he wasn't much more than an underpowered Spider-Man. Sure, he was blind and an accomplished professional, but his basic crime-stopper M.O. wasn't boldly original. Instead, it felt decidedly borrowed. Since he was not quite as popular as some of his contemporaries, writers have had to draw attention to him in different ways. Through this, Daredevil has gained the distinction of being a more tortured, mature character than most in the Marvel Universe. However, this need to break away has always been tempered by the safety of the Spider-Man narrative. Because of this, Spider-Man and Daredevil continue to share plot points, but rarely outcomes. Over half a century, whether it has been intentional or not, Daredevil has developed into the dark Spider-Man.

Daredevil's origin – like many of the popular Stan Lee created characters – is based upon a radioactive accident. Daredevil soon finds himself roving the sunny rooftops of Manhattan, yet his further adventures do not become the cartoon-friendly fare of Spider-Man. Even so, the similarities that persist are not without reason. Daredevil debuted less than two years after the first appearance of Spider-Man, and the comic-book industry has always looked to exploit a successful brand. Daredevil was different enough from Spider-Man to garner his own fans, but close enough to replicate the legitimately innovative narrative. Pair that with run-ins with the same rogues and a mutual lack of resources and the similarities only get stronger. For years, Daredevil languished as the shadow behind the true icon of Marvel. He lacked his own spark and would wait decades before a true, and long-lasting, legacy would be defined.

Daredevil hits his real stride with Frank Miller in the '80s. Though Miller kept the past intact, he immediately began to bring Murdock into the darkness. Miller's Daredevil didn't rove Hell's Kitchen because of his name; he did it because it was a crime-ridden slum. Miller changed how Daredevil was written, yet did something more admirable than that: he didn't change who he was. Miller may have inserted his own style into Daredevil's past, but the Spider-Man-like details remained. This had an unexpected effect – Daredevil became an alternate Spider-Man narrative. It is often said that super-heroes are the mythology of our time, and we all know that as stories spread, sometimes the details change. The basics of Spider-Man are universal, but our lives take different paths. Matt Murdock took a different path, yet a parallel one.

As discussed above, both characters had similar real-life beginnings, so let's analyze their narrative origins. Spider-Man is bitten by a radioactive spider in *Amazing Fantasy* Vol. 1 #15 (Aug 1962) and gains his powers, which are obvious and instinctual. Though he was part of a freak accident, he does not suffer any injury, only gains power. Once he can lift cars and jump over houses, what does this teenager do? He turns around and exploits the power. In his first origin story, this goes on for quite awhile, and Spider-Man becomes a television star. Though this specific plot point tends to be shortened now, the meaning comes across clearly. It is only when Parker's father figure, Uncle Ben, is gunned down that he feels – this is important – *guilty*, and changes his behavior. Guilt motivates Spider-Man's decision to become a hero. Because of this, Spider-Man is more likely to stumble upon problems than actively pursue them.

Daredevil stands in opposition to this. He too is caught in a freak accident in *Daredevil* #1 (Apr 1964), being exposed to radioactive material. This blinds and hospitalizes him. Now weakened and in the threatening environment of Hell's Kitchen, the young Murdock must toughen up and learn to perfect his burgeoning abilities. His father, Jack Murdock, dies after standing up for what he believes in. This motivates Murdock to pursue justice in all aspects of his life. He trains to become Daredevil, and though he does appear to have super powers, it is his discipline and ethics that drive his heroism. Even at their most

Daredevil and Spider-Man meet in *Daredevil* #16 (May 1966). Art by John Romita and Frank Giacoia. Copyright © Marvel Comics.

basic, Daredevil is the more mature of the two heroes. His motivations are certainly purer, though their clarity garners more violent responses. Daredevil starts out as a far more proactive figure in his crusade, and thus always teeters on the edge of going too far. Daredevil lacks the naïveté typically exuded by Spider-Man, and he therefore grows dangerously close to his opposition, in more ways than one.

During their early days, the relationship between their heroic and civilian lives plays out the most. Spider-Man keeps a secret identity, one that is rarely compromised – well, "rarely" in comic-book terms – and in recent years this has even required vast editorial changes to protect. Basically, Spider-Man lives his life in the hope that fighting with Doc Ock will not affect Peter Parker's life in the least. A lot of the time, Spider-Man's biggest concern seems to be missing a date with Mary Jane, or being late for dinner with Aunt May. Sure, Spider-Man's friends and family are threatened by his lifestyle and, like Daredevil's, have become the center of many turbulent situations for the hero, but it's Spider-Man's relationship with the criminal element that seems to soften the effect on his personal life. Spider-Man is a thorn in criminal's sides, but if a criminal isn't publically committing their crimes, chances are they aren't going to draw attention. Daredevil pursues villainy and therefore has a different dynamic with his enemies.

The greatest proof of this falls in one Daredevil story: "Born Again," serialized in *Daredevil* #227-223 (Feb-Aug 1986). In "Born Again," Matt Murdock's life is torn apart not by his own failings, but from the drug-fed desperation of an ex-girlfriend. The story comes from the basic idea that Daredevil is not effectively able to separate the heroic and domestic aspects of his life, and has quite a few loose ends floating around. Because of this, Murdock's former fiancée Karen Page sells the identity of Daredevil for drugs. The Kingpin is easily able to obtain the identity of his arch-nemesis and begins to deconstruct what he believes makes up Daredevil: his resources. Murdock is forced away from his friends and family and begins the slow crawl back. With his friends assuming Matt has died, they begin to piece their lives back together as well. Murdock finds himself on a journey that reveals that, while Peter Parker and Spider-Man are two sides of a coin, Daredevil is always Daredevil. With or without his costume, the resolve and perseverance he has exhibited all his life persist through the hardest of times. Murdock doesn't need the costume to help his confidence, and he never has. Thematically, one could argue that the reason Daredevil's identity is not as guarded amongst those closest to him – including villains – is that to not know the costumed part of his life is to not know him at all. People who know Peter Parker *do* know the genuine article; it's the costume that's the exaggeration.

Though Daredevil is more open with his loved ones, Parker and Murdock are both prolific daters. Actually, for a nerd and a broke lawyer, they do great. In the end, it seems only three loves hold any weight in each character's mythos. For Spider-Man, it's Gwen Stacy, Mary Jane Watson, and the Black Cat. For Daredevil, it's Karen Page, Elektra Natchios, and the Black Widow.

Beyond both having "Black" in their names, the easiest parallel to draw would be between the Black Cat and the Black Widow. They are the workplace romances. If either Matt or Peter weren't running around in spandex, they would never have had their fling with those dangerous beauties. Both are also challenges to the super-hero ethic, the Black Cat being a thief and the Black Widow being a spy and assassin. As shown in *Daredevil* Vol. 3 #8 (Mar 2012), this dynamic can even be transferred between the two heroes, when the Black Cat takes a shine to Murdock. Though both heroines retain their importance, neither romance stays in the forefront for very long, and both characters typically return to advisory roles. It's the other four women who define their lovers, and who – with a *little* abstract thinking – share parallels as well.

Spider-Man's first love is Gwen Stacy. Though the recent films have stated otherwise, Gwen became close with Peter shortly after high school during the early days of Spidey's web slinging, starting in *The Amazing Spider-Man* Vol. 1 #31 (Dec 1965). Though there's more to it, the important points are as follows: Gwen's father is killed during a battle between Spider-Man and Doc Ock; she blames Spider-Man. Peter's dual identity is compromised, and the Green Goblin captures Gwen. In *The Amazing Spider*-Man Vol. 1 #121 (Jun 1973), Goblin throws her off a bridge and, though Spider-Man attempts to save her, he fails. Peter's quest is reinvigorated and *once again* motivated by guilt.

Then we have Matt Murdock, who meets Elektra while training to become a crime-fighter – which we only find out years after the fact, in a flashback in *Daredevil* #168 (Jan 1981). They begin dating, but their relationship is interrupted by the death of Elektra's father at the hands of terrorists. She blames *herself*, and leaves to pursue a life of her own. She is reunited with Matt when they have both completed their training. They struggle with each other's choices, since they have both found what they believe to be the solution to the world's problems. Bullseye figures out that Murdock is Daredevil and, without knowing about their relationship, he murders Elektra for his own economic gain in *Daredevil* #181 (Apr 1982). She crawls to Murdock's apartment, and he is unable to save her.

Analyzing these two relationships reveals the disparity between our two heroes. Gwen Stacy's death, though horrific in its own way, isn't gory, nor does it include Elektra's struggle to see her love one final time. Gwen was the sweet, smart girl to match Peter Parker and (ignoring later stories that are typically ignored these days) maintains her purity as an idealized aspiration for Spidey. Elektra is that same perfect match to the more unified Daredevil / Murdock, though this connection is not sweet and is instead maintained because she is violent and over the top. She is brutally attractive and intelligent. The dark maiden for the dark... well, we'll go with "hero" and save *that* comparison for another time. When she returns from her training and encounters Murdock again, they are perfect matches in every way, including their sexuality. It should be no shock that this mix of sex and violence remains in her death. In an interview from *The Men Without Fear: Creating Daredevil* (video, 2003), Frank Miller characterizes Elektra's death at the hands of Bullseye as a rape and murder. The phallic sai defeats Elektra in both of her strongest attributes: her amazing physical prowess and her uninhibited passion. Elektra's death is not pure like Gwen's, because she herself was far from pure. Daredevil is motivated by her death, not as a lost ideal but as further proof of the dark world he fights against. Daredevil already knows what his ideals are; to motivate him he must only be reminded of the evil he faces. In this sense, Elektra's death is as great of a motivator as that of Gwen Stacy.

There are also strong similarities between Mary Jane and Karen. Both date their male counterparts early in their career but break it off, allowing the men to be with their true soulmates. Both were the most important female presence in the lives of our heroes after the death of their true loves. Hell, both even agreed to marry them, though Karen got cold feet. That said, the clearest parallel is their pursuit of fame. Both leave their hero to pursue careers as actresses. Mary Jane is very successful and returns to Peter only because she wants to. Karen, on the other hand, fails and then briefly becomes a porn star who slides into heroin addiction. She returns to Matt because she's sold his identity to the criminal underworld and legitimately has no one to turn to but him. And because he's a true hero, Matt accepts her. Karen would later die at the hands of Bullseye, in a scene reminiscent of Elektra's death, during Kevin Smith and Joe Quesada's "Guardian Devil" (which opened Vol. 2 in 1998). Though the scene is striking within that narrative, Karen Page's death has not retained the importance of Elektra's, which itself was reversed. While dreams seem to come true on the Spider-Man side, something always taints them when they encounter Daredevil. Mary Jane has often served as Parker's silver lining; Murdock lacks that person.

Daredevil and Spider-Man's villains often share many similarities thematically, though this isn't much of an arguing point because most of the super-villains developed in the '60s and '70s often do. Basically, they are either motivated by greed or by an obsession, which typically doesn't prevent them from displaying greed anyway. What can be more effectively discussed are two instances where villains have been successfully transferred between the two heroes and what effect that had on the villains themselves.

Wilson Fisk, the Kingpin, began as a Spider-Man villain. As Frank Miller put it, in *The Men Without Fear: Creating Daredevil*, he was portrayed as the "Jackie Gleason of Super Villains." Though this was certainly not the intent, a robust gentleman in purple pants can be easily dismissed. However, if you look to the real origins of the Kingpin, there's an interesting parallel between the two eras of the Kingpin's history that's often missed. In *The Amazing Spider-Man* Vol. 1 #50 (Jul 1967), our hero (in typical angst-ridden fashion) retires from crime-fighting. Fisk sees an opportunity. Parker, in his selfishness, essentially creates the Kingpin. Once again, motivated by *guilt*, Parker reclaims his mantle and defeats the newly crowned Kingpin of crime. Spidey and the Kingpin tussle multiple times over the years, and Fisk eventually "retires" from his position and flees the country. It's not until the Kingpin's wife, Vanessa, comes back to the United States that Wilson Fisk appears in *Daredevil* #170 (May 1981), over a decade after his debut. Here's the kicker: Vanessa comes back to New York to clear Fisk's name so his now-legitimate business ventures can proceed uninhibited. In order to do this, she enlists the help of *Nelson and Murdock* to do his legal work. It's only after her involvement with Daredevil that she's apparently murdered, and the Kingpin returns to his old ways. Thematically, it is Daredevil who creates *his* Kingpin.

Daredevil, in both his public and crime fighting personas, is now utterly entangled with the Kingpin, just as Spider-Man was in the Kingpin's first iteration. Jackie Gleason suddenly turns into a methodical and maniacal force of ruthless entrepreneurial aggression, the likes of which had never been seen before. Whereas the Kingpin had become a joke toiling against Spider-Man, when fighting Daredevil he suddenly amps up his operation to employ an "anything goes" stance. The Kingpin's more overtly dark persona is a direct result of his move to Hell's Kitchen. Kingpin no longer finds himself surrounded by human lizards and maniacal, flying industrialists. He's now in a world rapidly being populated by murderers. It's no coincidence that the two issues preceding the Kingpin's debut in *Daredevil* are devoted to establishing Elektra and Bullseye. Frank Miller wanted the audience to know that the Kingpin was now deadly serious business.

This wouldn't be the last time that stepping into Hell's Kitchen changed one of Spider-Man's foes. Enter Mysterio. If ever there was a stereotypical Spider-Man villain, he was it. Using Hollywood special effects to stun and confuse Spider-Man, Mysterio was little more than a spectacular thief; once his illusions had been dissected, he could do very little to stop Spider-Man. Though a founding member of the infamous Sinister Six, Mysterio became a joke amongst comic-book readers, much like Kingpin once was. This was until 1998, when Kevin Smith sought to re-invigorate the Daredevil franchise, which itself had been suffering from irrelevance for a good many years.

In Mysterio's move to Hell's Kitchen, he's transformed into a dying villain gathering his last resources. Though he first aspires to defeat his traditional nemesis, he realizes that the Spider-Man he observes is actually the briefly-tenured Ben Reilly. He turns his attention to Daredevil, seeing him as a "second stringer," an equal and natural enemy. He seeks not to gain wealth, or even any level of measurable power. Like the Kingpin, Mysterio seeks to destroy Daredevil and even starts (in "Guardian Devil") with a similar plan: buying the identity of Daredevil. From there, he uses his powers to pick at everything Daredevil holds dear, killing Karen Page by way of Bullseye, destroying Foggy's love life, and bringing Murdock's always-shaky faith in God back into question. Mysterio comes so close to destroying Murdock's ethics that the hero almost murders an infant. But Daredevil, who may get closer to darkness than others, can handle it. Defeated, Mysterio kills himself, admitting he has stolen the scene from Kraven. While certainly derivative of many runs – including Miller's, DeMatteis and Zeck's "Kraven's Last Hunt"[1] – "Guardian Devil" brought

---

[1] "Kraven's Last Hunt" ran in *Web of Spider-Man* Vol. 1 #31-132, *The Amazing*

Daredevil back to form by reestablishing the dark Spider-Man in a very literal way. Since then, many popular Daredevil narratives have maintained this style.

It's interesting to note that one of the most critically lauded Spider-Man tales is "Kraven's Last Hunt." In it, Peter finally seems to become the self-assured hero he should be at his age, and it's his villain, whose efforts have become obviously trivial, who ends the game. Earlier, we examined how Daredevil is more mature. It's possible that Spider-Man would pick up some of Murdock's traits if he matured more permanently. Spider-Man stories have dipped many times into darker topics, and some Daredevil stories have returned something of the levity of the pre-Miller Days (to notable success). This shouldn't come as much of a surprise. Change is refreshing to a franchise, and history has shown it's especially important within super-hero comics. But to maintain the "classic character," a writer must not contradict the essential elements of their success. In short, you can take Daredevil out of the darkness, but you can't take the darkness out of Daredevil. A touch of levity is also essential for Spider-Man. It has simply become who they are, and it will always return in some form.

"Light and dark" are not "good and evil." Spider-Man and Daredevil are opposites, but they seem to be on different sides of the same track. Daredevil's side is darker, sexier, and more visceral. Spider-Man has more light, more comedy, and maybe a little less pain. Through their lives, Peter Parker and Matt Murdock's paths have crossed many times, and they have become friends. They share tragedy, triumph, and an understanding of each other that other heroes can't replicate. Their parallel lives create a remarkable bond.

One fantastic and revealing encounter between Spider-Man and Daredevil takes place in *Daredevil* Vol. 2 #8 (June 1999). Spidey, *guilty* over the death of Mysterio, and Daredevil, disturbed by the chaos that ensues in its wake, meet on a rooftop. Murdock rants about how meaningless it all feels – how their roles are so often confused. Parker turns the conversation around with one point: "You saved that baby girl's life, Matt." And as Spider-Man swings away, Daredevil silently thanks him, reminded that no matter how close you are to evil, good still exists.

Daredevil and Spider-Man live on opposite sides of the same track, but they have the same destination.

Spider-Man Vol. 1 #293-294, and *Spectacular Spider-Man* Vol. 1 #131-132 (Oct-Nov 1987).

Daredevil and Punisher: Polar Opposites?

by M. S. Wilson

Daredevil and the Punisher – two men who couldn't be more different. Daredevil is a hero, concerned with fighting crime and helping people, while the Punisher is at best an anti-hero, only concerned with mowing down as many bad guys as possible. But are these men *really* so different? Or are they more alike than they seem at first glance? Closer inspection reveals as many similarities as differences. Their backgrounds, their motivations, even their personalities and methods turn out to be eerily similar. They could be opposite sides of the same coin.

An obvious place to start is with their respective backgrounds. What caused these two men to make the choices they have made? What factors brought them to where they are today?

In Daredevil's case, we know his story quite well. Born in Manhattan's rough Hell's Kitchen neighborhood, Matt Murdock's mother left shortly after he was born; his father, "Battlin'" Jack Murdock, a boxer, raised him. Jack was fairly successful as a fighter, though felt he had wasted his life. He wanted more for his son, so he urged Matt to concentrate on his studies. Matt wanted to please his father, so he studied hard and refused to openly join in the roughhousing so common in the neighborhood. This earned him the scorn of the other children, as well as the derisive nickname "Daredevil." However, Matt was more like his father than Jack knew. Matt would secretly go out at night and make mischief in the neighborhood (like stealing a nightstick from the local beat cop). Not wanting his dad to find out, Matt made sure to keep his face covered so he couldn't be identified. Matt put up with a lot from the bullies, but eventually reached his breaking point and fought back. Instead of being proud, as Matt had expected, his father was disappointed and actually hit him. This started Matt thinking about right and wrong, law and justice, and put him on the long road that would eventually lead to law school – and Daredevil.

The Punisher has a somewhat different background. We don't have nearly as much information about his formative years. He was born Frank Castiglione (his family soon changed their name to Castle) in Queens. As far as we know, his childhood was normal. Later, he studied for the priesthood, which suggests compassion and strength of spirit, qualities also noticeable in Matt early on. Frank never completed his studies for the priesthood, having quit when he realized he couldn't forgive sinners for their transgressions.

Matt began training in secret, honing his body as well as his mind. The mysterious man known as Stick trained Matt secretly, helping him in this endeavor. Sometime later, while Matt was in his teens, he saw a truck about to hit an old man in the street. Matt pushed the man out of harm's way, heedless of the danger to himself. The truck carried containers of radioactive material and one fell off and broke open, splashing into Matt's eyes. His heroic act cost him his sight, though he later found his other senses were heightened to superhuman levels. This made his training much easier, especially after Stick taught him to use his new abilities to enhance his fighting prowess. Matt progressed rapidly, in both his martial and academic studies. Eventually Stick left, having felt he'd taught Matt everything he could, and a disappointed Matt refused to embrace his "destiny" as the champion of Stick's fighting order.

Frank Castle, on the other hand, received all his training from the Marines. He enlisted and went to Vietnam, spending three tours of duty there and distinguishing himself in battle numerous times. He earned himself the nickname "the Punisher" for his ruthless and uncompromising methods in battle. He married a woman named Maria, and they had two children.

It's interesting to note that both men received nicknames early in their lives which they eventually adopted as *noms de guerre*. Obviously, their early experiences had a profound impact on who they would become.

Jack Murdock needed money to pay Matt's hospital bills and ended up getting involved with mobsters. A man known as "the Fixer" became a constant presence in Jack's life, using threats against Matt to keep the boxer in line. Jack won fight after fight, but the Fixer revealed to Jack his previous fights had been "fixed" and he was expected to take a dive. He might have done it, if it weren't for the fact Matt was in the audience cheering him on. He refused and went on to win the fight. Matt was proud, but that sense of triumph was tragically short-lived. The Fixer and his associates beat Jack Murdock in an alley, then shot him. Matt tracked down every person involved in his father's murder, ending with the man who'd pulled the trigger (Slade) and the Fixer himself. Matt chased the Fixer into the subway and cornered him, but the mobster suffered a fatal heart attack. Matt had avenged his father, but he realized there were many other criminals who might escape justice. His studies made him aware of the difference between law and justice, and he decided with his fighting skills and enhanced senses, he could help balance the scales in favor of the victims of injustice. He became Daredevil, champion of justice and protector of the innocent.

The Punisher's history is eerily similar. While on leave from the Marines, Frank and his family accidentally witnessed the killing of a mob informant in Central Park. The mobsters couldn't afford to leave witnesses, so they slaughtered the entire family – or so they thought. Frank Castle had survived, driven to the brink of madness by the loss of his family. Frank identified all the participants in his family's murder, but the police couldn't arrest them because they all had airtight alibis. Just as Daredevil had, Frank realized the mobsters would never be brought to justice through the system. He also concluded that justice sometimes has to transcend the law, and vowed to find justice for his family – albeit in a way different from Daredevil's – by killing all the people responsible. After killing everyone directly involved in his family's murder, he realized there were many other criminals who were involved peripherally. He decided to use his rage and grief to provide some measure of justice to other victims of brutality and injustice, dedicating himself to protecting the innocent and wiping out criminals wherever he found them, much as Daredevil did.

This is where we can see the most similarity between two. Both men suffered tragic loss, and – more tellingly – both reacted the same way, first trusting to the established system of justice to punish the wrongdoers, then realizing the system didn't always work and going outside of it in order to achieve true justice. Of course, their methods are not the same (Daredevil normally doesn't use lethal force), but their *reasons* for doing what they do *are* the same. Both Daredevil and the Punisher originally confined their vigilante actions to hunting down the killers of their family members, but later decided that wasn't enough. Each independently dedicated himself to the larger fight, the fight against injustice in all its forms, no matter the personal cost.

What can we learn from these disparate backgrounds? These two men seem at first to have nothing in common, yet upon closer examination we see some startling similarities. They both have a streak of recklessness in them, which causes them to take on seemingly impossible odds over and over again. They each also enjoy it, if not downright thrive on it. There's an interesting dichotomy within each man. Daredevil uses his costumed identity to rationalize breaking his promise to his father. After all, Daredevil is a "different" man from Matt Murdock, so it's okay to run around enforcing justice with might. The Punisher has declared numerous times that Frank Castle no longer exists; the person doing all the killing is only the Punisher. Obviously, the Punisher uses his activities as a catharsis, a way of venting the rage and grief that still burns within him over the loss of his family. Perhaps Daredevil's crimefighting serves the same purpose: a way of working off the frustrations of his early life, not just the murder of his father, but all the beatings and taunting and romantic frustration that have weighed down on him over the years.

The most striking similarity between Daredevil and the Punisher is that they both *care* so much. They might argue over methodology or even motives, but in the end neither could disagree about the fact they sincerely care about the fate of innocent people and want to help them in any way possible. This also illustrates the biggest contrast between the two: Daredevil believes *everyone* deserves a second chance and has the potential for good, while the Punisher believes criminals have already made their choices and eliminating them is the only way to prevent future criminal behavior. In a way, they may both be right. The Punisher's methodology says few hardened criminals are apt to reform, no matter how many chances they're given, while Daredevil's actions counter this with the idea that perhaps it's worth the effort for the small number who actually do reform.

Are Daredevil and the Punisher's philosophies and methods all that different? The most obvious contrast is in their attitudes toward killing. Taking away that one great divide, we can note several similarities. Both came to the conclusion (after personal tragedies) that justice and law are not necessarily the same things. Sometimes, in order to find justice, the law must be circumvented. Their exact methods of doing this are different, but that *belief* in justice is common to both. After all, Daredevil and the Punisher have each seen the worst humanity has to offer. Maybe that's why they've both fought the Kingpin so many times; he represents the opposite extreme, someone who twists the law to his own advantage and doesn't give a damn about justice. Daredevil might say the Punisher's brutal methods make him almost as bad as the Kingpin, but at least the Punisher's motives are pure, whereas the Kingpin only cares about personal power and control. Daredevil and the Punisher's philosophies are outward-looking, while that of the Kingpin is focused inward. Both vigilantes have also each seen some of the *best* that ordinary people can do: the Punisher when he was in the Marines, and Daredevil first with his father and then every day in Hell's Kitchen, as regular people try to get on with their lives without giving up hope or becoming criminals.

We're all familiar with the Punisher's *modus operandi*; his brutality is lethal. However, although Daredevil may not run around killing people, he's not exactly a choirboy either. Daredevil has beat suspects or informers to elicit information so many times that it's almost become a trope. There was a running gag to that effect about the plate-glass window at Josie's Bar being smashed every time Daredevil went there seeking information. DD has also subjected people to water torture and threatened to drop them from rooftops, to name only a couple examples. Later, he went as far as declaring himself "Kingpin of Hell's Kitchen" and (in the *Shadowland* crossover) cooperating with the Hand. Of course, he did all those things for the greater good, but the Punisher could claim the same excuse for his own methods. Both of them believe – to some extent – that the ends justify the means.

Of course, to really get an idea of these two individuals and their contentious relationship, we need to look at some of their actual meetings. Their first meeting was in *Daredevil* #183 (June 1982). In this initial meeting, the Punisher has heard of Daredevil and seems impressed by his reputation. He obviously respects Daredevil as a crimefighter and even suggests the two of them should work together, and they could accomplish a lot. Even at this early date, Daredevil is already horrified by the Punisher's indiscriminate slaughter of criminals. Commenting on the difference in their methods, Daredevil says: "Mine don't include senseless brutality. / Or wanton murder." So we see the dichotomy between the two already, and this split only gets wider over the years. The main story is about a kid named Billy, whose sister has overdosed on angeldust. Billy wants to track down the drug dealers and make them pay, but Daredevil convinces him to let the law handle them. Daredevil's fundamental belief in the justice system as flawed but necessary is illustrated in *Daredevil* #184 (July 1982), when he tells Billy: "We're only *human* Billy. We can be weak. We can be evil. / The only way to stop us from killing each other is to make *rules*. Laws. And stick to them. / They don't always work. But mostly they do. And they're all we've got." This encapsulates Daredevil's philosophy very well. It's a belief he'll keep throughout his career as both a lawyer and a super-hero.

The next meeting between Daredevil and Punisher is a crossover between *Daredevil* #257 and *Punisher* Vol. 2 #10 (both Aug 1988). In this story, Daredevil and the Punisher are each tracking down Alfred Coppersmith who, feeling like he'd been screwed over by the system after being fired from the company where he worked, started putting cyanide that company's products. Daredevil wants to stop Coppersmith, and the Punisher wants to kill him. When the Punisher finds out Daredevil is involved, he thinks to himself: "I admire his spirit, but his endlessly self-defeating liberalism is beneath contempt." They both track down Coppersmith and (predictably) end up fighting. As they pound on each other, they espouse their respective philosophy on crimefighting, while an entranced Coppersmith watches. Here we get an interesting outsider's perspective on the DD / Punisher split when Coppersmith thinks: "Coupl'a big bullies beatin' on each other to see who *wins* me, who gets to decide my fate. / So *stupid*. They think they got somethin' to argue about. But they don't 'cause they're the same guy. / There's no difference between the two of them. Both bullies, an' all bullies think *they're* the one that's *right*. / *Everybody* can't be right." Tellingly, from Coppersmith's perspective, Daredevil and the Punisher are one of a kind: each is part of the system that wronged him, and neither one is really better than the other.

The two vigilantes met again several times over the next few years. Their next significant meeting is in the "Dead Man's Hand" crossover, which featured Daredevil, the Punisher, and Nomad teaming up to fight a conglomeration of criminals meeting in Las Vegas to divide up the spoils after the fall of the Kingpin (in *Daredevil* #300). In *Daredevil* #309 (Oct 1992), Daredevil says he and the Punisher have a "healthy mutual dislike" for one other, which still seems fairly innocuous compared to the bitterness they would later show. In *Nomad*

Daredevil battles the Punisher on the cover to *Daredevil* #257 (Aug 1988). Art by John Romita, Jr. and Al Williamson. Copyright © Marvel Comics.

Vol. 2 #6 (Oct 1992) we get another interesting third-party take on the DD / Punisher dynamic when Nomad, observing the Punisher in action, thinks:

> His job is to make sure he never has to waste ammo on someone he fires at again. / Daredevil is repulsed by what the Punisher does. But the 'Devil has to know there's a sense of – finality – to Punny's methods. / Does it eat away at him – that his own methods – compassionate though they are – are flawed if you look at them logically and not emotionally?

An interesting question... could this explain why the Punisher tends to evoke such a strong reaction from Daredevil? Later in the same issue, when Nomad is contemplating killing the crimelord known as the Slug (whom the government has been blackmailing him to eliminate), Daredevil and the Punisher hover over Nomad's shoulders like the proverbial Angel and Devil, but with a twist: Daredevil takes the side of the angels, saying, "Think about what you're going to do. / How does this solve your problems? How does it wipe clear whatever you did in the past? / Will it make life easier for you in the future?" On the other side stands the Punisher, his white skull emblem looking vaguely angelic although playing the Devil's advocate: "It's the only answer! / The one you take out today won't hurt anyone tomorrow!" Nomad decides not to kill the Slug, but afterward wonders if he made the right call. The Punisher and Daredevil continue their debate and later, when Viper (who has temporarily allied herself with the Punisher) almost hits Daredevil with some stray rounds, Punisher chastises her. He and Daredevil may have their disagreements, but the Punisher obviously doesn't want him dead.

In the next few years, the two meet quite a few times and their relationship gets more and more bitter. In *Marvel Knights* Vol. 2 #2 (June 2002), the Black Widow says, during one of DD and Punisher's arguments: "You have done this so much, you could speak each other's words." Then in *Punisher* Vol. 4 #35 (Jan 2004) after Daredevil, Spider-Man, and Wolverine decide to hunt down the Punisher and bring him to justice, Daredevil shows he understands the Punisher's mind very well when he says: "The man has a code of ethics, one he follows as strictly as the three of us do our own. He will *not* take the lives of innocents." It seems no matter how large the divide between the two, Daredevil and the Punisher *do* understand each other's philosophies, even if they vehemently disagree over them.

The two met several times in the next few years, but their most significant meeting of this period (or possibly *any* period) was in Riker's Island Penitentiary. Daredevil's life had taken a severe downward spiral in the time leading up to this: Karen Page was savagely murdered, Daredevil's secret identity as Matt Murdock was exposed, and his partner and best friend Foggy Nelson had been (supposedly) killed. Matt was so fired up, wanting vengeance on Foggy's killers, that he ended up in the general population at Riker's, hoping to exact retribution. He was so despondent that he actually contemplated murder and even allied himself with the Kingpin. The Punisher talked to Matt, almost like an old friend, and helped shine some light on the darkness that filled Matt's soul. In *Daredevil* Vol. 2 #85 (July 2006), when the Punisher is about to kill another inmate, Matt yells for him to stop. The Punisher replies: "Now, *see?* An' I thought you didn't *give a damn* anymore." In *Daredevil* Vol. 2 #87 (Sept 2006), after a massive prison riot, the two cooperate to escape the prison. In a helicopter after the escape, Matt thanks the Punisher for helping him see how low he'd sunk, and that it was time to start the long climb back up. The Punisher replies: "You're hurtin' *a lot* right now Murdock, with *good reason.* / But you *don't* want to be *me.* / You needed to remember that." This may be the most telling moment in their entire convoluted and contentious relationship, a moment of mutual respect and understanding between two men who probably have much more in common than either one would care to admit.

Are Daredevil and the Punisher really opposites, or are they more two peas in a pod? The answer probably lies somewhere in between, but it does seem that the closer we look, the more they have in common. Both suffered tragedies. Instead of giving in to despair, each used his extraordinary abilities and drive, first to avenge their loved ones and then to help other victims. Both have a reckless streak and seem to thrive on danger, and both see themselves as being on a mission – doing something positive for the world – even though both have been called vigilantes (and worse) at various times. They use their crimefighting as a catharsis, to exorcise whatever demons haunt them, not just from the loss of their loved ones, but from the unconventional way they've led their lives. It's interesting that they see the differences between them, yet so many others – Nomad, Black Widow, Alfred Coppersmith – see the similarities.

Maybe Daredevil and the Punisher *can* see what we see – that they aren't so different, after all. They just have trouble admitting it to themselves. Perhaps they see one another as a dark mirror, a chilling reminder of what might have been. The Punisher started out a war hero, fighting for his country. If his family hadn't been killed he may have become a cop, firefighter – in short a *protector*; helping ordinary people every day much like Matt Murdock does. And what about Daredevil? He could easily have turned to the dark side, letting family tragedy and everyday circumstance grind him down, until it finally claimed his soul. Even Frank Miller, in the introduction to *Daredevil: The Man Without Fear* #4 (Jan 1994) said, "It's a wonder [Daredevil] isn't a villain." So maybe Daredevil detests the Punisher so much because he sees what *could* have happened (and could conceivably *still* happen) had he not had the strength to rise above his past and become the hero he is today.

From that perspective, the friction between these two men is understandable, even inevitable. After all, how would *you* feel if you looked into the eyes of someone you thought was your polar opposite and saw yourself staring back?

What Fall from Grace? Reappraising the Chichester Years

by Julian Darius

If you've heard of Daniel Chichester's run on Daredevil, especially his storyline "Fall from Grace," it was most likely in derision – and in passing. Some refer to it as the "motocross years," mocking Daredevil's armored costume during this time. Plenty refer to this material as part of the "grim 'n' gritty" trend in super-hero comics, as if Miller's work on *Daredevil* a decade earlier hadn't helped inaugurate that same trend. In large part because it's believed the changes this period wrought didn't stick, most Daredevil fans have learned that this period represents little more than an embarrassing chapter in Daredevil's longer history.

There's no doubt these stories aren't masterpieces. They're flawed. But they have impressive qualities, on their own terms. They also brought Daredevil, however briefly, to immense attention and popularity – in a fashion rivaled before only by Miller's work and afterward by Kevin Smith's.

Although Daredevil's new costume has been mocked, it was only one of three changes "Fall from Grace" brought. Another was the public revelation of Daredevil's identity, an idea later used to much celebration by Brian Michael Bendis. (This was nothing new for Chichester, whose earlier "Fall of the Kingpin" storyline has exerted a similar influence.)

But the change for which "Fall from Grace" got the most press was the return of Elektra. And that change wasn't undone. It's therefore a little odd to denigrate the "motocross years," based on other changes that were never likely to be permanent, while also enjoying subsequent Elektra appearances, as if those same "motocross years" didn't take a risk in making those appearances possible.

Finally, "Fall from Grace" didn't start the trend of big, "grim 'n' gritty" changes to super-hero status quos. Superman and Batman get that honor. "Fall from Grace" did perpetuate this trend, however – and here again, the storyline proved influential... not only on Daredevil but on super-hero comics generally.

Not bad for a comic no one cared about, before the much-maligned "Fall from Grace."

The Fall of the Kingpin

Some forget that writer Daniel (a.k.a. Dan or D.G.) Chichester had been on *Daredevil* for over two years before "Fall from Grace." Artist Scott McDaniel had been on the title for over a year prior. These weren't newcomers with no respect for the character. They were people who had honored the past and had told far more conventional Daredevil stories before they decided to radically change things up.

Daniel Chichester took over *Daredevil* with issue #292 (May 1991), following Ann Nocenti's tenure as writer. Although Nocenti had taken the title into more political territory, the series still carried much of Frank Miller's original tone. Super-heroes clashed on the cluttered covers of issues printed on cheap newsprint, at odds with the more sophisticated stories Miller brought to the title. In the early-to-mid-1980s, under Miller, that had been enough. However, by 1991, with the rise of graphic novels and high-production titles, with minimal covers and glossy paper stock, *Daredevil* looked out of place, neither sophisticated nor pulpy entertainment.

Chichester's first several issues continued threads left by Nocenti but which really went back to Miller, especially his development of the Kingpin as Daredevil's arch-nemesis. Miller's Kingpin arc never felt complete the way his Elektra arc did, but it too felt like it was heading somewhere definitive. In Miller's "Born Again" storyline, his last work for the monthly series, he brought Daredevil to his lowest point and had the hero consider killing his great adversary. Under Nocenti, the Kingpin shifted towards more legitimate business interests, at least publicly.

Chichester's early work on the title culminated in a sequel of sorts to "Born Again," in which Daredevil decided to finally bring down the Kingpin, whatever it took. He finally succeeds in issue #300 (Jan 1992), which culminates the "Last Rights" storyline and ends with a dethroned Kingpin relishing a murder and calling himself "a man… born again." Miller used "Born Again" to take apart Daredevil in order to reveal the true nature of a hero. Similarly, Chichester takes apart the Kingpin but leaves him oddly stronger, stripped of his airs of legitimacy along with his power. The result is a purer, more evil Kingpin.

Of course, while this was intended as a turning point in the story of the Kingpin, it doesn't look that way in retrospect. Fans, creators included, remember the Kingpin as a powerful gangster, and he inevitably returned to that position – only to be taken down again and again, in tales that effectively retold Chichester's "ending" to the Kingpin arc. This isn't Chichester's fault, any more than Miller could be blamed for the mishandling of Elektra under other writers. This has, however, diminished the reputation of Chichester's work.

At the time, "Last Rights" was understood as a major storyline in Daredevil history. These issues, #297-300, were collected as *Daredevil: The Fall of the Kingpin* – the first collection of *Daredevil* issues since Miller's "Born Again." Most of Miller's issues had yet to be collected. While such collections were slowly becoming more common, the very existence of *The Fall of the Kingpin* in collected form represented a major statement about the worth of the storyline.

Arguably, they represented the fulfillment of the narrative threads Miller had left. Of course, Miller's themes and images continue to influence new Daredevil stories to this day. *Daredevil* readers who began with Miller could have stopped with issue #300 and felt like Miller's story had come to some sort of completion.

It's telling, then, that Daredevil fans who love Miller and mock Chichester's later work tend to think Chichester's early work to be of good quality, to the extent that they're aware of it. Had *Daredevil* indeed been cancelled with #300, Chichester's stock amongst Daredevil fans would likely be in a very different place today.

Daredevil #301-318

But *Daredevil* wasn't cancelled. It plodded onward, as corporate comics tend to do.

Daredevil fought the Owl. He teamed up with Spider-Man. For three months, *Daredevil* crossed over with *Nomad* and *Punisher War Journal*. Glenn Alan Herdling stepped in to write two issues (#310-311, Nov-Dec 1992) which featured demons and tenuously tied into Marvel's silly *Infinity War* mini-series. With Chichester back, Daredevil battled an arsonist (#312-313, Jan-Feb 1993). He battled a new character named Shock, who made him remember Elektra (#314-315, Mar-Apr 1993). Even the villain Stilt-Man got a two-parter (#317-318, June-July 1993).

If none of this sounds particularly memorable, that's true. To his credit, Chichester offered a couple stories organized around interesting concepts, such as the time between murders in New York City (issue #304, May 1992) or exploring the New York subways as a setting (#316, May 1993). But a year and a half after the historic issue #300, *Daredevil* felt lost.

It had burned up the fuel left by Miller, but it didn't have a new direction. In place of one, *Daredevil* had turned into a pretty unremarkable title for the time, and sales were suffering.

In fact, these 18 issues featured one of the most dramatic changes in Daredevil history – a shift in artistic style. Miller and Klaus Janson had defined Daredevil's look during Miller's run. John Romita, Jr. had largely defined the look of Ann Nocenti's tenure. Lee Weeks, while rarely listed among Daredevil's best artists, had kept the title looking quasi-realistic and helped bridge the gap between Nocenti and Chichester. Then with issue #305 (June 1992), an unknown artist named Scott McDaniel took over as series penciler.

McDaniel's style was wildly expressive, compared to past *Daredevil* artists. His work in this period is strongly similar to the slightly later work of Mike Deodato, Jr. – another unknown who would, in 1994, achieve great popularity on DC's *Wonder Woman*. Both artists avoided detailed backgrounds and focused on figures, often depicted with exaggerated, melodramatic postures.

In fact, this was only part of a wider trend in comics art. The 1980s largely championed detailed, realistic artwork (e.g. George Pérez and John Bryne). By the early 1990s, the most popular artists (e.g. Todd McFarlane and Rob Liefeld) had turned towards highly exaggerated styles. Comics in general followed suit, and *Daredevil* was no exception.

However, such a style seemed uniquely ill-suited to Daredevil, who thrived in an urban, realistic landscape. Gods and aliens known for fisticuffs and explosions might lend themselves well to wild artistic styles. Daredevil was visually defined less by explosive, exaggerated forms and more by graceful flips from buildings, or by radar emanating from his figure and bouncing off the details of his landscape. McDaniel's style seemed to reduce Daredevil to just another Marvel super-hero title.

If *Daredevil* bucked the trends, it was more in the writing. After finishing his Kingpin arc, Chichester had shifted towards somewhat sillier stories – the Owl, Stilt-Man, etc. Perhaps he had attempted to bring the threads left by Miller to a conclusion, then continue in a new, lighter direction.

Like his "The Fall of the Kingpin," this too would be imitated. Chichester's successors would repeatedly swing towards the light-hearted, especially after periods of dark, realistic stories. Writers before Miller weren't always so serious, but Chichester seems to have been the first writer after Miller to deliberately and programmatically head in the opposite direction.

Unfortunately, this came at the wrong time. The exaggerated artwork that had become popular was often used to tell especially violent, extended stories. The realistic preferences of 1980s comics are rightly considered dark and violent, in contrast with what came before. But they were rarely gratuitous. In the exaggerated early 1990s comics, violence seemed its own reward. Readers wanted plenty of blood and casual murderers with knives for fingers, not Stilt-Man.

Therefore, *Daredevil*, after wrapping up Miller's story arcs, was busy imitating a popular artistic style uniquely unsuited to the content – yet going somewhat against the popular grain in terms of narrative content.

A radical change was in order. That change would come in issue #319 (Aug 1993). Issues #317-318 told the Stilt-Man story, which featured a good deal of humor and was almost certainly these 18 issues' greatest affront to then-current tastes. It felt as if Chichester and McDaniel were cleaning their palates before the following issue's big change.

The cover of #318 made this explicit. If the contents were somewhat silly, the cover was over the top. It has a cockroach devouring the Marvel logo. Every character on the cover had word or thought balloons, which bucked the trend against this practice, and all of them were humorous – or at least supposedly humorous. Daredevil, in a thought balloon, wondered, "Where are all the *'gritty'* writers when you *really* need them!!!" – a clear reference to the escalating preference for "grim 'n' gritty" comics. At the bottom of the cover, speech balloons coming from below the image – and representing the editors – worried that "this cover's gonna get us canned." In the bottom-right cover, an "editorial disclaimer" reassured readers, "Don't worry, we know it looks stupid, but we wanted to have some fun before we ruined DD's life – *again!*"

Daredevil #319

The cover of #319 couldn't have been more different. Mostly white, the cover featured an image of the Chrysler building rendered entirely in black. The title "Daredevil" was tiny, less than a quarter the normal size and positioned on the margins, cropped by the top of the cover. It was also entirely black, rather than the traditional bright red used for Daredevil's logo. Even the Marvel logo was rendered as a thin black outline. The only other text read "'Fall from Grace' prologue," announcing a multi-part storyline without any explanation or editorial pitch to readers. This lettering was almost as large as the title itself, suggesting that this new story wasn't the traditional Daredevil tale and making the issue look more like a mini-series than issue #319 of an ongoing series. The only color on the cover was the tiny figure of a man in red, presumably Daredevil, falling from the Chrysler building.

It was stark. It was minimal. It was sophisticated. It was striking. It was like nothing else on the stands.

It was also so different from the cover of the previous issue that it was hard to imagine these were covers of the same title, let alone covers separated by a single month.

In a single image, *Daredevil* told readers that everything had changed. No words could have been as effective.

This was a comic readers couldn't resist. And they didn't. The issue sold out almost immediately, and Marvel quickly produced a second printing with the whites and blacks of the cover inversed.

That cover was by Scott McDaniel, the title's regular artist. He had never produced an image like this before. He carried this new artistic style into the comic itself, where McDaniel's style barely resembled his previous work. McDaniel now frequently defined objects and spaces by their highlights, rather than rendering all their details. His figures were still exaggerated, but the

The striking, minimalistic cover to *Daredevil* #319 (Aug 1993) announces the title's bold new direction. Art by Scott McDaniel. Copyright © Marvel Comics.

overall effect had completely changed. Although his work would continue to evolve, he would never revert to his previous style.

This new look clearly resembled Frank Miller's recent art, especially on *Sin City*, where he also memorably rendered spaces through their highlights alone. McDaniel's art was in color, however, while Miller's *Sin City* work was black-and-white. In retrospect, the two artists' styles are instantly distinguishable, and it's clear that McDaniel adapted Miller's innovations into his own separate style. However, because both styles were so new and different at the time, many accused McDaniel of outright copying from Miller.

This accusation didn't hurt sales, however. Miller hadn't produced Daredevil artwork since his original run, outside of the 1990 graphic novel *Elektra Lives Again*. In lieu of Miller himself returning, even a copy seemed better than nothing. And because Miller's style had evolved since, his recent stylistic innovations were new to Daredevil. In its suddenly changed artistic style, "Fall from Grace" announced itself as a reinvigoration of the title along the lines of Miller's work – a return to boldness and relevancy.

Chichester had modified his writing style too. In his early, Kingpin-dominated issues, he had reached for poetic turns of phrase in his captions, sometimes to great effect. In the year and a half since, Chichester seemed to quiet this tendency, as *Daredevil* turned into a more standard-fare comic. Now, Chichester's more sophisticated elocutions returned with a vengeance. He certainly wasn't Alan Moore or Neil Gaiman, but he was juxtaposing poetic captions with panels in ways the average super-hero comic in 1993 didn't even attempt.

Both inside and out, the new *Daredevil* felt nothing like the standard super-hero monthly it had been the month before. Despite being printed on normal paper with the then-standard cover price of $1.25, these issues felt more like the kind of artsy, more sophisticated and experimental projects both DC and Marvel printed on better paper at higher cover prices.

"Fall from Grace" and Event Comics

The artistic overtones of *Daredevil*'s new direction were unique to that title, but the events of "Fall from Grace" took their cue from a wider trend. By *Daredevil* #319 (Aug 1993), American comics had already embraced radical changes to the status quo as a way of bringing in new readers and garnering attention for super-hero characters.

A year before, the four Superman titles faced flagging sales and seemed out of step with the public's increasingly violent tastes. So, at the end of 1992, DC killed off Superman to unprecedented fanfare and sales. In early 1993, DC replaced the dead hero with four alternates, eventually bringing back the original – although in a mostly black costume for a time and with longer hair that stuck around for years. The Superman titles became bestsellers, and their stories shifted markedly towards violence.

In the middle of 1993, Batman went through a similar event, as the new villain Bane broke Batman's back and the new anti-hero Azrael became the new, more violent Batman who wore an armored costume. This new status quo continued for about a year, during which "Fall from Grace" was published.

Such storylines would become increasingly mocked in later years. It's true that they frequently seemed to arise out of nowhere, rather than flowering inevitably from long-standing characters and narratives. It's also true that these events were staged to increase sales. But they were exciting. And they arguably represented the biggest change to how super-hero stories were told since super-hero stories began.

Super-hero comics had always resisted change, not unlike sitcom TV. For the most part, stories were episodic and, no matter how dramatic, returned to a status quo by the story's end. Once, this had been based on the premise that super-hero comics were read mostly by children, who might miss an issue on the newsstand. With the rise of comic stores and an aging readership, soap operatic change seeped in on titles like *Uncanny X-Men*. Occasional big changes occurred, particularly around DC's *Crisis on Infinite Earths*, but the status quo on any given title rarely changed dramatically.

After the death of Superman and the breaking of Batman, comics overreacted in the other direction. Radical change seemed to generate radical sales. The status quo wasn't mandatory anymore; it was the enemy. All bets were off, and virtually every major super-hero would be put through major changes.

"Fall from Grace" (*Daredevil* #319-325, Aug 1993 - Feb 1994) was the first Marvel imitator of this trend, soon dubbed "event comics." By the end of the storyline, Daredevil's status quo would be radically changed, and press promoted this fact from the story's start. As soon as the prologue issue sold out, the storyline was immediately understood as part of this wider, "event comics" trend, for which it would serve as an important test case.

The astonishing success of "Fall from Grace" demonstrated that the "event comics" formula could work at Marvel too. But it also demonstrated that such stories could catapult a second-tier (arguably even a third-tier) title to bestseller status. This wasn't a simple matter of the character's popularity; it was at least as much a question of format.

Superman and Batman had multiple titles, letting readers get new installments of their status quo-altering stories multiple times a month (if not always weekly). The excitement over these stories was in large part based on a fascination with reading what happens next, which generated impulse buys. Some of these readers felt these stories were guilty pleasures, and most of them weren't regular readers of the titles involved – hence the boost in sales. It was "Fall from Grace" that demonstrated comics readers would wait a month for the next chapter of such a story.

Before "Fall from Grace," status quo-changing events were a way of getting new readers for the top tier of super-hero franchises, especially at DC. Afterwards, this model was understood as applying to everything.

About halfway through "Fall from Grace," Wolverine got the adamantium pulled from his body in *X-Men* #25 (Oct 1993).

By the end of "Fall from Grace," Green Lantern Hal Jordan's home city and entire extended cast were destroyed, culminating in him turning decisively evil in *Green Lantern* #50 (March 1994) and leading to his replacement as Green Lantern.

That same month following the conclusion of "Fall from Grace," *Captain America* #425 (March 1994) began a long-running story in which Captain America found that the serum that gave him super-powers was killing him. He got a new, armored costume and readers awaited his permanent replacement (which never materialized).

By this point, such radical changes had already become so common that stories could play against reader expectations. Thus, *Flash* #92 (July 1994) introduced a character clearly designed as Flash's replacement, and Flash was apparently killed three months later. This was all misdirection, however, on the part of writer Mark Waid, who didn't like these violent event comics.

A few months later, while *Daredevil* concluded "Tree of Knowledge," its follow-up storyline to "Fall from Grace," *Wonder Woman* #90 (Sept 1994) began a storyline in which Wonder Woman was replaced by the more violent Artemis.

About the same time, Marvel began Spider-Man's infamous "Clone Saga," explicitly created to imitate DC's Superman and Batman stories. Harkening back to a forgotten 1975 story involving a clone of Spider-Man, the new story brought the clone back, confirmed that he was the original (and the Spider-Man readers had known since 1975 had actually been the clone), and had this new character replace Peter Parker as Spider-Man. Because it sold so well, Marvel strung the story out for two full years, ending it in late 1996 (after Peter Parker was revealed to be the original all along).

Such storylines continued for some time. A year after "Tree of Knowledge" concluded, DC killed off and replaced Green Arrow, in a story organized around *Green Arrow* #100 (Sept 1995).By then, the "event comics" fad was fading. Many titles, including *Daredevil*, had seen sales drop after the initial excitement. Later super-hero comics would occasionally use tactics learned from the "event comics" fad, but that period of super-hero history was spent.

Most fads are derided after the fact, and most agree that the editorially mandated attempts to grab sales rather than tell intrinsically honest stories led to a shallow period of drama on the many pages of super-hero comics. However, many "event" storylines have received a nostalgic rosy tint. Even Spider-Man's "Clone Saga," once so scorned that even Marvel mocked it in print, has come to be remembered fondly by some, although more for its ambition than its execution.

"Fall from Grace" hasn't fared nearly as well as most. To be sure, its narrative is sometimes a mess. It has too many characters, including unnecessary guest-stars like Venom and Morbius. It also has a serious problem with transitions between scenes featuring Daredevil and ones featuring Matt Murdock. Too often, Daredevil's allies and villains seem on pause until the next Daredevil sequence – which resumes matters from the previous Daredevil sequence's business, as if no time has passed and Daredevil didn't leave and return.

Yet "Fall from Grace" has some stunning visuals that deserve to be placed alongside Miller's own work. It's a work of art, not something reducible to its "events."

And those same denigrated changes to the status quo have had lasting importance. Sure, it's easy to focus on what "failed" and reverted to the status quo, such as Daredevil's costume. This is by far the element most mocked by critics of the storyline – precisely because doing so is so easy and cheap.

"Fall from Grace" also brought Elektra and other elements from Miller's work back into the Marvel universe. While we can debate the ethics of such a choice, Elektra's return was never undone, and it allowed many good stories (as well as a not-so-good Elektra motion picture). It's hard to imagine the Marvel Universe without Elektra and the Hand running around, and that goes back to "Fall from Grace."

The storyline also revealed Daredevil's identity to the public. Although this was later undone, like Chichester's earlier "The Fall of the Kingpin," it would also be imitated by later creators. In fact, the first year of Brian Michael Bendis's run – by far his most celebrated work on Daredevil – revolved around these same two story ideas.

Elektra Returns

Daredevil #319 reintroduced John Garrett, the S.H.I.E.L.D. espionage agent composed of mostly cybernetic parts. Miller created Garrett for his celebrated *Elektra: Assassin* (1986-1989), in which Garrett featured prominently, but the character hadn't been seen since. Because of the wild nature of the mini-series, which had been published by Marvel's Epic imprint and sold exclusively in comics shops, some had even speculated that *Elektra: Assassin* shouldn't be considered in continuity. It certainly had no impact on any other Marvel title. "Fall from Grace" brought that mini-series into continuity for the first time.

Even the Hand, created by Miller and inextricably bound to his Elektra arc, had only rarely been seen since. The evil ninja organization had appeared in the 1982 *Wolverine* mini-series, illustrated by Miller, and had occasionally appeared in subsequent *X-Men* and *Wolverine* stories. But the organization hadn't appeared in *Daredevil* after Miller's original run – until Chichester's early issues, leading up to his "The Fall of the Kingpin" storyline. In *Daredevil* #319, Chichester and McDaniel introduced the Snakeroot, an even more savage organization that had co-opted the Hand and come to form its inner circle.

But the real, Miller-related surprise came on the final page, which showed a sai driven through a man's chest, suggesting that perhaps Elektra had returned as well.

Even the hint of Elektra's return sent shockwaves through the comics community. The character had always been a fan favorite, and her arc was by far the most fondly remembered aspect of Miller's original run. "Fall from

Grace" might be mocked for the new costume it gave Daredevil but above all, Elektra's return was the far bigger "event" for comics readers at the time.

Despite her popularity, Elektra hadn't been in the pages of *Daredevil* for over a decade. After his original run on the title (which ended in late 1982), she had appeared only in *Elektra: Assassin* (1986-1989) and in the graphic novel *Elektra Lives Again* (1990), both by Miller himself. Reportedly, this was because Marvel, through *Daredevil* editor Ralph Macchio, had verbally promised Miller that no other writer would be allowed to use the character – a promise Marvel violated by permitting her return in "Fall from Grace."

Miller was vocal about his disapproval. He was busy preparing his extended retelling of Daredevil's origins, in the mini-series *Daredevil: Man without Fear* (#1-5, Oct 1993 - Feb 1994), which would be published alongside the final five issues of "Fall from Grace." The two combined to create a kind of Daredevil fever not seen since Miller's "Born Again." Then, in protest over Elektra's return, Miller announced this would be his final work for Marvel – a vow he's kept ever since.

Poetically, the storyline that gave *Daredevil* its most dramatic new direction since Miller appeared alongside Miller's swan song for these characters.

For its part, Marvel claimed that it couldn't be bound by Macchio's promise to Miller, which had occurred when the company was privately held. It had since become a publicly-traded company, accountable to shareholders, and it felt that it couldn't be bound to a verbal promise an editor had made years before. A decade had passed, Miller's output was sparse, and Marvel had a current creative team eager to use the character. Elektra represented a potentially lucrative commodity, and her usage in the two decades since clearly illustrates this to a greater extent than anyone at Marvel could have reasonably guessed.

Of course, that doesn't make Marvel's decision ethical, and it's a choice that's still debated in comics circles, seemingly every time the character is used prominently.

There's also an artistic argument to be made, in which Miller as *auteur* contrasts with the collective model embraced by corporate American super-heroes.

Marvel's decision also didn't account for the growing graphic novel market. Nor could the company anticipate the later digital comics market. In those environments, vast amounts of monthly production count for less than a single celebrated work. An additional Miller work might sell well in perpetuity, whereas a decade of forgettable monthly comics, starring Elektra or not, have little lasting sales potential. In this way, ethics and high-art values may well be smarter, even from a purely financial perspective, in the long term.

These are real concerns, about which reasonable people may disagree. The one position that can't be held is that Elektra's return was somehow radically disharmonious with what Miller had established.

Elektra's famous death (in *Daredevil* #181, Apr 1982) was occasioned by her choice not to kill Foggy Nelson, thereby at least partially redeeming her by having her choose her love for Matt over her duty as an assassin. Beginning in the very next issue, Miller played several times with the idea of her resurrection. This culminated in the penultimate issue of Miller's original run (the extra-long *Daredevil* #190, Jan 1983), in which the Hand tried to resurrect Elektra but found themselves unable to do so because her soul was now pure, perhaps as a consequence of Matt's love.

That issue began and ended with a framing sequence that suggested that, after the main events of the issue, Elektra had in fact been resurrected. Now wearing white instead of her traditional red, she climbed a snowy mountain, echoing both her ninja training and religious ascent. The captions suggest that she wished to hide her return from Matt Murdock – implicitly to allow him to grieve for her, perhaps because their personalities and violent lifestyles meant they could never be a couple. Readers speculated this might represent a kind of stark, warrior afterlife for Elektra, but this was mere conjecture.

That's where Miller left Elektra. His *Elektra: Assassin* was deliberately ambiguous as to whether it took place before her death or starred this resurrected Elektra – or even should be considered as part of continuity at all. Reportedly, Miller saw it as a flashback to before her death, but this might explain why she wore red, not white, and was the assassin we knew, rather than showing signs of having been purified.

As he had during his original run, Miller, in his stunningly brilliant *Elektra Lives Again*, further played with the idea of Elektra's return, focusing on how Matt continued to be haunted by her memory. It too was ambiguous and ended with Matt believing his visions of her were only hallucinations.

In fact, Miller's original deal with Ralph Macchio wasn't *really* that no one would use Elektra. It was that no one would bring her back except Miller. Perhaps that's partly why he left her resurrection so ambiguous. If she had definitively returned, Marvel could have argued that Miller had opened the door for others to use the character.

But while acknowledging the ambiguities involved, Elektra had effectively already returned to life in *Daredevil* #190.

Letting another writer reintroduce her formally might have been unethical, but it wasn't a violation of Miller's work. Elektra living but exiling herself from Matt arguably represented the best conclusion to her story. Corporate superheroes are rarely given definitive endings, however, and at least her return didn't dishonor what had come before. In fact, Miller had himself played with the possibility of Elektra's return since the issue following her death.

Other long-dead comics characters have returned with far less explanation. At DC, Hal Jordan, Jason Todd, and Barry Allen have all returned with the weakest of explanations, in ways that dishonored past material. In the case of Bucky Barnes, martyred World-War-II sidekick to Captain America, writer Ed Brubaker argued that Bucky's death had first been depicted in a later, retroactive story anyway. He also pointed out that many past Captain America stories played with the idea of Bucky's return – a criterion Elektra also meets.

Moreover, Chichester explicitly brought Elektra back in a way consistent with Miller's material, especially Elektra's apparent resurrection in *Daredevil* #190.

After readers saw the sai at the end of *Daredevil* #319, Daredevil began finding similar evidence. In issue #321 (Oct 1993), Daredevil finds holes in a wall and identifies them as having been left by a sai. In issue #322 (Nov 1993), he finds an actual sai in a dead man's back.

That same issue depicts the Snakeroot's attempt to resurrect Elektra using Garrett's cyborg memory of the violent Elektra he knew. In the next issue (#323, Dec 1993), we see that the Hand has succeeded in reconstructing Garrett and in bringing to life a purple, zombie-like version of Elektra called Erynys.

The sais weren't explained until the storyline's penultimate issue (#324, Jan 1994), which reveals that Stone has been wielding them, not Elektra. Stone was a part of the Chaste, the Hand's opposite – a group of good ninjas that included Stick, the character Miller invented as the person who had trained Daredevil. Stone had a role in the crucial *Daredevil* #190, helping Daredevil confront the Hand's plan to resurrect Elektra. Here again, Chichester honored Miller's earlier work.

Elektra is revealed, on the final two pages of *Daredevil* #324 (Jan 1994). Art by Scott McDaniel, Hector Collazo, and Michael Avon Oeming. Copyright © Marvel Comics.

This revelation made the sais we'd been seeing simple misdirection. The only living Elektra was apparently Erynys, a perversion based on Garrett's memory of the assassin he knew. As the penultimate issue draws to a close, Daredevil confronts Garrett and Erynys, only for them to run away as a new figure arrives: Elektra herself, clad in white instead of red.

McDaniel's beautiful rendering of Elektra, in that issue's final double-page spread, is worthy of Miller himself. His new style fit Elektra like he'd created it simply to draw her.

In #325 (Feb 1994), Elektra implies she's been on the mountain (seen in #190) since her resurrection. This suggests that *Elektra: Assassin* was indeed a flashback and that Elektra's appearance in *Elektra Lives Again* might really have been a hallucination. Elektra explains that she's only returned because the Snakeroot was creating Erynys. Elektra, who redeemed herself before her death and was purified (in #190) by Matt's love, breaks down emotionally at the thought that Erynys represents the violent, amoral assassin she's struggled to leave behind.

In the issue's climax, Elektra battles Erynys, and Daredevil delivers the killing blow, by way of one of Erynys's stylized sais. As Erynys dies, Elektra says she's reabsorbing the darkness in herself from Erynys. It's hokey, but so too was Miller's use of souls, as seen in the Hand's power of resurrection, in the reference to Matt's love somehow purifying Elektra's soul, and in *Elektra: Assassin*.

That said, Chichester rushes matters in ways that diminish the power of Elektra's return. For example, Miller had spent multiple issues and an entire graphic novel exploring how much Elektra's death haunted Matt, so we might expect the couple would be given some space to reconnect after her appearance at the end of #324. Instead, the pair shift into the mode of a conventional team-up, with only occasional dialogue referencing their situation.

Elektra also isn't granted the appropriate space to explore her emotions. Issue #325 last shows her weeping at how she's "lost," having just absorbed the part of herself Erynys represents. Then, instead of returning to this, the story shifts to Matt's concerns, neither giving Elektra another scene nor even showing where she goes. (As already noted, Chichester seems to have trouble with transitions.)

The execution of Elektra's return was less than perfect, but not without its merits. Whether or not it represented unethical treatment of Frank Miller, it honored his work. It may have been an "event," but Elektra's return certainly wasn't done without regard to what Miller had established.

The New Costume

In issue #320 (Sept 1993), Daredevil's costume was torn to shreds in a fight (with a sadomasochistic villain who enjoys being hit). By the end of the issue, Daredevil's wearing only half of it, suggesting that's how much he's managed to salvage. In the opening pages of issue #321 (Oct 1993), he abruptly makes a new armored costume, in order to stand more punishment during fights. To make matters worse, this appears to be a flashback ending with Daredevil fighting the same demon he was fighting at the end of the previous issue, with no explanation as to the costume change. Did Daredevil leave the fight, make his costume, and come back? Who knows?

While hardly the most graceful of narrative executions, the new costume itself made a lot of sense. Daredevil's red spandex suit was always silly from a practical perspective. He might have been more of a gymnast than Batman, but both heroes got into plenty of fistfights, in which some sort of shielding would be essential. Daredevil's new costume made sense, and it reflected the long trend towards realism in super-hero stories.

Comics, however, are a visual medium in which cool images often trump logic, however regretfully. For example, super-hero stories rarely attempt to explain the presence of capes, which might enhance visuals but would only get caught in things (such as villains' hands). Daredevil's red outfit is a classic design of streamlined simplicity (reminiscent of the Silver Age Flash or Green Lantern). The armored costume had many separate areas of padding, each of which could be red, dark blue, or white. The resulting visual was far less impressive, logic be damned.

In issue #323 (Dec 1993), we see that Daredevil's club can break apart, revealing a concealed chain, thus converting the club to nunchaku. The club can also extend its length, becoming a full-length staff. Improbable though this may have been, it at least represented an improvement to Daredevil's traditional limited arsenal.

Matt Murdock Exposed!

In issue #323 (Dec 1993), we're introduced to the offices of the Big Apple Advocate, "the *bottom* of the *barrel* in small press *newspapers*." There, a reporter named Sara Harrington has submitted a story that claims Matt Murdock is Daredevil. She used to intern with Ben Urich of the Daily Bugle, who long-term readers know uncovered Daredevil's identity but chose not to run the story. Her notes are in Urich's handwriting, indicating she stole his work. Although the floundering newspaper can't confirm the story, it chooses to run it anyway, because it needs the sales.

In the next issue (#324, Jan 1994), Daredevil's shown a discarded copy of the paper with the headline "Matt Murdock is Daredevil?" Matt briefly confronts Urich who explains how this happened. In the story's final issue (#325), Harrington and Urich are part of a mob that breaks into Murdock's apartment but finds a Braille map that seems to confirm Murdock's blindness. We soon learn Matt planned this, to discredit the original story, but the idea that he's Daredevil is still out there.

In the final issue's epilogue, the FBI has arrested Sara Harrington, based on a tip from Urich. How the FBI accumulated this evidence, without also authenticating that the files she stole were Urich's and thus legitimate, isn't adequately explained, although they apparently arrest her for phone fraud rather than breaking into Urich's computers. (When she committed this phone fraud, or how the FBI didn't uncover her real crime, remains unexplained.)

Urich then pens his own piece praising Murdock and claiming the lawyer isn't Daredevil. Matt visits Maggie, the nun from Miller's "Born Again" storyline, to consult about a new name to adopt, indicating that he's abandoning his Matt Murdock identity.

Like the story's other plots, the exposing of Daredevil's identity seems stilted in execution. But like them, it also followed up on past stories, specifically Urich knowing Daredevil's identity. And in a genre in which superheroes identities are typically known by many intimates yet rarely leaked to the public, this plot represented a realistic development. "Event comics" changed their characters' status quo, but rarely did they do so in such a logical way that stemmed from already-established elements.

"Tree of Knowledge"

"Fall from Grace" continues fairly directly into "Tree of Knowledge." Like its predecessor, it's a bit of a mess, with lots of characters and some odd transitions between scenes, but it's generally clearer than "Fall from Grace."

This improvement starts with the very first pages of issue #326 (March 1994), which begins the storyline in about as dramatic a manner as possible: with the burial of Matt Murdock.

Apparently, after the conclusion of "Fall from Grace," Matt hadn't simply chosen a new civilian identity, becoming "Jack Batlin" to honor his boxer father. Matt's arranged a funeral for himself, during which Hellspawn, the shape-shifting demon who died during "Fall from Grace," is buried in Matt's coffin. To protect them, Matt hasn't told the truth to Foggy Nelson or Karen Page, his on-and-off girlfriend, both of whom believe Matt dead.

"Tree of Knowledge" thus begins dramatically as we watch Matt's friends and allies mourn. Perhaps the saddest reaction is that of Karen Page. The most dramatic, though, is Wilson Fisk, the former Kingpin whom Matt dethroned, who spits into Matt's grave.

Confronting some criminals, Daredevil takes and brandishes their gun. The captions tell us Matt does so consciously, to encourage people to believe this new Daredevil is a separate person – and definitely not Matt Murdock, despite what the newspapers have said. It's a startling image that recalls how Batman controversially brandished a gun in *Detective Comics* #327 (May 1964), which also was intended to start a new era for its character.

McDaniel's new style continued to develop. More lines are rendered purely with color alone, without inked lines to hold the color. McDaniel also uses more close-ups and dramatic poses. The combined effect is often masterful, with several stunning panels.

The Theme of Technology

The mid-1990s were a key moment in the history of technological change, as internet terminals migrated from college campuses into homes. Most fiction of the time ignored this new reality, but "Fall from Grace" hinted at it by stating that Sara Harrington stole Ben Urich's files by breaking into his computer, rather than taking his physical notes (although she seems in one scene to have those, too). "Tree of Knowledge" responds more ambitiously to this new technology. Its main villains, the Silicon Pirates, are described as technological terrorists, which has subsequently become a real security concern.

Some of this looks pretty silly now. Kilobyte could only be used as a super-villain name when "kilobyte" still sounded like a somewhat esoteric word, though it quickly became antiquated as the world forged ahead into terabytes and beyond. Names like Bitmap or Emoticon, while silly, seem remarkably ahead of their time. Characters talk about the free exchange of information, data encryption, and how technological advances could lead to surveillance of private citizens.

"Tree of Knowledge" sometimes even has a vaguely *Matrix* feel, with technophiles in flamboyant costumes hanging out as part of underground society. In issue #330 (July 1994), Chichester even seems to link this with the then-growing rave culture, giving us a club where such technophiles party. There, his captions tell us:

> Industrial music mixes machine clanks, electronic feedback, random radio noise.
> The sounds a culture makes as it comes unglued.
> Strobing light and sound trigger synapses in the brain.
> The human body becomes a hack site, flesh and technology forging a strange, new alliance.

While the story rarely reaches such heights, when it does, it seems closer to *Neuromancer*, William Gibson's influential 1984 cyberpunk novel, than the average 1994 super-hero schlock.

"Tree of Knowledge" even thematically acknowledges the role of pornography in this new technological era. Pornography has driven advances in art and media going back to the printing press, and it's well known to have heavily influenced the internet revolution. Pornography has since pioneered streaming video, online payment systems, and data encryption. "Tree of Knowledge" implicitly acknowledges this through Karen Page, who was exploited sexually around the beginning of Miller's "Born Again" storyline. Now, she's tempted by a high-pressure offer to help manage an innovative pornography business. The company even seems to be offering an interactive virtual girl for computer desktops, a product that didn't become commonplace until a decade later.

In practice, the Silicon Pirates, run by the long-established terrorist organization HYDRA, do far more traditional terrorism than anything online. But here too, "Tree of Knowledge" was ahead of its time. The story features a lot of loose talk about whether the government should, in response to this terrorism, implement some form of martial law and ignore certain civil rights, which in retrospect strongly recalls the American response, less than a decade later, to 9/11.

The Failure of "Tree of Knowledge"

Despite its positive aspects, "Tree of Knowledge" was regarded as a failure. In part, this was due to problems also present in "Fall from Grace," such as a meandering plot with frequent guest stars (here including Captain America, Black Widow, Iron Fist, and Gambit).

However, "Tree of Knowledge" lacked the elements that made "Fall from Grace" feel so revolutionary. Obviously, Daredevil couldn't adopt a second new costume, nor get his alter ego exposed again. "Tree of Knowledge" didn't so much carry these story elements forward as presume them to be the new status quo. For example, Ben Urich and Sara Harrington are dropped completely. In short, "Tree of Knowledge" failed to capitalize on what made "Fall from Grace" attract so much attention.

Nowhere is this more evident than in the treatment of Elektra. In the storyline's first issue, we see her, appropriately wearing a mix of her classic red outfit and her purified white one. There, she is rejected by the Chaste because she's absorbed Erynys's essence. Consequently, she can't return to the mountain with them as planned. She appears occasionally thereafter, culminating in the final pages of the storyline's final issue (#332, Sept 1994), in which she and Matt essentially part ways. But she never gets involved in the storyline's events, and her brief appearances amount to little more than resetting her character following her return.

Thus, the character who represented the greatest appeal of "Fall from Grace" basically sits out of its sequel.

Complicating matters, *Daredevil* began to run late. To avoid skipping an issue of a top-selling title, issue #328 (May 1994) was a fill-in by writer Gregory Wright, with McDaniel illustrating only the cover. Labeled an "interlude" to the storyline, it's a lackluster issue guest-starring Silver Sable.

There must have been some miscommunication, because the previous issue ends with Daredevil and Captain America about to face off. In the fill-in, there's no reference to this, and those two super-heroes work together. Readers might have guessed the fill-in was meant to take place between pages late in the previous issue, leaving the heroes' confrontation to Chichester and McDaniel. But when they returned (issue #329, June 1994), they made no reference to that cliffhanger, leaving readers to wonder what had happened.

Fill-ins almost inevitably dilute titles, but such amateurish mistakes were catastrophic to reader confidence. "Fall from Grace" and "Tree of Knowledge" worked because they felt *special*, more like the kinds of auteur-driven stories then being printed in better formats. The mundane fill-in seemed to illustrate that Marvel didn't understand it was this special, auteur feeling, not simply Daredevil's new costume, that made the title such a sudden hit.

After the fill-in, McDaniel's art seemed to deteriorate slightly, as if rushed to meet deadlines. His new style peaked around the separation between the two storylines, then began to lose a bit of its detail and toning.

Making matters worse, the storyline ran an extra issue. Issue #331 (Aug 1994) billed itself as part "V of V" but ended in a cliffhanger that continued into issue #332 (Sept 1994), billed simply as "Tree of Knowledge, finale." Including the "interlude," "Tree of Knowledge" ran seven issues, as long as "Fall from Grace." The interlude had compromised the story's artistic and narrative consistency. And many fans wanted more Elektra, yet received only a couple of uneventful pages an issue.

During this time, Marvel also published *Daredevil Annual* #10 (1994). Its main story, also written by Greg Wright, starred Elektra as fans wanted to see her – back in action. But like the fill-in issue, the quality wasn't there.

Daredevil only sold after its creators turned it into an experimental artistic title. Elektra had only been written by Miller, outside of Chichester and McDaniel. To see her reduced to a conventional story felt sacrilegious – and misjudged, given her relative absence from "Tree of Knowledge." It was enough to make even fans of "Fall from Grace" suspect that Miller might have been right about her return, after all.

"Root of Evil"

After "Tree of Knowledge," Chichester and McDaniel left *Daredevil*. In lieu of a letters column in the next issue (#333, Oct 1994), Chichester explained that the creators were focusing on a project starring Elektra.

The choice made sense on several levels. It would avoid the creators rushing, and would avoid diminishing Elektra by letting other creators use her.

But this choice would also allow Marvel to capitalize on the popularity of Chichester and McDaniel. When the four-issue Elektra mini-series appeared, it would be on glossy paper with embossed, cardstock covers, published under the "Marvel Select" banner, which focused on such higher-profile projects. Each issue would feature 32 pages, plus front and back covers and nice inside covers, all without ads. It would be priced at $2.95 an issue – then twice the standard issue price.

This certainly was a step up for Chichester and McDaniel, but it also reflected the quality of their work, which felt more like one of these glossy mini-series than the standard super-hero fare.

In fact, going back to "Fall from Grace," Marvel had already tried to capitalize on *Daredevil*'s newfound success. Issue #321 (Oct 1993) featured a wraparound cover mostly composed of glow-in-the-dark ink (normally white), justified as representing what Daredevil sees with his radar. This raised the cover price to $2.00. Issue #325 (Feb 1994) was priced at $2.50 because it contained extra pages. Not quite double-sized, it would normally have been priced at $2.00, but Marvel apparently sought to cash in on the title's sudden popularity. None of the issues of "Tree of Knowledge" had such extra features, but with issue #328 (the fill-in issue), the standard cover price rose to $1.50.

After the announcement of the Elektra project in *Daredevil* #333 (Oct 1994), issue #334 (Nov 1994) featured a new four-page Elektra story by Chichester and McDaniel. Issue #335 (Dec 1994) featured another text piece with a couple illustrations, followed in #336 (Jan 1995) by a three-page Elektra story by Chichester and McDaniel.

When the Elektra mini-series (#1-4, Mar-June 1995) appeared, six months after the final Chichester / McDaniel issue of *Daredevil*, it was officially titled *Elektra* (the first time any publication could boast this), although the cover made it look as if the title were *Elektra: Root of Evil*.

Here, McDaniel's art returned in force and continued to evolve. Printed on quality paper that more effectively captured color, the omission of inked lines between colored spaces now looked much better. McDaniel also began adding patterns around panels in a way that accentuated the page as a separate unit of meaning. This technique was extremely rare in 1995, although it would later attract attention on titles such as *Fables*, as illustrated by Mark Buckingham. McDaniel also varied his style for Elektra's flashbacks, including one in issue #4 that was designed to look like a child's drawings. By the end of the series, McDaniel's style had grown more exaggerated, essentially becoming the style he's used ever since.

The story was less successful. It depicted Elektra assembling her own team of new characters to battle the Snakeroot. It could be hard to follow, and the flashbacks to Elektra's earlier life revised what Miller had previously established in ways that didn't seem to add much. The story ends with Elektra visiting her father's grave, ostensibly coming to terms with her past.

This really was the first solo Elektra story, outside of the short, black-and-white story Miller had done. Daredevil and Nick Fury make short appearances in the first issue, but the story really belongs to Elektra. While better solo Elektra stories would come later (especially with the series launched in 2001 under the Marvel Knights imprint), this mini-series was effectively the first.

Chichester and McDaniel never did a follow-up series, nor returned to *Daredevil*.

Daredevil after "Tree of Knowledge"

By then, of course, *Daredevil* had moved on. While Chichester and McDaniel prepared the first *Elektra* series, *Daredevil* ran a five-issue storyline (#333-337, Oct 1994 - Feb 1995) entitled "Fathoms of Humanity." Or "Humanitys Fathom" (no apostrophe), if one believed the cover — which suggested the comic couldn't even get its own titles right. One could also point out that the story's title lacked the Biblical overtones of the titles Chichester had used since issue #319.

"Fathoms of Humanity" was written by the aforementioned Greg Wright, with solid but conventional pencils by Tom Grindberg. It was widely seen as a drop-off in quality, and sales began to dip.

Another five-issue storyline followed (#338-342, Mar-July 1995), this one without even a name of its own. Artists, none as compelling as McDaniel, continued to change, while the writing was credited to Alan Smithee – a name used by writers when they want their own name removed. Even featuring the Kingpin, as well as more attention on Daredevil's neglected supporting cast, couldn't get readers interested.

The next issue (#343, Aug 1995), entitled "Recross," is notable for having been written by Warren Ellis, then still in the early stages of his career, and for not featuring Daredevil in costume.

This was only a fill-in, however, before Marvel took Daredevil in a new direction. Two months after the *Elektra* mini-series ended, the direction inaugurated with "Fall from Grace" was already coming to an end.

With issue #344 (Sept 1995), *Daredevil* was folded into Marvel's new "Marvel Edge" imprint, featuring the company's slightly more "edgy" characters. These titles were printed on better paper, which was rapidly becoming more commonplace. For the occasion, Daredevil became more violent, his stories infused with a tougher tone that felt appropriate to the character.

For the occasion, *Daredevil* received a new permanent creative team: writer J.M. DeMatteis and penciler Ron Wagner, both capable creators who already had memorable work to their credit. With their very first issue, they introduced a villain wearing Daredevil's original yellow costume. In the very next issue (#345, Oct 1995), this villain tore up Daredevil's armor (while not being worn), forcing him back into his red costume. By the villain's defeat in issue #347 (Dec 1995), Matt Murdock has been revealed to be alive. Subsequent stories would continue to play with the character's multiple costumes and civilian identities, but the old status quo was essentially restored.

The new direction inaugurated with issue #319 (Aug 1993) had descended into lackluster content and then been repudiated, a mere two years later. For those who derided that new direction from the beginning, this was the ultimate evidence that it had been a bad idea all along. For those who detested the "event comics" phenomenon, *Daredevil* represented not only the first Marvel character and the first non-A-list character to get such treatment, but also the first time such treatment had failed.

But of course, it hadn't failed.

No, the new direction didn't last – outside of Elektra's return. But if that's how eras are judged, half the super-hero comics in history would get a failing grade. Everything changes. Sometimes, it changes back. The new direction certainly had flaws – and was mismanaged by Marvel, from the standpoint of quality control – but it was also dynamic and exciting, including some brilliant elements and moments. McDaniel's innovative style, Elektra's return, and Matt Murdock's burial all continue to stand out.

"Fall from Grace" was an "event comic," produced by long-term Daredevil creators, that helped encourage further such "event comics." It played a key role in this period of comics history. Moreover, it played a key role in Daredevil history, too.

The new direction also brought a whole new readership to Daredevil – many of whom were too young to have read Miller's work, unless they happened upon the few and incomplete collections then available.

When Bendis later brought down the Kingpin, he was borrowing from Chichester's "The Fall of the Kingpin" arc. And when Bendis revealed Daredevil's secret identity to the public, he was borrowing from "Fall from Grace." That most readers now prefer Bendis's version doesn't mean his precursors deserve derision.

When any creator besides Miller uses Elektra, he or she owes a certain debt to "Fall from Grace" and that first *Elektra* series. There would be no further Elektra in the Marvel Universe without "Fall from Grace."

You can love it or hate it, or some combination of both. You can even call it the "motocross years," if it makes you feel cooler. But we ought to be able to agree on one thing: warts and all, it's fascinating.

.22 Caliber, a Girl's Gun: Vanessa Fisk and Freedom of Action

by Kevin Thurman

Calling *Daredevil* a feminist work may sound a bit weird, but after a close textual reading of Bendis's early run on *Daredevil*, it is clear that the most ambitious and indeterminable figure there is Vanessa Fisk. While the male characters tend to take up more "screen time" than others, it's the incorruptible character of Vanessa Fisk that stands heads and tails above the rest. This is not to say she is seen a lot through the run, but the impact she makes on the story is in many ways the only reason the story exists.

It's easy to read Bendis's run and chalk it up as one of the best crime comics ever written, but this is also an undervaluation of the characters within the run and the roles they play. While the length and breadth of Bendis's run can be seen as something of a game being played between super-heroes and crime figures, it's the understated and often brutal character interactions that go unnoticed. This isn't to say they are ignored or forgotten; they are just too often overlooked in lieu of the grander game and characters.

Without a character like Vanessa Fisk setting things in motion from early on, the story would never have played out the way it did. Vanessa is like a phantom that haunts *Daredevil* still to this day. Bendis never made her a damsel in distress or a pawn. Instead, Bendis wrote Vanessa as the wheels, cogs, and machine by which the story turned.

While not unprecedented in *Daredevil* (after all, look to Elektra or Typhoid Mary for more female characters who acted of their own will and did not define themselves based on who was saving them), Vanessa was no pawn. She had power and the will to carry actions out. She had what is sometimes in existential philosophy called "agency," meaning she handled her power and used it according to her own wants / needs.

Agency can seem such a big, high-dollar word, when in fact it is such a simple concept. All we are talking about is that these characters act according to their own rules and not some predetermined role like most female characters in comics. Of course, there are examples anyone can find to show the opposite, but the overall comics culture is one that puts women in the place of pawns, manipulated by male heroes and villains alike for dramatic purposes. For once, a high-calibre writer like Bendis turns this practice on its head.

Shooting a man in the head seems like such a cliché to spur a story into action. But what if it's a family member shooting another family member? Still something of a cliché, but we are getting better. Now, what if it was a mother shooting her *only* son in the face for her son's treacherous actions against her husband, his father? Now we have something interesting. After all, this is now the action of a wife / mother taking her life into her hands and deciding what is more important. And the role she plays throughout the story is neither wife nor mother but something else of her own creation.

Known as the Kingpin, Wilson Fisk was the biggest crime syndicate in NYC and growing. He, alone, was a one-man criminal organization. When a two-bit thug comes to town and starts muscling for power because he feels he deserves it, this still should not alarm someone as powerful as the Kingpin. But when one stands alone the way Wilson Fisk did, it was only a matter of time before he fell.

The interesting part is not the fall of a powerful man, but the rise of a free woman. The problem of many characters in *Daredevil* is that they are all stuck together. Fisk can't make a move against Murdock / Daredevil and vice versa. The only way to truly attack the other is through subterfuge or waiting and hoping the other makes a mistake. Once Sammy Silke (the two-bit thug mentioned earlier) comes in, he seems to set the story in motion by murdering the Kingpin and then outing Daredevil's identity to the feds. This is simply an appetizer for what is to come.

See, one of Silke's main conspirators was Wilson and Vanessa's son, Richard Fisk. Their only son. This is one of many aspects that makes Vanessa so fascinating. She was willing to avenge her husband's murder by callously killing her own son. This is not like characters stuck together playing some form of chess. These are emotions and actions being carried out by a woman of her own volition. There is Shakespearean weight to these pages.

So many things happen during Bendis's run that it is easy to forget the early machinations that got it all started. After all, there are many people murdered during his run, so it can seem a bit ludicrous to give such importance to the small role of Vanessa Fisk. Even the characters themselves seem to joke about how negligible the murders are. When Murdock and Foggy Nelson, as well as the FBI, discuss Richard Fisk's murder, they describe the weapon used to kill him as a .22 [caliber], "a girl's gun" (*Daredevil* #32 Vol. 2, June 2002). It's almost as if Bendis is making a joke of the action. Yeah, one insignificant character shooting another. One woman. Shooting her own son in the head. And all anyone can comment on is the gun size and how it is seen as a feminine gun. However, it was more than enough to kill the main men who betrayed her husband, the Kingpin – including her son.

To say it's a girl's gun is really just a throwaway insult. After all, isn't this how far too many women are treated in real life? Almost as if she were some woman suffering PMS and went nuts, but no real damage was done. After all, it was just a "girl's gun," as they call it. There's something deeper being said here about Vanessa's actions and how they can be interpreted.

What are clearly the actions of a woman taking the story into her own hands are instead derided. The subtext of the joke says she's just a woman, and therefore this is nothing big that she has done. Obviously, this is almost completely antithetical to the overall impact of murdering her own son – and a few other men. But Bendis does not let his characters go quietly. Instead, to top it off, Vanessa actually meets with Matt Murdock and gives him a parting gift: the name of the federal agent who ratted Murdock out. If this were a game, it is now being played according to her rules. She has decided the course for several characters and not the other way around.

Now, what Murdock does with the name (scaring the agent by hanging outside his window at night) is actually more passive than anything Vanessa Fisk

"A girl's gun" did in Richard Fisk. From *Daredevil* Vol. 2 #32 (June 2002). Art by Alex Maleev. Copyright © Marvel Comics.

does. She not only murders and gives Murdock the name of the agent, but also helps her husband escape the country. Going back to the idea of agency, it should be obvious that Vanessa is the definition of existential agency. She has a power she is enacting based on her own will and plans. There are no men or super-heroes chiding her to take a different path. There is simply Vanessa and what she wants, which is her husband's safety and dignity.

To explain more fully why a word like "agency" is important, what we mean when talking about agency is the will and the responsibility that comes with the action(s) in question. After all, Vanessa was never brought to a court of law and forced to atone for crimes of murder. Instead, Vanessa took responsibility for her own actions and how they played out. In the panel in which Richard realizes he is about to be killed, there's a look of pure terror on his face. This is necessary, since it shows the reader that Richard and Vanessa both know why this is happening, and why it's necessary for Vanessa to shoot him.

Vanessa is Richard's mother and she, above all others, had a deep understanding of who Richard was and why she must kill him. She was both creator and judge presiding over him. It's hard to imagine a tougher scenario to showcase the agency of a character than this. Hell, in many ways she was one of the only characters granted some form of agency, but that's not to say Bendis writes two-dimensional characters. No, Bendis is a writer in the style of David Mamet or Aaron Sorkin, a writer who crafts deliciously inexhaustible characters who are more subject to conditions in their lives than they are simply actors in a narrative, free of larger context.

Moreover, much like the two writers mentioned, Bendis is also a character in touch with how women are portrayed and seems hellbent on changing it. So while everyone can call a .22 caliber gun a girl's gun, just remember it can make people dead just as easily as any other gun. Especially when handled by someone as willful as Vanessa Fisk, who is neither heroine nor murderess but simply a person.

When Things Fall Apart in Hell's Kitchen: Postcolonialism in Bendis's Daredevil

by Jon Cormier

In Brian Michael Bendis's run on *Daredevil*, the "illusion of change" offered reflects characteristics of postcolonial theory.[1] It isn't Daredevil or his main antagonist, the Kingpin, who are the driving force in Bendis's revision of the status quo but previously unknown or unacknowledged outsiders. These "others" cause greater change precisely because they have no vested interest in the continuing narrative of Daredevil and the Kingpin. These new characters are not simply created to be agents of change for an author's run on the series, but are vital to defining just what the main narrative is and how it should be presented. These "others" don't just allow for change within the main narrative, they allow for change in how the narrative is presented. If the core dichotomy of *Daredevil* is Daredevil and the Kingpin, then these "others" represent Hell's Kitchen itself. Hell's Kitchen is not merely the setting for the stories, it is the fulcrum on which Daredevil and Kingpin are balanced, and these

---

[1] The illusion of change is the idea that superhero comics promote and promise big lasting change but will always restore everything to the original status quo. This is particularly evident in how heroes and villains return from the dead.

"others" are as much a part of it as are our feuding leads. With Bendis, they finally get a bigger voice in the narrative and upset the accepted balance.

Laying the Groundwork: Setting the Scene Bendis Inherits

Most readers of super-hero comics are generally comfortable with the idea of good opposing evil as a driving dichotomy of the genre. In *Daredevil*, particularly since Frank Miller, this trope is predominantly the struggle between Daredevil and the Kingpin on the streets of Hell's Kitchen. This battle, sometimes swinging in favor of Daredevil and sometimes swinging in favour of the Kingpin, remains balanced and fairly static in order to maintain the illusion of change. In fact, their constant opposition to one another goes beyond MacGuffins and plot to become one of the defining aspects of this title itself. The battle between Kingpin and Daredevil is never questioned as being essential to the comic. Their opposition is the hegemonic discourse[2] at the core of the comic *Daredevil* itself, not just of the various plots where it is obvious. Villains like Owl and aspects like the ninja death cult the Hand have added flavor to the story, but the main narrative remains the struggle between good and evil in Hell's Kitchen. The two main players in that location are Daredevil (representing good) and the Kingpin (representing evil), regardless of whom the actual villain of the month may be.

In turn, this core struggle defines the space Daredevil and the Kingpin inhabit. They both see Hell's Kitchen as a space they can define and ultimately control by having their worldview adopted (or imposed upon) the residents. Because this struggle is presented to the reader as the main narrative of the comic, both Daredevil and the Kingpin can be cast into the role of colonizers coming to an untamed wilderness. Daredevil inherits the role of a religious colonizer, while the Kingpin becomes a military and economic colonizer.

Daredevil swings into the depths of the urban wild much like a Jesuit missionary trying to convert the natives. It's not just Murdock's actual religion that places him in this role but the way in which his actions are driven by a moral code, specific to him, which he uses to fight what he sees as a moral decay in the residents of Hell's Kitchen. Murdock's moral code comes from the promise he made his father to be a better man, and in trying to keep that promise, Murdock uses Catholicism to help him define what that promise

---

[2] Hegemonic discourse is something that has become so imbedded in a culture that there doesn't appear to be an alternative. Nobody asks, "Why is it this way?"

actually means. But it's the personal moral code Murdock believes in, and uses Daredevil to enact, that places him in a religious colonizer role. His actual religion is a reflection of this religious colonizer role rather than a defining factor behind it. Daredevil is there to convert the ignorant to his worldview with all the implications that involves.

The Kingpin, on the other hand, represents a combination of the military and economic forces of colonialism. He simply overwhelms his opposition with force and / or the resources at his disposal. His role in the hegemonic discourse of Hell's Kitchen is best defined by FBI special agent Driver when busting the Owl: "But see, what made Wilson Fisk a genius is that he incorporated his business so *completely*, so *strategically* into the fabric of the city… / that it was near impossible for us to find a way to point to the place where the *legitimate* and *illegitimate* business separated" (*Daredevil* Vol. 2 #45, May 2003). To the Kingpin, Hell's Kitchen is merely a resource-rich wilderness he will use to fill his coffers, and when the natives get restless he will ruthlessly dispose of anyone opposing him.

Where the Kingpin and Daredevil differ from traditional colonial forces is that they both originate from the place they are trying to colonize. Unlike the European settlers coming to North America and expanding westward into what they saw as fertile lands of opportunity, Daredevil and the Kingpin are trying to colonize their homeland. Both men try to define themselves by expanding their own worldview in the place in which they grew up. By trying to accomplish this while opposing one another, they in turn define the space itself. Hell's Kitchen is presented to the reader as the place where Daredevil and the Kingpin fight, and others are caught in the middle.

While Hell's Kitchen as a setting is one of the defining aspects at the core of the Daredevil mythos, the residents (other than heroes and villains) are presented more as an afterthought. They are as much a part of the setting and scenery as the low-rise brownstones, the docks, and Josie's bar. The main roles presented for residents are as innocents whom Daredevil tries to protect, criminals in the Kingpin's employ, or some combination thereof (e.g. a junkie using drugs imported by the Kingpin's gang). The residents of Hell's Kitchen are presented as wanting to take part in the hegemonic discourse by lining up behind one of the two parties who provide the main narrative of the comic. In this status as present but not participating directly, the residents of Hell's Kitchen become what Gayatri Spivak termed "subalterns."[3]

Alternately, if it wasn't for the residents of Hell's Kitchen, Daredevil and Kingpin wouldn't be who they are. This is not just in terms of their growing up in the neighborhood, but in terms of how the residents are the people both Daredevil and Kingpin lump together as "others," either as victims (those who need saving) or consumers (of the criminal empire). By having a group of people present but not allowed access to the main narrative, Daredevil and Kingpin are afforded the narrative freedom to define themselves and their roles as colonizers.

Inner City as the Wild West

With Daredevil and the Kingpin as colonizers, the inner city locale of Hell's Kitchen takes on the role of the wild and untamed frontier of urban frontier theory.[4] Fundamental to the inner city as a frontier to be colonized are the subaltern natives. The residents of Hell's Kitchen are used to support just how essential Daredevil and the Kingpin are to the comic's narrative. Their struggle is important and not just because it is the focus of the book; it is important *and* the focus of the book because their struggle is separate from what everyone else is doing. The "everyone else" of the comic is used to highlight how essential this fight between good and evil is to the world of super-hero comics, not to show whether this conflict can benefit the residents of Hell's Kitchen. The residents have their own narrative and their own worldview separate from both Daredevil and Kingpin.

When faced with this creation of Hell's Kitchen, Daredevil takes on a garrison mentality.[5] Daredevil is isolated from a cultural centre and besieged by

---

[3] Subalterns have no access to the key discourses within a culture, but their presence is essential for defining the culturally dominant players. De Kock, Leon. "Interview with Gayatri Chakravorty Spivak: New Nation Writers Conference in South Africa." *ARIEL: A Review of International English Literature* 23(3). 1992. Pages 29-47.

[4] Urban frontier theory is a response and adaptation, proposed by such theorists as Richard C. Wade, Sharon Zukin, and Daniel Elazar, of Frederick Jackson Turner's "The Significance of the Frontier in American History." The core notion is that the inner city replaced the natural frontier as the wilderness of America.

[5] The garrison mentality as used by Northrup Frye to define Canadian literature. Frye, Northrop. "Conclusion to a Literary History of Canada." *The Bush Garden: Essays on the Canadian Imagination*. Toronto: Anansi, 1975.

a hostile landscape, particularly Hell's Kitchen under the Kingpin's influence. Daredevil remains isolated because he is not a public hero, like the Fantastic Four, and not a team player like an Avenger. He has friends and confidants like Luke Cage, Iron Fist, and Spider-Man, but they too reflect his commitment to a street-level vigilantism rather than the public. Daredevil is besieged by the Kingpin's criminal empire, not just through costumed assassins like Bullseye, but through the Kingpin's unseen influence – aggression and control towards the residents themselves. To combat this unknown and unknowable worldview, Daredevil sets up a formally immature worldview through which Murdock shows a deeply moral discomfort with the "uncivilized" element of Hell's Kitchen. This separation Daredevil sees between himself and the subalterns means he reduces them to something he can fight for, rather than as people with their own worldview who are perfectly capable of managing on their own.

When seen as a colonizer with a garrison mentality, Daredevil can only win his eternal struggle with the Kingpin by separating the residents of Hell's Kitchen from their own values and cultural background. Only by creating a homogenous worldview does Daredevil stand a chance to win the hegemonic discourse over to his side. Only when he gentrifies Hell's Kitchen can Daredevil "win." However, throughout Bendis's run, Daredevil is constantly confronted by not just new or revised villains but the residents of Hell's Kitchen themselves.

Brian Michael Bendis and Ben Urich

In their hegemonic discourse, Daredevil and Kingpin lose sight of the fact that they need the residents of Hell's Kitchen to validate their struggle. Without these people, their struggle would have no border, no witness, no audience, and nobody willing to buy into their cultural structures. However, because the residents, in the role of subalterns, have been left out of the predominant cultural discourse, they are also in a prime position to subvert it. Bendis uses this situation to great effect to shake up the established narrative that has been presented to *Daredevil* readers prior to his work.

It's people who don't buy into Kingpin and Daredevil's dominant culture who end up affecting change in Bendis's run. It is an outsider, Mr. Silke, who manages to take down the Kingpin and return the New York criminal empire to its more traditional values. Daredevil's identity gets passed to the FBI by this same outsider and released to the press by another outsider, FBI agent Driver, who doesn't buy into Daredevil's worldview, even if they are fighting on the same "good" side the comic presents. Even more telling is how the residents of Hell's Kitchen themselves seek the blood of the heroes trying to protect them once identities are revealed. Matt Murdock says it best, in *Daredevil* Vol.2 #40 (Feb 2003), when waiting for the jury to deliberate: "They want blood. Everyone wants blood." And not just Murdock's blood; the trial of the White Tiger shows that a number of the residents are sick and tired of having someone else decide what's right and wrong for them, and being forced into a position that requires super-heroic protection. They don't appreciate being placed into Daredevil's formally immature structures. They don't like being treated as victims needing saving from themselves, simply because they aren't Daredevil.

These minority voices, that reinvent both the Kingpin and Daredevil, ultimately revise and reinvigorate both for Bendis's run. When faced with his identity being made public, Matt Murdock is ready to quit his personal mission, as he realizes a lot of the public isn't predisposed to his worldview. However, this temporary challenge to his status quo only manages to further entrench him into the role he created for himself. When the case against White Tiger ends tragically, Daredevil manages to find the real cop-killer and doesn't beat him physically but appeals to the criminal's moral nature, inspiring him to do the right thing. Daredevil further strengthens his adherence to his role of a religious colonizer by converting this character to adopt the worldview Daredevil has for the people he protects. Even when faced with an overwhelming rejection of his worldview and when the siege he finds himself in has gained momentum, Daredevil just shores up his structures and fights back in the only way he knows how.

It isn't only Daredevil who's rejected by those left out of the hegemonic discourse. After being shot, left for dead, and effectively removed from power, Wilson Fisk's colonialism is reinvented by the same people he never considered worthy of letting take part. His wife, Vanessa, takes over his criminal empire and is capable of dismantling it more effectively than Daredevil ever could because throughout the history of the comic she has constantly been left out. She has no connection to the construction she is presented with and feels no attachment to the world she was intentionally left out of by the Kingpin.

When Vanessa Fisk takes over Wilson's empire, she dismantles it by selling it to the forces of gentrification. In *Daredevil* Vol.2 #36 (Oct 2002), she sells Fisk Tower to Donald Trump in the ultimate move of blandly gentrifying anything associated with Hell's Kitchen. Much like the real-world Hell's Kitchen being marketed as Clinton by real estate agents in order to remove the historic association with crime, Mrs. Fisk does her best to remove the comic's hegemonic requirement of a criminal empire for Daredevil to fight against. By removing one party of the hegemonic discourse, Bendis sets up Daredevil to have to deal with the "others" and the place he created for them by his own actions.

With the core "evil" from the narrative removed, Daredevil is left to deal with his own issues. Sure, the narrative creates a struggle over who will fill the power vacuum left by Kingpin's departure, and Daredevil continues to oppose criminal activity. But his main conflict is with the reality the residents of Hell's Kitchen present. Murdock struggles to recognize his own role in their creation and rejection of him as a hero. The residents who are in line with Daredevil continue to be so, but as others come into conflict with that reality, Murdock is navigating territory he hasn't focused on in the past.

In "Wake Up," Bendis's first story arc (in *Daredevil* Vol 2 #16-19, May-Aug 2001), the comic is at its least rigid and formal in terms of presenting the story to the reader. When the focus of the action is not Daredevil (and the Kingpin), the narrative can free itself from the formally rigid framework that Daredevil himself presents to the reader. The artwork has more open, flowing, and borderless layouts, with sketchy figures more evocative than realistic. It is given more freedom to define itself, rather than the rigidity of super-heroic narrative constraints. The narrative is presented in its own way to reflect the protagonist's differing worldview from that of Daredevil. The ongoing narrative of *Daredevil* follows a more stable and rigid presentation that reflects Daredevil's garrison mentality of formal immaturity that reinforces social norms. There are nice little boxes that people fall into, much like super-hero comics present the action in nice little boxes to the reader.

When the focus shifts from the hegemonic discourse of *Daredevil*, the presentation of the narrative itself shifts away from familiar structures. The presentation of the comic itself is defined on different terms than the status quo usually presented month-to-month. This in turn helps further differentiate the hegemonic discourse of Daredevil and the Kingpin from the subaltern "others" of Hell's Kitchen. The story of Leap Frog's kid shows Daredevil from a different point of view and reflects how his actions are affecting the characters generally presented to the reader as background setting. Yet this story in particular has Ben Urich, the old Daredevil consort, as the protagonist. This is a man who has been ever-present in the narrative yet never allows himself to be defined by the struggle between Murdock and Fisk.

Really, the voice of Hell's Kitchen is Ben Urich, as he's the only one seeking out these stories and trying to present them as a valid option to be listened to. He becomes the filter through which Hell's Kitchen gets a voice rather than being reduced to resources for Daredevil and the Kingpin to levy against one another in their continued war over who rules the new frontier. Ben Urich is the cipher through whom all the voiceless "others" can be heard by the hegemonic discourse, not just between Daredevil and the Kingpin, but between comic and reader as well. Yes, Ben Urich gets caught up and used in the narrative fight between Daredevil and the Kingpin, but he remains solidly devoted to being heard on his own terms rather than keeping in line with one of the other. And while Urich and Murdock respect one another and have a level of friendship, they are not unquestioning allies against Kingpin. Urich remains his own man with his own judgements and worldview, one which places him in a position to align with everyone else in Hell's Kitchen. He is on their side more than simply trying to tell them what is best.

Throughout his run as writer on *Daredevil*, Bendis creates his "illusion of change" by shifting the focus away from the hegemonic discourse of Daredevil and the Kingpin onto Daredevil's relationship to the residents of Hell's Kitchen. With the Kingpin removed, Hell's Kitchen goes back to its own definition of classic crime, either with Mr. Silke or later with Anthony Bont's return. Rather than submit to the gentrifying forces of Daredevil and the Kingpin, Hell's Kitchen rejects both of them on their own terms. Matt Murdock is forced to justify his choice to be Daredevil to the public on their terms. Bendis provides a nice bookend for this idea with his first story arc, focussing on Leap Frog's son, and having Murdock attend a support group for people talking about Daredevil's actions in "Decalogue" (*Daredevil* Vol. 2 #71-75, May-Sept 2005). This change in focus, from the Kingpin to Hell's Kitchen's own residents, means Daredevil's immediate attention isn't on one hard target but spread out to a community. Murdock recognizes his creation of Hell's Kitchen, stating:

When Things Fall Apart in Hell's Kitchen: Postcolonialism in Bendis's Daredevil

Matt Murdock explains his colonial agenda to the residents of Hell's Kitchen. From *Daredevil* Vol. 2 (Sept 2005). Art by Alex Maleev. Copyright © Marvel Comics.

> When I was just a boy, this city – it took my father from me and it took my mother and it took everyone I have ever loved. And to sit here and to listen to your stories – that are just like mine.
>
> I would *never* in a million years have wished any of this on *any* of you. I just want you to know that.
>
> I'm trying so *hard* to keep these kinds of things *away* from you... and they just *keep coming* in every direction
>
> [...]
>
> Listen to me...something needs to be *built* – I need to do more than fight people, I need to *build* something so strong *they* can't attack it. All that stuff with the Kingpin. *That's* why I said what I said. Not to run the city. Or to lord over people... I just want to build something in *place* of Wilson Fisk that we can actually *live* in. We need to rebuild out lives.
>
> And *no one* is going to help us. Not the cops, not the feds, or the heroes. It's just *us* here.
>
> This is why I am doing what I am doing and why there are so many people ready to take me down. Because the people who made money off of what Wilson Fisk built – who made money off of our misery and our misfortune... they miss that money. And they can't sell this new thing.

Murdock tries to align himself with Hell's Kitchen and show how together, under his influence, they can oppose the worldview offered by Wilson Fisk. They define themselves and he attempts to convert them to his worldview by showing his connection to their world.

Going into "The Murdock Papers" (*Daredevil* Vol. 2 #76-81, Oct 2005 - Mar 2006), the final arc of Bendis's run, Murdock has managed to finally recognize the position in which he's placed the residents of Hell's Kitchen and tries to align himself with them. Daredevil's initial actions are to stop an armed robbery, and he's met with applause and acceptance from the public. This shows how Murdock has moved from oppressing Hell's Kitchen by his will (i.e. declaring himself the new Kingpin) towards aligning himself to their needs and perspective. Yet this story arc goes about reestablishing the hegemonic discourse between Daredevil and the Kingpin. Furthermore, this process is initially brought to the reader through the perspective of Ben Urich, who is granted time with the Kingpin.

The ultimate result is that the balance between the Kingpin and Daredevil is reestablished; however, Daredevil gets removed from Hell's Kitchen. With Matt Murdock off in prison and the Kingpin back in town, the status quo exists once more – although slightly modified. The conflicting worldviews are back at the core, but the voice of the "others" gets removed once again as the narrative setting moves out of Hell's Kitchen and into Ryker's Island, allowing Matt Murdock to colonize another wilderness full of unruly inhabitants. It's as if Matt Murdock is put on trial, not for being Daredevil but for upsetting the status quo of his own book by sliding towards a point of view that aligns more with the natives than one strictly opposing the Kingpin, though equally oppressive to Hell's Kitchen itself. To establish the status quo of *Daredevil*, the actual voice of the people must be sidelined so it (and they) can act as the background setting for the action between protagonist and antagonist. Hell's Kitchen can fill a void and present interesting voices that oppose both Daredevil and the Kingpin, but both characters need to step back into their roles as colonizers for the change presented in Bendis's run to be illusory. By again gaining the narrative spotlight, Daredevil and the Kingpin send the voices of Hell's Kitchen into the periphery, and *Daredevil* once again becomes a narrative of colonial conflict over a space full of voiceless "others."

Daredevil: Intermediate Super-Hero Filmmaking

by Geoff Klock

    Daredevil launched onto the screen at a crucial moment in comic-book movie history. Super-hero movies had just begun the decade they would dominate at the box office, but the learning curve was steep and the people who made them were still figuring out what worked and what didn't. It took decades of misfires, with Roger Corman oddities and camp crusaders, before super-heroes could finally be taken seriously on the silver screen. It had to be done right, and there were sure to be missteps along the way.

    Eventually, *The Dark Knight* would gross over a billion dollars. But back in 2000, hot on the heels of surprise hit *Blade* – a film no one really saw as having blockbuster potential -- *X-Men* got the ball rolling. *Blade 2* followed, and *Spider-Man* wasn't far off. Super-hero movies built up speed, and the engine was being redesigned and expanded as fast as the coal could be shoveled in. This trend built at Marvel until they had a stable of cinematic titles: three more Spider-Man movies, four more X-Men movies, two Fantastic Four movies, two Ghost Rider movies, two Punisher movies, two Hulk movies and four other films -- *Iron Man*, *Iron Man 2*, *Thor*, and *Captain America* -- that would lead into *The Avengers*.

    Somewhere in the middle, not a blind experiment but not a guaranteed success, came *Daredevil* (2003). Written and directed by Mark Steven Johnson, *Daredevil* is generally considered a critical failure. However, it is a failure with a surprising amount of style and personality. Moreover, it was an important part of the "how to make a super-hero film" learning curve. It is worth looking at what works and what doesn't work, if we want to understand the super-hero movie generally.

There are five main points to analyze wherein *Daredevil* takes on some major issues that can make or break a super-hero film. In ascending order of importance, they are: costumes, Easter eggs, a manic scene-stealing performance, screenplay structure, and finding a very human connection in very insane territory.

Costumes

Daredevil fixed a large problem that reared its costumed head in *Spider-Man*. Peter Parker, the Amazing Spider-Man, has a mask that covers his face, and so did his film antagonist, the Green Goblin. This resulted in something that unfortunately resembled *Power Rangers* – a children's show where American actors would talk face to face, then suit up, covering their faces and thus allowing footage from the original Asian TV show to be integrated; all the American actors had to do at that point was voiceover work. *Daredevil* improved on *Spider-Man* by making sure the hero got out of that mask as often as possible, especially in the final scene. The bulk of the last battle in *Spider-Man* involves masked antagonists. Daredevil's final confrontation with the Kingpin is handled face to face, as it should be. Every successful super-hero movie afterwards would follow suit, allowing actors to act with their faces as much as possible. One instance of perfect understanding this growth is in the great villain Obadiah Stane in *Iron Man* -- and how little time he spent encased in a giant suit of armor.

Yet *Daredevil* also ran into a problem with the costume that was unfortunately unique to the character. In the comics, you don't usually think of the costumes as being made out of anything – they are just color applied to naked bodies. This is a trope readers accept and do not question, nor do they ever need to. However, for a movie you have to go with some kind of *material*. Adam West's Batman had silk. Tim Burton's Batman had rubber. Nolan's Batman had Kevlar. The X-Men had leather. However, *Daredevil* ran into a problem using leather. Daredevil is blind and so has a mask with no eyeholes, making the ensemble look very much like bondage gear (even more than these things usually do). The connection between Daredevil's Catholicism and what

Daredevil (Ben Affleck) and Elektra (Jennifer Garner) do battle in 2003's *Daredevil*.

appears to be bondage gear could have been interesting, but *Daredevil*'s style makes it difficult to make much of the observation. Cinematic audiences would have to wait until *Watchmen* made even more explicit than *Batman Forever* the idea of super-hero gear as fetish-wear.

Daredevil's costume is spandex in the comics, but the movie goes for a more realistic feel. This level of realism, however, might be its biggest failure. The leather never really translates into what we think of as we see Daredevil swing from buildings and leap into the night. Admittedly, the red spandex would have looked just as silly, but the film's costume aims for a level of adult that is never truly achieved.

Elektra takes 96 minutes to show up in costume – nearly the length of the 2000 X-Men movie. When she does, her costume is black where the comic-book outfit is red; it has no head covering, and has leather pants where the comic has a skirt. Elektra fans would have to wait until the opening scene of her own movie to see her in an outfit closer to the comics. The decision on the part of *Daredevil*'s costume designer was to go for something more realistic, and it makes sense for the world of the movie. The result is good without being remarkable.

Bullseye demands a costume from the Kingpin in the middle of the movie, but the moment is merely a joke. For the length of the movie, he wears a black snakeskin coat over a black tanktop. The outfit, especially that coat which is often accompanied with rattlesnake sounds on the soundtrack, is much more effective than the one in the comics, where Bullseye appears in a black, skin-tight body suit, including a mask with white trim. *Daredevil* makes another smart move with the comic-book character's trademark white bullseye on the forehead. If costumes in comics are really just color applied to naked bodies, than the movie takes this concept straight onto the screen for Bullseye's logo: he has a set of concentric circle scars on his forehead – literally a bullseye design on flesh – where it's located on the comics version's costume. This allows the actor to act without a mask, and it implies someone totally disturbed, whereas the comic-book version would just seem silly in a live action movie. This is exactly the kind of translation that needs to be made from the page to the screen.

A Manic, Scene-Stealing Performance

Colin Ferrell's gleefully mannered and over-the-top performance as Bullseye is the best thing about *Daredevil*. He growls, he bugs his eyes, he has these strange sleepy, fey moments when his eyelids seem to almost close, and then he is again wide awake and growling. He holds objects like a weird stage magician, and he is introduced winning a darts game in a bar by hitting the bullseye every time (once even splitting his earlier dart down the middle). He kills an annoyingly talkative old woman he is seated next to on a plane with a peanut – and then orders more from the stewardess, who just thinks the old woman is sleeping. He sniffs people like an animal and recoils from the smell of a rose. He points to the mark on his forehead in a theatrical way, with a flourish of his hands and an ironic bow. He stands on his motorcycle, and at more than one point in the movie (including when simply going up the escalator at and airport) holds his arms outstretched with his palms open, as if receiving applause from some invisible audience.

Ferrell's performance seems to exist in its own pocket universe, or a different movie, isolated from everyone else in *Daredevil*, and it suggests that this is not just the actor – the character seems to be mugging for an audience in his head. The song playing when Bullseye is introduced is a bouncy ironic rap that includes the lyrics "top of the morning to you," and this points to the most important part of the Irish Colin Ferrell's performance: he genuinely seems to be having fun being Bullseye, and says so to the Kingpin, when asked if it was really necessary to kill a bodyguard.

For contrast, look at the particularly egregious *Thor*, in which the villain is Loki, the God of Mischief. In the movie, Loki has the ability to ruin gods just by talking to them and should revel in his power, as Iago does when he is able to ruin Othello simply through the power of his language. Among people who should have been the first to figure this out is director Kenneth Branagh, who actually played Iago in just this way, opposite Lawrence Fishburne. But he needn't have gone to Shakespeare for inspiration – Colin Ferrell would have done just fine.

Ben Affleck gives Daredevil a bit of a playful smirk, which is good but is often drowned out by super-heroic bombast. Of Elektra, the AV Club's Keith Phipps writes, "The role needs a steely, inhuman reserve, and Garner's innate likeability works against her. Even when she's taking aim with a bow and arrow, she looks like she might be thinking about kittens." Ben Affleck and Jennifer Garner are great in the rom-com moments, but unremarkable action figures elsewhere. Joe Pantoliano and Michael Clark Duncan are fine, but they appear to be in very different movies – the first a quiet procedural, the second a cartoon.

No one comes close to competing with Colin Ferrell for attention, but this is not a problem. A single stand-out, crazy performance has worked for super-hero movies before and after. Marvel villains, in the comics, were initially set up as grand figures of malevolence. Ferrell's performance is in an excellent line of twitchy, crazy, overly intense super-hero bad guys including Willem Dafoe as Norman Osborn, Mickey Rourke in *Iron Man 2*, and Nick Nolte in *The Hulk* at Marvel, as well as Jack Nicholson and Heath Ledger decades apart as the same Clown Prince of Crime. It's something that should have been picked up on by Doctor Doom in *Fantastic Four*, for example, but was sadly ignored in favor of a more subdued and less memorable performance. *Daredevil* holds up a tradition in this area that super-hero movies ignore at their peril.

Easter Eggs

Comic books have a coterie audience, a small and knowledgeable fan base. The films have huge budgets and need to appeal as widely as possible. Just as the smartest kids' movies have jokes for the parents that go over the kids' heads (see Pixar for genius examples) comic-book movies have Easter eggs to please the long-time fans. Comic books, especially Marvel in the '60s, grew more popular due to the interconnectivity shown through Easter eggs in the books; the same now works for the movies. Many new fans were surely introduced to the X-Men in *X-Men: First Class*, but it was still a cute moment when the shape-shifter Mystique, played by Jennifer Lawrence, wonders if Magneto would not prefer her when she gets older – and morphs into Rebecca Romijn, who played the older Mystique in the first three films. That was aimed at pleasing people who saw the earlier movies. *Iron Man 2* has a moment for more die hard fans: Tony Stark is looking to invent a new element, creates a machine to do so, and uses Captain America's shield to prop up a part, not realizing (as long-term fans will) that the shield is made of the material he is trying to invent. There are also more "meta" Easter eggs involving comic-book creators – Stan Lee's cameos in Marvel movies, for example, or writer / artist Walter Simonson appearing in the banquet scene at the end of *Thor*.

On this meta Easter egg front, *Daredevil* is absolutely out of control: no less than eleven Daredevil comic-book writers and artists are name-checked or given cameos. A young, blind Matt Murdock prevents Daredevil co-creator Stan Lee from stepping into oncoming traffic, and a client of Murdock's, never seen, is also named Lee. Kevin Smith, who wrote *Daredevil* comics, plays a lab assistant named Kirby, after comic book genius Jack Kirby, who drew *Daredevil*. Father Everett is named for Bill Everett who co-created Daredevil. The rapist is named Jose Quesada after Joe Quesada, who drew the *Daredevil* comics that Kevin Smith wrote. Bullseye kills a man with a pen to the head, and when we see the deceased man's face hit the pavement, we recognize him as Frank Miller, Daredevil's most famous writer. The boxers who populate the world of Matt Murdock's dad are all named after *Daredevil* writers and artists: he falls asleep watching a fight on TV where the winner is Colan, named after Gene Colan; he is supposed to take a dive in a fight with John Romita; a thug named Kane is named after Gil Kane; the fixed fights he wins are against Miller, Mack, and Bendis (named after Frank Miller, David Mack, and Brian Michael Bendis – the last being the writer on *Daredevil* at the time the movie came out).

When Bullseye tells the Kingpin he wants a costume, it's a cute moment – he's asking to be made into a super-hero character, as if he isn't one already – but the name-dropping in *Daredevil* is dead silent if you are not aware of it... and far too loud if you are. Stan Lee, a character named Lee, and one *Daredevil* writer playing a character named for a *Daredevil* artist is too cute and starts to feel like the shibboleths of a too-nerdy club. Compare this to a pitch perfect in-joke in *Captain America* (2011), in which the Red Skull makes a crack early on about the cosmic cube and how "The Fuhrer is too busy digging for trinkets in the desert." Like the name-dropping in *Daredevil*, if you don't get it, it goes right past you without bothering you. Unlike *Daredevil*, it is an Easter Egg that has more of a chance with a movie-going audience, as it is a reference not to a comic read by a handful but to a huge movie, *Raiders of the Lost Ark* (1981). It also functions as a joke for the very in-the-know nerds, because *Captain America* director Joe Johnston is often more known as an art director on *Raiders* than as a film director in his own right. *Daredevil* tries to pile on the in-jokes, but future movies have learned that a little goes a long way, especially if that little can be recognized by a bigger group than the comic book fans.

Screenplay

Many super-hero films pick up speed in the sequel because they are finally on the other side of that pesky origin story. *Daredevil* begins with Matt Murdock wounded in a church and confessing to a priest. He relates his origin tale – the son of a boxer father, blinded by radioactive waste, using new senses to avenge his father's death – and we are shown this sequence almost as a montage. Getting the details out and down quickly is a smart move. As we know from *Spider-Man* and *Hulk,* origin stories that look satisfactory on the comic-book page can be *very* goofy in a film (radioactive spiders and bombs that transform rather than vaporize). These origin stories are often quite clunky because, although super-hero comics are currently aimed at college-educated men, their origins often hearken from a time they were aimed at 12 year-olds. The hero we went to the movie to see can take *forever* to show up – the *Hulk* has nearly 40 minutes of realistic father issues before the radioactive poodles are ripped up by a giant green monster. *X-Men* put the origin story off until its fourth installment, a decade later.

Daredevil deals with the origin quickly, but given the egregious drag that follows, the origin may have been better handled not in a sequence but in a wordless montage under the opening credits. *Daredevil*'s main weakness is in its screenplay structure, which absurdly waits until the 80 minute mark to establish the central conflict that should have appeared at 30: the Kingpin sending Bullseye to kill Elektra's father, which turns Daredevil and Elektra's budding romance into war and sets Daredevil against Bullseye and the Kingpin.

Up until that point, the film meanders, often cute and often frustrating. After the origin story, we get Daredevil murdering a rapist who, as Matt Murdock, he was unable to convict in court – a shockingly serious plot point that is ignored, despite what should be a serious impact on the character as a whole. We then get Matt Murdock taking up a court case involving Dante Jackson, played by Coolio, being framed for a crime he did not commit (in the Director's Cut). Daredevil flirts with Elektra. Ben Urich, played by Joe Pantoliano, gets the clues that lead him to uncover Daredevil's identity. All of this appears unconnected, and none is especially urgent. Urich is picking up information he will not realize the significance of until very late in the film. The script structure is a handful of unconnected threads for most of the movie.

Looking over the whole film, it feels as if *Daredevil* wants to take a realistic tone with its reporter, court case, and businessman villain, but it also needs the super-heroic swagger of Bullseye and Elektra. Add the origin story, and you have a movie that is over-burdened. In a comic book, you can slowly introduce these elements, with an issue about the reporter and another about Bullseye, before putting it all together. Movies rarely have the time, nor their audiences the patience. Ultimately, *Daredevil* ends up feeling like two or three films stitched together.

We realize the film's attempt to hold the diffuse strands of its first half together when we return to Daredevil wounded in the church, confessing to the priest, and remembering that this is the frame. The chaos is bookended, and so placed, however haphazardly, into some kind of structure. All of the information in the first chunk of the movie was supposed to answer the burning question of who Daredevil is and how he came to be wounded in the church. The problem is that there's so much unconnected stuff going on that it is too easy to forget about the frame story until you return to it 105 minutes later – an entire movie has gone by without a reminder.

Once Elektra's dad is killed, the movie snaps into focus, getting the clear through-line it needed to establish earlier. The fights among Daredevil, Elektra, and Bullseye at the end of the movie have clear motivations, and each leads to the next. Elektra, for example, fights Daredevil because Bullseye has made it look like Daredevil killed her father. Daredevil fights Bullseye because Bullseye killed Elektra. And killing Bullseye leads straight into the final battle with the man who set all of this into motion, the Kingpin.

Daredevil sets up the Kingpin as the figure behind all the crime its hero confronts. The origins of this concept go back as far as Satan, who many Christians see as the author of all evil. In literature, the idea is primarily associated with Professor Moriarty. Sherlock Holmes said crime was like a vast web and that web had a center and that center was Moriarty. It's a common idea in films because it provides crude but easy satisfaction. All of the ills can be traced to a single figure who, can be defeated in a one-on-one battle, which is much more heartening than, say, *The Wire*, or real life, where the evils of this world have no simple origin. They are diffused throughout vast bureaucratic systems, and the people who do evil seem mostly harmless until they are assembled into this malevolent machine.

Daredevil takes this idea of a central mastermind to the nth degree. Just as a paranoid person *needs* there to be a central villain to make this chaotic world full of random evil make sense, *Daredevil* needs the Kingpin to be the central villain to make its chaotic screenplay, full of disassociated plot points, hold together. It was the Kingpin who hired Bullseye. The Kingpin is behind the Dante Jackson frame job. The Kingpin is behind the murder of Daredevil's dad. It is implied that Daredevil's help exposing the Kingpin is a big part of why Urich doesn't expose Daredevil's identity. *Daredevil* barely holds together as a screenplay, and the reveals at the end about the Kingpin are mostly important because it is the screenplay's last-minute bid for unity and coherence.

Daredevil's handling of the origin story is smart and in line with what comic books did in the old days — a few panels with origin and then on to the action. *Daredevil*'s meandering story is also in line with what the comics do, but this is an area in which a movie should *not* be like a comic book — a movie needs a very focused through-line and cannot get away with picaresque stories like comic books and TV shows can.

Humanity

The real triumph of *Daredevil* — its lasting legacy for the Marvel super-hero film — was one that would have been hard to guess at the time: John Favreau's Foggy Nelson. Favreau's easy-going, improvisational-feeling, super-casual performance was a major part of what would make Marvel super-hero movies great. Comic books are deeply insane. As comic book pundit Chris Sims puts it on Comics Alliance:

> A "gritty crime story" [at Marvel comics] is one where a blind lawyer ninja dressed as the Devil fights a massive Sumo wrestler with a cane that shoots

lasers, who employs both a Major League Baseball pitcher who killed a batter with a fastball and the blind lawyer ninja's girlfriend, the daughter of a diplomat who herself became a ninja, died and came back to life, and was once replaced by an alien shape-shifter.

You *need* a regular guy to anchor all the insanity, much of which is present in the movie. Ben Affleck cannot be the human anchor, since he's dressed in fetish gear, and neither can Elektra, since, again in the words of Keith Phipps, she looks "like the world's deadliest hooker."

Favreau learned the value of this regular human anchor playing Foggy Nelson in *Daredevil*. When Murdock tells Foggy the girl's name is "Elektra Natchios," Foggy responds, "Well, she sounds like a Mexican appetizer." He describes the office they both work in thusly: "This place doesn't look like a law office, okay? It looks like the set of goddamn *Sanford and Son*. Every time I walk in here, I'm waiting for Lamont to walk down the stairs." Foggy teases Matt about the seeing-eye dog that ran away from him ("What does that say about your emotional availability?"), and they talk about alligators in the sewer and *Fight Club*. This is how actual people talk, and this kind of charm makes it easier to swallow when the crazy hits the fan.

When Favreau directed *Iron Man,* he put this humanity into the whole movie and most of the characters. Tony Stark has the same easy-going charm, as does Favreau's own Happy Hogan. But the real inheritor of this is Clark Gregg's Agent Coulson, whose normal, informal, go-with-the-flow humanity anchors the insanity not just of *Iron Man* but of the entire Marvel Cinematic Universe that we see through Coulson's eyes. As comic-book fans, we are used to it, but the casual moviegoer needs to be walked through this deeply strange place. In *Thor,* you have a Norse God punching FBI agents, which is weird enough. Now watch the trailer for *The Avengers*, and imagine you have never read a comic book. You will see the film is clearly about a World War II veteran and a cyborg who have teamed up to fight a wizard who attacks present-day New York City. You need Agent Coulson. In *Iron Man 2*, Coulson tells Tony Stark, "If you try to escape, or play any sort of games with me, I will taze you and watch *Supernanny* while you drool into the carpet." When the Destroyer shows up in *Thor* and an agent asks Coulson if it's one of Stark's, he replies, "I don't know. Guy never tells me anything." Whatever situation Coulson is in, he accepts it and acts normally, is game for anything, and travels from film to film – which teaches the audience how they should approach the material. Without Favreau's discovery of the humanity of Foggy Nelson, the Marvel Cinematic

Universe simply does not work, and though many people seem to have forgotten about *Daredevil*, this remains its legacy.

Daredevil's Legacy

Is *Daredevil* a success? It is certainly not remembered fondly by most people, or even most comic book fans, and it failed to produce a sequel (outside of *Elektra*), which is the mark of success in the super-hero film arena. However, *Daredevil* reminded moviemakers early that a super-hero movie is not about fancy costumes but about the people beneath – and that you need to see those people's faces if you want your movie to work. The film held up the venerable tradition of committed and crazy super-hero villains. It showed that when adapting comics, some storytelling techniques translate and some do not. Even when its story lacked urgency, the movie never forgot two central tenets of moviemaking that hosts of movies totally abandon: stories should be fun, and they need a human center. In a world in which Michael Bay makes literally a billion dollars showing piles of metal punching piles of metal while Victoria Secret models stare at green screens blankly, it's wrong to forget about such a plucky and oddly influential movie as *Daredevil*.

Works Cited

Branagh, Kenneth, dir. *Thor*. Writ. Ashley Miller, Zack Stentz, Don Payne, and Michael Straczynski. Perf. Clark Gregg. Paramount, 2011. DVD.

Favreau, John, dir. *Iron Man 2*. Writ. Justin Theroux. Perf. Robert Downey, Jr and Clark Gregg. 2011. Paramount. DVD.

Internet Movie Database. Web. 14 Jan. 2012. imbd.com

Johnson, Mark Steven, dir. *Daredevil*. Writ. Mark Steven Johnson. Perf. Ben Affleck, Jennifer Garner, Colin Farrell, and John Favreau. 2003. Marvel. DVD.

Lindsay, Ryan K. "A Short History of Marvel Movies." *The Weekly Crisis*. Ed. Kirk Warren. N.p., 30 Apr. 2010. Web. 9 Jan. 2012. www.weeklycrisis.com/2010/04/short-history-of-marvel-movies.html

Phipps, Keith. "Elektra." *The AV Club*. N.p., 18 Jan. 2005. Web. 14 Jan. 2012. www.avclub.com/articles/elektra,4724/

Sims, Chris. "True Stories of "The Core Marvel Universe"." *Comics Alliance*. N.p., 24 Nov. 2009. Web. 29 Dec. 2011. www.comicsalliance.com/2009/11/24/true-stories-of-the-core-marvel-universe

The Only Way is Down: Brubaker's Saga as '70s Cinematic Noir

by Ryan K. Lindsay

Cultural knowledge indicates that Daredevil is the noir character of the Marvel Universe. This assumption is an unchallenged perception that doesn't hold much water under any major scrutiny. If you add up all of *Daredevil*'s issues to date, the vast majority are not "noir." Mild examination exposes Daredevil as one of the most diverse characters who has ever been written across a series of genres, from swashbuckling romance, to absurd space opera, to straight up super-heroism and, often, to crime saga. Daredevil gets play in nearly all corners of the realm of narrative, and yet the mind often reverts to considering him a noir character.

While *Daredevil* has often been a crime book – some would argue this is when he is at his best – and there have been bleak moments peppered throughout his history, his actual incidences of true noir are few and far between. Noir is not just crime, a distinction often misunderstood. Noir is a sub-genre of crime, predicated on one larger factor – there are no happy endings. If you won't pull the trigger at the end of your tale, you have not created a noir story; you've simple told a crime tale.

The most accurate representation of Matt Murdock inhabiting a noir world is when the love of his life, Elektra Natchios, dies in his arms – one of Marvel's most shocking moments (in *Daredevil* #181, Apr 1982). Though Daredevil exacts a form of revenge upon Elektra's murderer, the heart of the tale is Elektra's demise – a bleak ending for their love. It crushes Matt for a long time after – with him even digging up her body in the very next issue and cradling her dead face once more. Such a dark act represents the prime example of Daredevil as a noir character, but perhaps also the only example.

Frank Miller's follow up tale, years later, of the bleak destruction of Matt Murdock as a man in "Born Again" (Daredevil #227-233, Feb-Aug 1986) feels like a noir tale and even holds the utter desolation well past the halfway mark of the narrative. It could have become a noir masterpiece, yet lacked conviction as it approached the finish line. This doesn't lessen the story – though it could be argued excising Nuke from memory would lift that storyline into the realm of perfect – but it removes the tale from the noir column. If you look through Daredevil's darkest moments, they never stick the landing into the inky depths, because that's so rarely what comics do. Comics are a perennial second-act medium, and ending on a bleak note means you might have to start on one as you cycle through, and that's no place to jump into the next arc.

Daredevil was a book (and character) darker than most, but he was not a true noir player until Ed Brubaker took over the title. Under Brubaker's determined direction, Daredevil became a hero analysis akin to a pulp '70s flick, full of the unending knowledge that the world is going to beat you down. Every time. You can divide Brubaker's 52-issue run into two noir sagas – of which the first (itself made up of three segments) will form the majority of this analysis – and both are informed more by the anti-heroes and worlds of '70s subversive filmmaking than by super-hero comics of the preceding four decades. These films represented a noir turn, in which it wasn't just the main character who was doomed to failure, it was the entire world, and during his tenure Brubaker certainly showed that no matter where Murdock went, darkness would find and embrace him tightly.

"The Devil in Cell Block D": A Scorsese-Style Noir

The gauntlet was thrown down in the very first pages of *Daredevil* Vol. 2 #82 (Apr 2006) – it was time for true noir. The very first panel, the base building block of Ed Brubaker, Michael Lark, and Stefano Gaudiano's brutal masterpiece, is a bleak establishing shot. Hell's Kitchen stands tall against the night rain. "It's not a nice place anymore." Upon entry to this tale, we need to

Ed Brubaker begins his run by announcing his noir intentions. From *Daredevil* Vol. 2 #82 (Apr 2006). Art by Michael Lark. Copyright © Marvel Comics.

forget what we know or think we have an understanding of. This time, things are different, and you're told this up front. Of course, no one ever really thought of Hell's Kitchen as a great holiday destination, but the idea that it isn't a safe location for anyone is a disconcerting thought.

The austere introduction heralds a small-time crime: nine staccato images of violence showcase hoods robbing a mob poker game for $500. A gun, a brutal impact, scattered cards, broken glass, and rooftop jumps: this is the new status quo. Not a cape to be found, just raw human atrocities. By this stage, the scene is set, and the turn of the page portents the chills to come.

Daredevil drops out of the rain and into the scene. This double-page spread is the Rosetta Stone for everything else to come. Our intrepid hero appears normal in frame, yet everything else is canted at a Dutch angle. The world is awry, our hero is straight, and the two are adversarial at all times. Such angle play is a standard film-noir trope and used to great effect here. Adding the slanted rain to this scene only further conjures up connections to film noir. The final aspect is the chiaroscuro lighting of the piece: the world is shadowed, and Daredevil's blood red uniform stands out from the darkness. The term chiaroscuro means "light-dark," and the intent here is to show the dichotomy between hero and setting. Instead of holding our hero in the illuminated brightness of righteousness, we are delivered a horned avenger of Hell's Kitchen, whose color more often represents death and danger. He is this visually placed in opposition to the rot that has taken hold of his town. Here is a hero who matches his world, a hero who might not fit the general definition of heroism (especially as it applies to super-heroes) but a man who stands firmly for something.

This is all established in three pages. Brubaker, Lark, and Gaudiano are going to drag Daredevil down, and there will be no coming up for air.

The next building block of the story is the wrongly incarcerated man. While Daredevil fights injustice in the city, Matt Murdock sits alone in a jail cell. It's a great trope (a man unjustly imprisoned), and it also sets up a deep mystery from the outset – who is Daredevil, if Murdock is serving time on a bunk? Brubaker drops the super-hero swagger from the comic and grounds Murdock and Daredevil in the dirty corners of noir and pulp.

Super-heroes might not be Scorsese's regular stock in trade, but this grounded element certainly is. Once we see all of Brubaker's elements established, we soon also note the tone being delivered. Matt Murdock is offered up as a man – a flawed and troubled man. We can thus draw parallels between this spandexless man and some of the leading men from Martin Scorsese movies in the 1970s – particularly Travis Bickle from *Taxi Driver* (1976). Bickle is a man without fear. It makes sense to view Murdock through the lens of Scorsese's films because Scorsese was a man deeply entrenched in Catholicism – even entering a seminary in 1956, though eventually deciding upon cinema as his vehicle to shape the world. He was conflicted about his faith, something Murdock completely understands.

Taxi Driver is about a man trapped – a man who does not see a future of reward or success. The movie is an examination of what happens to a man when he loses faith. Brubaker has taken Murdock and destroyed his faith completely – he does this early on in his run. Much like Scorsese's cinematic assessment of Bickle, Brubaker is mainly concerned with what happens to Murdock next, once everything is stripped away. These men are rubbed raw to their base elements, and so we see reactions both brutal and visceral.

The prison machine, the grinding engine of the system where super-heroes send their defeated villains and never think about them again, suddenly turns its gaping maw on Murdock and it doesn't respect what it sees. The system is too corrupt to reward the man who is Daredevil for what he has selflessly done for so long. Nothing carries over; this is just a blind man in a hell made up of shivs in the yard, toilets coated in detritus, fists in faces, and a hierarchical structure that loads Murdock with a dangerous burden on already slumping shoulders. From the outset, things are bleak – unrelentingly so. This is extremely reminiscent of Bickle's return to America, after fighting for his country in a war across the world. He receives no applause, nor help, and such a bleak reception eventually warps him into bringing this violence back home to unleash on the unfair world around him.

Miller said it best through the Kingpin: "A man with nothing to lose is a man without fear" (*Daredevil* #227-233, Feb-Aug 1986). Brubaker sets his stage with this concept in mind, as Murdock is separated from his wife, treated terribly by prison personnel and inmates alike, and finally set up to hear the dying heartbeats of his best friend. Foggy Nelson is stabbed during a legal visit and Murdock's world becomes drowned in blood. The man is isolated and brought low, and Brubaker doesn't seem to have much of a plan to allow him to rise above the adversity.

Violence quickly characterizes this run, much as it did cinema in the '70s. Movies finally made explicit the blood and pain of the world on their screens, after years of subterfuge and intonation. Scorsese was certainly a proponent of bringing realistic violence onto the screen. He didn't peddle in glossy action, and his outbursts yielded sloppy blood spatters and nasty deaths. Super-hero comics are so often a genre in which fisticuffs are traded but never actually gauged with any realism. Spider-Man should be able to crush men with one punch due to his strength; when Cyclops and Wolverine scrap, there should be more than just torn spandex and scraped skin. Daredevil spent years trading blows to little avail, yet in this run each pounding collision of flesh means something. The blood is sticky and the screams resonate through your spine.

With Foggy murdered, it's interesting to note the first blood we see is on Murdock's fists, and it happens while alone. Murdock punches a wall, repeatedly, while imagining himself at Fogwell's Gym talking to his father. Murdock's first violent outburst is to self-harm. Before anything else, he blames himself for Foggy's death. He punishes himself, internally and externally, and then he moves this radius out to include the other criminals with whom he is now trapped. Bickle is a man who holds his hand over an open stovetop flame, as if to prove himself worthy of understanding that which he will soon dish out. These men loathe themselves as much as what they perceive to be their only course of action on an unfair playing field.

Murdock is sent to general population – laid low with the fiends – and he becomes an avenging blur administering rough medicine some might see as justice, but which others could just as easily construe as punishment. As Daredevil, Murdock struggled for arcs with the Owl, under writer Brian Michael Bendis, yet Brubaker only needs seven panels to show how Murdock can truly deal with this loser of the criminal set, once all restraints are removed. With Owl's teeth knocked out and blood spattered on the floor of his cell, Murdock steps past social and personal boundaries without a care. He is exceptionally quick to adapt to the darkness that the world around him presents.

Comic heroes usually uphold their own standards, yet Brubaker allows Murdock to sink well below them. His retribution is far more prolonged and aggressive than the grief forced upon him by others. In *Daredevil* Vol. 2 #84 (Jun 2006), he tracks the source of Foggy's death to Hammerhead and works on systematically tearing him down, in a fight that is difficult to describe as fair. Murdock collapses his hardheaded foe easily, finally administering a blow to his nerves that makes him feel immense pain. He internally admits: "It's the kind of move Daredevil usually avoids... it's torture." He knows this is a dark path yet is beyond caring. He is beyond fear, and that concept obviously pertains to his thoughts upon his soul as well.

This concept of retribution through violence, of rebirth through blood, is what ties Murdock and Bickle together. Their anger is vented and what they see of the world is swept clean, but a real solution is not found. These are false actions that only lead the characters down darker paths. This is a delusional progression and one that we are shown doesn't actually help the man inside.

The dark path winds ahead of Murdock, and there seems no reason to apply any brakes. Murdock contemplates killing Wilson Fisk, one of his oldest foes. He realises that he even *wants* to do it. As a moral character, the end is within reach. This is in line with Bickle's spiral toward an assassination attempt on a U.S. presidential candidate. Both men could use retributive violence to stitch up their long and sad tales. Everything is in place for Murdock, but one person's intrusion proves to be Murdock's salvation. Long an adversarial soldier in the same war, Frank Castle joins the fun in prison, and he plays the role of the cynic. He's hardened by years of murdering scum, yet he has enough respect for Murdock not to want to see him go the same way. His mere presence shows Murdock what he truly is and what he should be doing. These two men have long been similar. Castle is what Murdock could have been with one sidestep along the journey, and so Murdock realises he must pull up. The last thing he wants is to be Frank Castle, so his salvation comes in the form of comparison.

The prison storyline sets the scene for a stripped-down Matt Murdock – and Daredevil. His birth in blood is necessary in order to make him a more finite target. His best friend taken away, his wife isolated, and his secret identity stripped, Murdock becomes the focus. Spandex and roof-flipping might still be part of his repertoire, but we now cannot forget the man within the suit. We understand this isn't about a super-hero; it's about a man. Just a man.

Murdock resembles Travis Bickle more than he does any spandex hero we've seen before. He wants to change the world in other ways but has to resort to violence to make his impact. He's aggressive, unhinged, internally struggling, and determined to do whatever it takes to find his own victory. And in the end, no matter what we're shown, we don't see any true victory in sight. The lesson is: we are all broken and wrong – every single one of us.

"The Devil Takes a Ride": A Polanski Parable

You understand the noir soaking Brubaker's run when you analyse Murdock's actions upon finding freedom outside the prison. His first thought is to throw himself into the case, follow the next lead, and not to settle back into any form of normality with his wife. We don't even see a panel of him enjoying his return to her; he simply rejoins the hunt, and that's how the world will always be for this man.

This atmosphere of determination and personal ignorance is heartbreaking, but the worst part is that it makes sense as a response. Why be good when the world is such a bad place and all it gives you are terrible things? As we enter the second arc of Brubaker's run, in *Daredevil* Vol. 2 #89 (Nov 2006), the tone shifts slightly. The prison was full of obvious examples of the worst of society. Upon release, things should get better and yet do not. No matter where Murdock goes, the world is a broken place and one we know he won't be able to fix.

This tragic mood feels straight out of the reels of Roman Polanski's cinematic offerings of the '70s. It makes sense to analyse Murdock's extensive world through the haze of Polanski's world view because, by the '70s, Polanski had already suffered the kind of tragic loss you only read about in ridiculous fiction. The maniacal cult surrounding Charles Manson killed Polanski's pregnant lover, Sharon Tate, in the home he shared with her. This gruesome situation would forever shape Polanski's feelings about the world. Thinking about *Chinatown* (1974) is an effective way to see how Daredevil's explorations into the world, under Brubaker, show how his negative worldview stretches beyond Hell's Kitchen, particularly after understanding how rotten he is inside.

The change of location to Monaco offers up some gorgeous establishing shots. The "cinematography" of Lark / Gaudiano makes this globetrotting tale feel immersive. With the wife firmly out of mind, it doesn't take long for a new femme fatale to wander into scene – even if this one appears to be unwitting to some degree. Lily Lucca becomes an engaging character the more Brubaker peels her layers away. She is an aggressively powerful woman while also being the patsy of her own story. Any suggestion of ownership in relationships is staged or inaccurately placed. Lily is a pawn, and her greatest strength is in not believing it.

Another woman in such a perilous predicament is Evelyn Mulwray in *Chinatown*. She is another damsel caught in the web of depravity the world so effortlessly lays down. These women want nothing but control, yet find it wrested from them every time.

Lily has been given a perfume, by a shadowy benefactor, that makes men smell whatever their heart desires. Murdock gets close to her and smells Karen Page, not his wife. He's already on the run from his current life. When the temptation of his past is put in front of him, he doesn't know how to respond. It's as if his internal moral compass is broken, or at least a little swayed. The deepest truths and desires within Murdock conspire to make his life a misery.

The entire tale of "The Devil Takes a Ride," spanning issues #89-93 (Nov 2006 - Mar 2007), plays out like a super-heroic Roman Polanski movie. The European locales offer a decidedly Polanski vibe, but there are also the themes of inner turmoil and revenge. Murdock becomes a Jake Gittes trying to help a female who can't help herself. The trail leads through some villainous tropes — offering Tombstone and a new Matador a chance to deliver the fighting we need — and the culmination becomes a conversation between Murdock and a very bitter and rotten old lady. The matriarch of Daredevil's decline is Vanessa Fisk, Wilson's former wife.

The entirety of issue #92 is devoted to the final reveal of Vanessa's motivations, the layout for her future (and final) actions, and the overall denouement of this small slice of Brubaker's overall tale. In a medium in which costumed villains cackle maniacally while trying to poison water supplies, Vanessa Fisk wants retribution against one half of the duo that ruined her life. She is pragmatic in her drive and measured in her delivery of malice. The two settle their feud, and their tale, through conversation. No one wants to see a super-hero punch a sick woman, and the low-key nature of this conclusion makes it simmer even more deliciously on the back burner. It may feel like Murdock wins, but he caused the spiralling descent of Vanessa Fisk and he's responsible for the ills that perpetually plagued her. If we focus too strongly on our leading hero, we neglect to realize we have just witnessed the noir demise of another player on the stage. How can he feel victorious in the poignant defeat of a lady who should have been given the chance to remain innocent?

This, however, is only the second act of Brubaker's great noir. Prison stripped Murdock down, what feels like a victory against Vanessa Fisk — as she dies and exonerates him with her final actions — is a streak of sunshine breaking through a perennially bleak sky, yet the machinations in place for the final reel, in which Murdock will face the biggest challenge, the true directing force of everything that has come before. In this titanic struggle, he will have no option but to lose – because this is noir. The reason the loss still kicks the reader so hard is because, above noir, this is a comic book. The heroes nearly always win in comics, even if only on a moral ground, yet here Murdock is completely destroyed. In fact, he never even stood a chance.

The momentary reprieve, at the end of "The Devil Takes a Ride," is the apex of relaxed happiness for Murdock. He returns to his wife, his identity is once more protected (at least legally), his best friend rises from the dead (he had been hiding in Witness Relocation), and life finally seems to have settled back into a groove. The "big bad" seems defeated, and this is where Murdock's mistake lies. Vanessa was simply a pawn, and the true evil steps up to distract Murdock once more, while Brubaker executes his *coup de grace*.

"Without Fear": A Peckinpah Massacre

Daredevil's world is drawn into the shadow once more in a brilliant scene in *Daredevil* Vol. 2 #95 (May 2007), in which he intercepts street level thugs mid-crime. In Hell's Kitchen, Daredevil clearly has the upper hand, and as he exhibits this dominance, one of the thugs changes his behavior. Rather than be caught, to be held and questioned and broken down, he guns down his partners and looks Daredevil square in the eyes as he turns his automatic weapon upon himself. This drastic display of commitment to not being caught offer a visceral scene but also a major hint at who's pulling the strings on this whole caper. These men were too afraid to be caught.

The violence of this arc is most disturbing because it involves blatant images of death and destruction that feel irreparable. When the thugs are shot, they aren't coming back. It is no ruse; it is fatal. The main distraction for Murdock is the relapse of Melvin Potter into his old ways as the Gladiator. He dons his costume and descends upon an open marketplace, using his wrist blades to wantonly attack and slay in a massacre the likes of which he had never committed before.

The primitive nature of these acts calls to mind the glorious studies of violence that Sam Peckinpah filled a career creating. This final act of Brubaker's noir owes much to *The Wild Bunch*, a 1969 movie that helped lay the blood-smeared foundations for the violent cinema in the 1970s. The film, and Brubaker's final arc of noir, are so bold because of their intrepid depiction of brutality and realism of violence. When people engage in hostility, there's a good chance they will die in terrible ways.

Hell's Kitchen descends into Peckinpah's Wild West not through narrative but through excessively meticulous and ostentatious violence. As crime takes over, innocent people are not safe, and only might can meet might. You can hear the words of Peckinpah covering the action in this tale: "Well, killing a man isn't clean and quick and simple. It's bloody and awful. And maybe if enough people come to realize that shooting somebody isn't just fun and games, maybe we'll get somewhere" (*Playboy*, Aug 1972). The severity of violence in "Without Fear" is matched with the ramifications of these actions. Much like the '70s finally accepted and understood the consequences of violence that changed the tone of a decade, *Daredevil* as a comic finally rises above super-hero tropes and shows us the terribly truthful resolutions of situations filled with hostility.

If the man behind the brutality of *Straw Dogs* (1971) is going to be any influence over this arc, you have to worry for the fate of Milla Donovan. Murdock has already seen several lovers die, and so when Gladiator steals into the night with Donovan, in *Daredevil* Vol. 2 #98 (Aug 2007), we can only assume the worst. She is thrown off a building, and when Murdock swings down to save her from this, he doesn't yet know he's already lost the battle where she's concerned. His relationship is about to hit a noir dead end.

The downfall of Daredevil comes from the enemy's understanding that he must present an opponent Daredevil cannot punch into submission. He must act first, ensure his victory, and then revel in the unwinding of his own genius. There are no Bond-villain moments of exposition to give the hero a chance at turnaround success. Daredevil was damned from the start, and the worst blow is that he never figured it out.

With Daredevil's defeat certain, Mr. Fear finally steps forward as the major contributor to the bleakness of Murdock's landscape. The Man without Fear up against the manufacturer of fear. Fear's costume holds the regal pomp of previous incarnations, yet also feels functional. The realism is on display as much as possible while still referencing super-hero tropes. The appearance and actions of Chico and Merv on the street, peddling Fear's toxin, also feel like a '70s movie. Even Fear's duped henchmen and building of a fortress of excess around himself offers an "Enter The Dragon" type of model, making a villain feel larger than life.

The intricacy of Fear's plan, the pure audacity and elaborate nature of it, places him as a noir mastermind. He thought every step through before he even began. Noir is a slow and inevitable march to darkness, and Fear has ensured from the first moment that this march is indeed inevitable, because there's nothing Murdock can do to save himself from this plan. He's quite literally doomed to this failure.

In the downward spiral in *Daredevil* Vol. 2 #103 (Feb 2008), Murdock refuses to give up. His wife is poisoned with Fear's greatest and latest gas, his informants on the street aren't delivering enough, and his options are running out. In the middle of a spandex comic, our red hero attacks another stooge who's recuperating from a slicing Daredevil delivered earlier. Fancy Dan says he won't talk, and Daredevil threatens to "rip out every one of those stitches and see what's inside." The few rules left are shattered and forgotten. We always knew a man without hope was a man without fear, but it appears he's also a man willing to do "whatever it takes" — or so he tells a chained up Ox after hitting him with a speeding cab and lighting up a butane torch.

The ultimate step of this noir parable is the decimation of Matt Murdock as an actual hero, as someone who acts heroically. Murdock exploits situations, goes further than possibly needed, and acts based on emotion rather than fact or reason. Murdock is forcibly altered by his situation and surroundings, and in this respect Fear has already won. The villain is running away with the victory, and the clock is counting down for Daredevil to turn the tables.

After abusing Ox's nerve clusters so as to emulate torture by fire, Daredevil wonders why he doesn't feel worse about it. He's conditioned against violence, even when perpetrated by himself. Years of villains pulling these stunts against him have finally opened up the option that he can do it himself. He doesn't feel bad about it — but he *does* feel bad about *not* feeling bad about it. Social judgements might keep him in line, but his own personal code has ceased to do so. Milla's case worsens, and when Murdock finds out Ms. Lucca was the instigator, he sneaks into her house and chokes her. Though technically involved, Lucca is no more than a pawn, which ostensibly makes her innocent, yet Murdock attacks this woman in the night with vehemence. Our hero is gone. The only question then becomes: "What will be left of the man?"

If "The Devil in Cell Block D" broke Murdock down, and "The Devil Takes a Ride" showed Murdock that the entire world is broken and no one man can fix it, then "Without Fear" is the moment in which these two elements mix to produce the only response any man can muster: violence. Men and violence broke Murdock down, and it's these same things that make the world such a corrupt and injust place. Finally, as he slips into the noir cycle and becomes what he loathes, Murdock becomes a violent man.

The showdown between Daredevil and Mr. Fear, in *Daredevil* Vol. 2 #105 (Apr 2008), is perfect final-reel fodder. Daredevil is obviously the better at combat, yet he cannot win this fight. He beats Fear down, severely, and the response from the villain is "I *love* that you think *you've* won." Typically, at the end of a super-hero story, the hero beats the villain into submission and the status quo can be restored in time for the coda. Fear has ensured this cannot occur because he built a failsafe into his plan: there never was any antidote, and every person he has infected with his toxin will remain in their terrible state. Donovan will never recover. Daredevil loses, and hard.

This terrible down note leaves Murdock's life in a mess. He confines his wife to a hospital, where all they can hope to do is care for her indefinitely, with no hope of recovery. Another love has yet again been painfully lost. Another life has been ruined because of him. The villain not only succeeded with his plan but now resides in Ryker's Island prison, enjoying an easy existence because every crim and screw in the establishment inherently fears him. He's going to wait out, and enjoy, his sentence, and when he's ready he'll just walk out, because that's the control he has. He's unstoppable, and that's the ultimate failure for any hero. Fear represents the wave of violence in the world that cannot be stopped. Peckinpah saw this as an absolute, and his heroes were rarely able to "solve" the world around them. Their endings were often just as bleak.

Brubaker closes the trilogy with a panel of Murdock sitting on his bed, his hands clasped, his head down. Everything was wagered, all was lost. A hero contemplates his future and finds a bleak landscape instead of blue skies. The next step is so rarely analysed in the super-hero genre: what is the end game for any of these heroes? Murdock avenged his father's death directly in his very first issue, yet never gave up the chase. Like the gunslingers in *The Wild Bunch*, perhaps Murdock dreams of "pulling back" after the next tussle. He seeks a nebulous goal. He'll know it once he grasps it, and until then he's locked into high gear and moving forward. This is a doomed mindset and one engineered to breed failure.

This isn't Fair; This is Noir

Brubaker spends over three years ensuring Matt Murdock's world finally feels true noir. The bleak trilogy of "Devil in Cell Block D," "The Devil Takes a Ride," and "Without Fear" is merely just the start. True noir and its terrible conclusions really have no end. After Murdock is laid low, Brubaker spends the other half of his run detailing Murdock's actions while firmly grounded at the lightless bottom. There is no ascent for this character – at least, not on Brubaker's watch.

Matt Murdock does want to get on with his life – or what's left of it. He tries his best, yet it only leads to more terrible things. Dakota North, his intrepid private investigator for the firm, is beaten and shot because of a case in the "Cruel & Unusual" arc (*Daredevil* Vol. 2 #107-110, Jul-Oct 2008). The whole situation might work to make Murdock see some sort of golden light in the form of judicious pursuit, and North doesn't die. But the story still leads downward after he has sex with her. His wife – locked up, psychologically uncontrollable, afraid – is innocent, yet he betrays her in the worst way a husband can betray a wife. Murdock becomes the ultimate Peckinpah lead, as he asserts his male dominance over a submissive female.

If Murdock is the "hero" of the series, he certainly spends a good deal of it not fulfilling the basic and simple criteria of that role. He's not only fallible but consistently fails. Life isn't going to suddenly become better for him; he needs to *be* the change in the world he wishes to see. It becomes apparent that he's not capable of this, and Brubaker has the spine to take this to its logical conclusion.

After losing his moral center and cheating on his wife, Murdock is presented with a situation that could either make or break him. A villainous assassin guild, the Hand, approaches Murdock and asks him to be its leader. It's a final step down, and he's reluctant to take it, since it would signify his end as any sort of hero. He could possibly take the role and become an anti-hero, somewhere on the level of Frank Castle, but he knows this slippery slope isn't the sort of situation with many opportunities for heroic deeds. Murdock turns down this opportunity, because he isn't interested in digging any deeper down.

Enter Wilson Fisk, who finally got away from New York, from Matt Murdock, and from the seemingly endless cycle of violence and possessive destruction his world had been consumed by. In *Daredevil* Vol. 2 #116 (May 2009), he winds up on the Costa Da Morte, where in the midst of a deathly system inured toward crippling you on every level, he finds happiness. More importantly, he finds peace. He meets a girl, they become a simple unit, and then the past catches up with him. The Hand, scorned by Murdock, put Fisk back into play merely as a pawn to trigger an oppositional response from the man they truly want to lead them. In a serene situation, Murdock becomes the cause for unrest. He is the villainous force, even if not consciously. Don't most villains see themselves as the good guy?

A union is formed between former bitter enemies, yet both know it can't last. Usually the villain eventually betrays the goodwill of the hero, and here that cliché is flipped. Murdock is more than happy to play the lesser man sooner; he sells out Fisk and steps forward to lead the Hand so that no one else can. He can sell this as a magnanimous gesture all he likes, but the truth is that Murdock becomes the leader of a clan of ninja who kill for money. There's no way to spin this as heroic.

Much like Popeye Doyle in the final minutes of *The French Connection* (1971), Daredevil has turned a corner and possibly become the villain. Or proved that any man who sides with violence is an enemy to peace. Daredevil is willing to do whatever it takes to find what he deems a victory and leave the collateral damage for later.

As Murdock descends the stairs into the inner sanctum of the Hand, home of his own future villainy, he does so with a smile. He understands that, as a hero, he has lost. Even when he did good, or found a victory, it usually ended in dead loves or injured friends. His track record as a good person has consistently yielded more terror, not only in his world but in the geographic ripple around it. Murdock might be blind, but he sees this and he accepts his changed fate. In *Daredevil* Vol. 2 #500 (Oct 2009), he slips deeper into the earth and thinks, "I *deserve* whatever awaits me below."

This is the end; there is no last minute turnaround here, no victory to be found or even hoped for. This is noir on its purest level. Brubaker holds his ground and doesn't yield to the conventions of the genre. After more than three years, Brubaker departs the title with Matt Murdock lost. This is his comment on super-heroic fortitude — it must eventually lose because the enemies are too great. One man cannot resist the temptation to change under the strain of the storm.

For a blind man, the world just became a darker place.

About the Contributors

Tim Callahan started his writing-about-comics career with Sequart.org and the posts that would become the foundation of *Grant Morrison: The Early Years*. He would go on to contribute essays to future Sequart publications and find a home as a weekly columnist for Comic Book Resources and Tor.com, along with working as a regular contributor to *Back Issue* magazine and Comics Alliance. He is currently working on several graphic novel projects which should be released before his kids go off to college.

Jon Cormier lives and works in Ottawa, Ontario. He once had a comics blog called "hynoray." He is working on his first independent comic project.

Julian Darius holds a Ph.D. in English and an M.A. in French. He founded Sequart, for which he wrote *Improving the Foundations: Batman Begins from Comics to Screen* and *Classics on Infinite Earths: The Justice League and DC Crossover Canon*, along with several other works and a multitude of material for Sequart.org. He is also a fiction author.

Matt (Matias) **Duarte** is an avid reader and occasional writer who currently lives in Valencia, Spain, with his wife. English teacher by day and professional time-waster by night, he enjoys reading all types of comics and books, though he particularly enjoys fantasy and science fiction. Other interests include video games, football, punk music, and finding excuses to avoid writing when he knows he should be doing that instead.

Stéphane Guéret and **Marie-Laure Saulnier** are both physics teachers. **Manuella Hyvard** teaches biology and **Nicolas Labarre** is an associate professor in American sociey and culture, with a specialty in American comics. Though nominally divided between scientists and comics specialists, they share an abiding curiosity for all things scientific and for popular culture. They all live and work in Western France, between Le Mans and Bordeaux.

As a child, **Christine Hanefalk**'s favorite super-hero was Superman, due in equal parts to Christopher Reeve's iconic portrayal of the character and the easy access to Superman comics translated into her native Swedish. As an adult, it was a chance encounter with Daredevil that pulled her back into the world of comics and opened her eyes to a completely different breed of superhero. In late 2007, Christine decided to combine her profound love of the character of Matt Murdock with her passion for writing by creating the Other Murdock Papers, a Daredevil-centric website. Since then, she has set out to prove, one blog post at a time, that there is no topic pertaining to the Daredevil title or its characters that is not worthy of a deeper look.

Forrest Helvie lives in Bristol, Connecticut, with his wife and two sons. He is also working on completing his doctoral dissertation, which is focused on the relationship between American literature and comic-book super-heroes. He served as a panelist at a number of conferences discussing his research in comics and won the 2012 Lent Award in Comics Studies from the National Popular Culture Association. In addition to his work in comics scholarship, Forrest is a full-time professor of developmental English at Norwalk Community College in Connecticut.

Geoff Klock is the author of *How to Read Superhero Comics and Why* and *Imaginary Biographies: Misreading the Lives of the Poets*. He has a fancy doctoral degree in English from Oxford University and teaches Composition, Brit Lit 1, and Film as an Assistant Professor at the Borough of Manhattan Community College, City University of New York. He treats horses good and is friendly to strangers.

Ryan K. Lindsay writes comics and about comics. He's launching *Ghost Town* from Action Lab Entertainment, the mini-series *Heist*, the phenomenal *Fatherhood* from Challenger Comics, and has a *My Little Pony* one-shot from IDW. He's had short stories published by Image / Shadowline and ComixTribe. He's also had essays published in *Criminal*, *Godzilla*, *Horror Factory*, and a smattering of sublime Sequart tomes. He is Australian. Hit him up on @ryanklindsay and ryanklindsay.com for words daily.

Vinny Murphy hails from Clarkstown, New York, and holds a B.A. in English from St. Thomas Aquinas College. Though this is his first widely published work, he has contributed to numerous projects such as Sequart.org, Mancouch.com, and most recently *The Rockland County Times*. In between covering local town board meetings, he was once able to slip "Avengers Assemble" into a headline, an accomplishment he mentions frequently. He is a life-long fan of all things super, spacey, or groovy, and maintains that the most under-appreciated art form in the world is pro-wrestling.

Will Murray has been a Marvel Comics fan since he purchased *Fantastic Four #4* in a drug store back in 1962. 30 years later, he created the mightiest mutant in the Marvel Universe, Squirrel Girl, with legendary artist Steve Ditko. He has contributed to *Alter Ego, Comics Scene*, and a host of similar magazines, and regularly pens introductions for the Marvel Masterworks series. Currently, he writes the Wild Adventures of Doc Savage novels for Altus Press.

Henry Northmore is a journalist working in Edinburgh, Scotland. He used to write a blog for Sequart.org from the perspective of a U.K. comics aficionado, but spends most of his time as Assistant Editor at *The List*, Scotland's leading arts and entertainment magazine, alongside freelance work for the likes of *Scotland on Sunday, Shock Horror*, and *The Dark Side*. Specialist subjects include all the major food groups: comics, horror movies, video games, and rock music.

Kevin Thurman was born and raised in Texas (he asks that you please not hold this against him) and migrated to Alaska, where he lived for a few years. Finding himself in Santa Fe, New Mexico, he soon discovered Uatu the Watcher working in a tortilla factory. They traveled cross country to Illinois, where he presently lives with his wife and the brain of JFK, which he keeps in a jar in the pantry. He is the co-author of Sequart's upcoming *Voyage in Noise: Warren Ellis and the Demise of Western Civilization*.

M. S. Wilson a house painter / handyman with literary aspirations. He lives in Saskatchewan (central Canada) and loves comic books, all forms of SF / fantasy, and gorillas (not necessarily in that order). He used to write a column (The Peter David Factor) on Sequart.org. He's single and spends his time reading, playing video games, and contemplating his next writing project.

Also from Sequart

TEENAGERS FROM THE FUTURE: ESSAYS ON THE LEGION OF SUPER-HEROES

MUTANT CINEMA: THE X-MEN TRILOGY FROM COMICS TO SCREEN

AND THE UNIVERSE SO BIG: UNDERSTANDING *BATMAN: THE KILLING JOKE*

GOTHAM CITY 14 MILES: 14 ESSAYS ON WHY THE 1960S BATMAN TV SERIES MATTERS

IMPROVING THE FOUNDATIONS: *BATMAN BEGINS* FROM COMICS TO SCREEN

Grant Morrison: The Early Years

Our Sentence Is Up: Seeing Grant Morrison's *The Invisibles*

Curing the Postmodern Blues: Reading Grant Morrison and Chris Weston's *The Filth* in the 21st Century

Classics on Infinite Earths: The Justice League and DC Crossover Canon

Keeping the World Strange: A *Planetary* Guide

Minutes to Midnight: Twelve Essays on *Watchmen*

For more information and for exclusive content, visit Sequart.org.

www.ingramcontent.com/pod-product-compliance
Lightning Source LLC
Chambersburg PA
CBHW032106090426
42743CB00007B/260